Dear Jacob

A MOTHER'S JOURNEY OF HOPE

Patty Wetterling with Joy Baker

MINNESOTA
HISTORICAL
SOCIETY PRESS

The publication of this book was supported though a generous grant from the Eugenie M. Anderson Women in Public Affairs Fund.

Minnesota Historical Society Press,
345 Kellogg Blvd. W., St. Paul, MN 55102-1906.

mnhspress.org

The Minnesota Historical Society Press is a member of the Association of University Presses.

Manufactured in Canada

10 9 8 7 6 5 4 3 2 1

International Standard Book Number
ISBN: 978-1-68134-314-3 (paperback)
ISBN: 978-1-68134-318-1 (e-book)

Library of Congress Control Number: 2024946538

Find a reader's guide to *Dear Jacob* at www.dearjacobbook.com.

"For nearly three decades Patty remained steadfastly convinced that her son would reappear one day, and that her family would put their nightmare behind them.... The mother of four turned her agony into action, becoming a passionate advocate for missing children. [*Dear Jacob* is] the story of... how she coped with the truth, as well as her comforting friendship with Joy Baker, the blogger who helped bring Jacob's killer to justice ... the book contains moving letters Patty penned to her long-missing son."
   —*People* magazine

"In the end, *Jacob's Hope* gives hope to all of us. As Patty Wetterling shows, terrible things happen but the human spirit survives."
   —*St. Paul Pioneer Press*

"Nearly impossible to put down. Patty's thoughtful and open approach allows readers to glimpse the Wetterling family's story from the inside."
   —*Mankato Free Press*

"Following Jacob's abduction, Patty and her family were thrust into a world of unimaginable pain. Each riveting page of this book reveals glimpses of a mother's unwavering devotion to her son and her commitment to bringing Jacob home. Patty continues to honor her son's legacy as a physical embodiment of *hope* and provides a lifeline for families searching for their own missing children."
   —Michelle DeLaune, president and CEO,
   National Center for Missing & Exploited Children

"If you've ever doubted the tenacity of a mother's love, this book will convince you. It conveys the terror of an abduction, the gift of cherished memories, and the importance of promoting a legacy of hope. In addition, this extraordinarily inspirational book shows all professionals the need to provide empathetic, trauma-informed care."
> —Sharon W. Cooper, MD, coeditor of *Perspectives on Missing Persons Cases* and *Medical, Legal and Social Science Aspects of Child Sexual Exploitation*

"I am so deeply touched by Patty Wetterling's candid account of Jacob's tragic story. I found myself holding my breath with anticipation through much of this book. I cried often, but they were tears of inspiration. It takes so much dedication to become the dogged trailblazer that she is. Patty is a courageous person, and I admire her greatly."
> —Pat LaLama, investigative journalist

This memoir is dedicated to Jacob
and all who share the hope

{ Chapter 1 }

In 1989, I was thirty-nine years old and beginning to wonder what I wanted to do with the rest of my life. I felt fortunate I'd been able to stay at home with our kids for the past thirteen years, but now that they were all in school full time, I finally had a chance to pause and dream a bit about future possibilities. My fortieth birthday was approaching, and I found myself yearning for meaning and a renewed purpose. Who was I? What did I want to do next?

A friend gave me the name of a career counselor she knew in St. Cloud and recommended I make an appointment with him. "Just warning you, though," she cautioned. "He doesn't mince words."

I was fine with that. I needed someone who would be straight with me and encourage me to imagine possibilities. I made the appointment.

A few days later, I found myself being escorted into this man's office. The room was windowless, stark, and serious, with dim lighting, dark paneling, and an oversized wooden desk that appeared too big for the space. There were no files on the desk, no photos on the walls—just a framed diploma and a counseling license. As the very busy counselor rose to greet me in his very businesslike suit and tie, I began to lose what little confidence I had mustered while waiting in the reception area. What was I doing here?

"Hi. I'm Patty," I said, stepping forward to shake his hand.

"Nice to meet you, Patty," he said, taking my small hand in his and shaking it with a firm grip. "Have a seat."

He directed me toward a dark brown leather armchair, then settled into a matching one across from me. At just over five feet tall, I had to sit forward on the chair so my feet didn't dangle.

"So Patty, what brings you here today?" he asked me.

I took a deep breath.

"Well . . . I guess I'm looking for a little direction. For the past thirteen years, I've been a stay-at-home mom—which I love," I added quickly. "But now that my kids are all in school full time, I've been considering going back to work."

"Do you have anything specific in mind?" he asked.

"No, not really. I'm looking for something, but I'm not sure what," I answered.

"What are you good at?" he asked me.

I hated questions like this. Obviously, if I knew the answer, I wouldn't be here right now. I started babbling.

"Well, I have four amazing kids. Amy is thirteen, Jake is eleven, Trevor is nine, and Carmen is seven. I love being their mom, and I'm really involved in their lives and all their activities."

He smiled. "So, what *else* are you good at, besides having babies?"

I gave him a sideways glance, put off by his implication. I wasn't just *having babies*. I was *raising children* and *managing a family*. Was he joking? I couldn't tell, but one thing was certain: he wasn't mincing words.

I shifted uncomfortably in my chair. What *was* I good at? I took another deep breath and continued.

I told him about graduating as a math major from Mankato State College in southern Minnesota. I'd also picked up minors in education and psychology to go with it.

Next, I told him about student teaching in Monterrey, Mexico, during winter quarter of my senior year.

"I taught math to seventh, eighth, and ninth graders," I explained.

"Did you speak Spanish?" he asked.

"Yes. I had four years in high school, so it came back pretty quickly. It helped that my host family in Monterrey only spoke to me in Spanish."

He seemed to be eyeing me differently now.

"After graduating from college, did you go on to pursue a job in teaching?" he asked.

"Yes, but not a traditional one."

I explained how, at twenty-one years old, I'd taken a job teaching math aboard a ship at the Harry Lundeberg School of Seamanship in Piney Point, Maryland. The young men I taught were training to become merchant marines.

"These guys were *tough*," I explained. "A lot of them got sent to Harry Lundeberg through the court system. Judges told them, 'Either go to seamanship school, or go to juvey.' It was my job to get them to pass the math portion of their GED."

"And did they?" he asked.

"Almost every one," I said proudly.

Next, I told him about my second job, teaching at Kent Junior High School in Palmer Park, Maryland.

"Midway through the year, the school was forced to implement a de-segregation plan, and they started busing in thousands of kids from all across the district. The new kids didn't want to be there any more than the neighborhood kids wanted them, so things got pretty ugly. Tensions built, so eventually we had to wait for the police to arrive so they could dismiss school each day and lock the doors behind us. Everyone had to leave, even the teachers."

He was listening intently now and encouraged me to continue.

I rambled on about being a soccer coach, PTA president, entertainment coordinator for the Millstream Arts Festival, insurance processor for my husband Jerry's chiropractic business, landlord and general repair person for our rental property . . .

He stopped me.

"Okay. But what do you really *love*?" he asked.

"Kids," I said, without a moment's hesitation. "I love kids."

"Well, there you go," he answered.

I returned home and started to put some serious thought into going back to school. With my minor in psychology, I had often dreamed about becom-ing a high school guidance counselor. It would require two more years of college to obtain my master's degree, but with our busy family schedule I wasn't sure I could handle the commitment. Instead, I decided to complete the necessary paperwork to renew my Minnesota teaching license, just in case an opportunity presented itself.

Just before school started that fall, I noticed Jacob was holding things closer to his face whenever he tried to read. I made an appointment to have his vision checked, and since school was starting in a few weeks, I figured we could do some back-to-school shopping at the same time. I treasured one-on-one time with each of our kids and tried hard to carve out special mo-ments like this.

We headed to JCPenney at Crossroads Center mall, and I watched as Jacob browsed the usual racks of sports jerseys and sweatpants. He was a natural athlete who could pick up any sport with ease, and the clothes he wore reflected it.

"We should probably try to find something for school pictures," I suggested.

After a few moments, Jacob held up a long-sleeved black shirt with a yellow collar. It had shooting stars, planets, and comets on the front.

"How about this?" he asked.

It wasn't something he would normally wear, and it was definitely not something I would have picked out for him. I realized this was a new milestone for Jacob, as his own sense of style was just starting to emerge. I was happy to be sharing it with him.

"Looks great," I said. "Do you think maybe we should try to find something besides sweatpants to go with it?"

He laughed, his bright blue eyes sparkling.

"Fine," he conceded. "But what I *really* need is a new pair of Air Jordans."

"Yeah, right," I laughed.

Jacob loved everything Michael Jordan—especially since the two of them shared the same birthday. He had posters, basketball cards, magazines, a #23 Chicago Bulls jersey, and even a Michael Jordan cover plate for the light switch in his and Trevor's bedroom.

We found a pair of jeans, then made our way to the shoe department. Jacob made a beeline for the Nikes and picked out a pair of white high-tops with a black swoosh. His feet were already bigger than mine, and though he was still about an inch shorter, I knew he would soon be looking down at me. Jacob was growing up. Literally.

"How about these?" he asked.

The store clerk found a pair in the right size, and when Jacob finally got them on his feet, he took a few steps, then quickly pivoted and faked a jump shot.

"Can I get them?" he asked excitedly.

I had to smile at his unbridled joy.

"Okay," I answered. "Let's go."

I paid for the shoes and we were on our way.

When we finally made it to the eye appointment that day, we both learned what I already suspected. Jake needed glasses.

"Can I get contacts?" he asked the optometrist, without missing a beat.

I turned to him, surprised. I guess I had assumed he was too young for contacts, but the optometrist had no problem with it. We put in the order, and about two weeks later we headed back to the mall so Jake could learn how to wear them.

My eyes watered as I watched him put the contacts in and take them out while the optometrist assisted him. I didn't have any experience with contacts myself and was sure I wouldn't be able to handle wearing them, but Jake was amazingly adept at it.

"This is a big responsibility," the optometrist told him. "You'll need to take them out and clean them every night, and you need to make sure your hands are clean whenever you handle them."

"I will. I can do it," Jake said confidently.

He wore them out of the optometrist's office, so happy and amazed at how much better he was able to see. He couldn't wait to get home and shoot some hoops to try them out.

In early October, I got a call from Kevin Blanchette, a good friend of ours and a math teacher at St. John's Prep.

"How would you like to teach at the prep school?" he asked me. "They're looking for a part-time geometry teacher who can start soon."

"Yes, definitely!" I jumped at the chance. Part-time sounded perfect, and St. John's Prep was just eight miles west of us, in Collegeville.

"Who do I talk to?"

"Well, me actually," Kevin said. "I'm head of the math department, so you'd be working for me. The dean of students is the one doing the hiring, so I'll set up an interview with him and call you back with a time."

The interview went well. Afterward, I was given a tour of the classrooms, the underground tunnels that connected the school to the dorms, the athletic fields, and the amazing view that overlooked the lake.

It all felt so right, and it ignited a spark in me that I hadn't felt in a very long time. The more I learned about the school and their Benedictine values of "listening with the heart," the more I knew I would fit there. I was ready to step outside of my comfort zone and take this next big step on my life journey. I eagerly awaited the job offer.

A few weeks later, on Saturday, October 21, both Jake and Trevor had hockey practice. On our way home, I could tell something was bothering Jacob.

"What's wrong?" I asked him.

"I can't skate in these new skates!" he finally said in frustration.

"You're a good skater, Jake. You just have to get used to them."

"No, I'm really slow! I need to be faster to play forward!"

Jacob's friend Aaron Larson had decided to try out for house league that fall instead of travel team, and Jacob had decided to join him. They had both played on a travel team the previous year for the St. Cloud Youth Hockey Association, and on that team, Jacob played full-time goalie. But on house league, all the players got equal playing time and took turns rotating among positions. At first Jacob had been fine with the switch, but now he suddenly felt like he wasn't fast enough or good enough. I knew he was worried about not making the same team as Aaron and it really bothered him. Nothing I said or did could lighten his mood.

That night as I was catching up on laundry, Jacob followed me into the living room.

"Sorry I was so crabby today," he apologized. "Do you want to play a game or something?"

Jacob was always sensitive about hurting other people's feelings, and I knew he was trying to make up for it. I thanked him for the apology, but declined his offer. I had so much to do, juggling schedules, laundry, meals, dance, hockey, basketball, friends, sleepovers . . .

"I can't right now," I told him. "I really need to catch up here."

"I just want to do something that makes you happy," he said.

"Thanks, Jake," I said. "But not tonight. I really have a lot to do."

If only I had a do-over. I will regret those words forever.

{ Chapter 2 }

On Sunday, October 22, 1989, the high temperature was predicted to be in the low 70s—a good twenty degrees above average and one of those perfect, late-autumn days that Minnesotans relish. Jerry and Jake both loved to fish, so they got up early, hooked the boat up to the Chevy Suburban, and went to try to catch some keepers. I was happy they were taking advantage of the beautiful weather before having to put the boat away for the season.

It was MEA weekend in Minnesota. For teachers, this meant a professional development opportunity, as the Minnesota Education Association (MEA) held its annual conference in St. Paul. However, for kids and their parents, MEA meant extra days off from school and a long weekend for family fun.

The kids had been in school for over six weeks by now. Amy was in eighth grade, Jacob sixth, Trevor fourth, and Carmen second. Ever since Jake had come home with his new pair of Nike high-tops, Trevor had been begging for his own pair. As brothers, they were not only best friends, but also fierce competitors. Whatever Jacob got, Trevor usually wanted too.

So, when Trevor and Carmen woke up that Sunday morning, the three of us drove to Crossroads Center in St. Cloud. Amy, our official teenager, chose to stay home and sleep in. She had plans to stay overnight at a friend's house later, so that was okay. I figured she could use the extra sleep.

We quickly found the Nike high-tops at JCPenney. Trevor tried them on and we were out the door in record time, anxious to get home in time for the noon kickoff of the Vikings game against the Detroit Lions.

Sundays in the fall were all about the Minnesota Vikings. By kickoff, the six of us—all dressed in purple—crowded in front of the TV, cheering, eating, and willing them to win. Carmen danced around with pom-poms, while Jacob gave the play-by-play. He was amazingly talented at this, and often

7

gave a play-call analysis, only to have the TV announcer repeat the same thing moments later.

At halftime, I set out some munchies while Jerry and the kids headed outside to play a game of O.D.—Offense-Defense. It was a game they invented with their friends and played in the grassy area of our cul-de-sac. One side got four plays to try to score a touchdown, while the other side played defense. After four downs (or a score), they switched sides. Jerry was the all-time quarterback, and Carmen was the all-time "hikest." Inevitably, other kids from the neighborhood also joined in.

I absolutely loved days like this in our peaceful little circle, and the unseasonably warm weather made this one especially glorious. As Amy and I walked down the driveway to watch the kids play, our next-door neighbors, the Jerzaks, walked over to say hi.

Merle and Scottie Jerzak lived right next door in a Spanish-style house with stucco siding and beautiful outdoor gardens. Their daughter, Rochelle, was less than a year older than Amy, and they'd been best friends ever since we moved to the cul-de-sac five years earlier.

We moved to St. Joseph in 1976, following Jerry's graduation from Palmer College of Chiropractic in Davenport, Iowa. "St. Joe," as the locals called it, is just outside the larger St. Cloud metro area, and with a population of only three thousand or so at that time, it had a small-town charm we really loved. From its friendly residents and historic downtown buildings to its vibrant college-town atmosphere, we knew this was a place we wanted to call home.

We found a turn-of-the-century Victorian home in the middle of downtown St. Joseph with beautiful woodwork, a bay window with a window seat, old-fashioned radiators, and a large attic on the third floor. To save money, we remodeled the first floor of the house for Jerry's chiropractic office and converted the second floor and attic space into our living quarters.

For seven and a half years, we lived above the chiropractic office. Amy had been born in Davenport, but Jacob, Trevor, and Carmen were all born during this time. I absolutely loved being only steps away from the grocery store, meat market, parks, shops, and other conveniences. However, with patients coming and going all day long and four busy (and growing) kids, both Jerry and I wanted to move somewhere a little more spacious and private.

In the fall of 1984, we found exactly what we were looking for. It was a wood-sided split-level tucked back into the woods of a newer development called Forest Manor, just two miles away. The eight homes on our cul-de-sac were full of kids, and Amy, Jacob, Trevor, and Carmen all loved having so many new friends. They spent countless hours playing in the yard, hanging out at the neighbors', building forts in the woods, and riding their sleds down Chocolate Chip Hill. It was a fun, busy neighborhood, and so different from living right downtown.

After the Vikings game, Jacob begged for one more chance to skate before hockey tryouts.

"I need more practice on the new skates. Can we go? Just for a little while?"

Jerry agreed to take the boys to the arena for open skate while I stayed home with the girls and did more laundry.

"I need to let Dave and Vicki know if we're coming tonight or not," I said to Jerry. "What do you think?"

Our friends Dave and Vicki Glenn were hosting a dinner party at their new home in St. Augusta. It was a wrap-up meeting for St. Joseph's annual Millstream Arts Festival, and as entertainment coordinator, I felt I should attend. Another committee member, Steve, had been at the Glenns' house all day, preparing an amazing multi-course meal.

"It's up to you," Jerry said.

"I think we should go."

Since Amy would be gone at her friend Erin's house, we asked Jacob if he would mind babysitting Trevor and Carmen for a few hours while we went to the party. He was in sixth grade, and though we'd never asked him to do this before, we knew we wouldn't be gone long and figured they would be fine staying home and watching videos.

"Sure," Jake replied. "Can Aaron come over?"

I figured that was even better. Now we would have two very responsible sixth-grade boys watching over our fourth grader and second grader.

The clock was ticking as Jerry arrived home with Jake. Trevor had hockey practice after open skate, so we'd made arrangements with another family to drop him off when they were done. While Jerry hurried off to trade his sweatshirt for a sweater, I called and ordered a pizza for the kids for dinner. We left around 5:30 PM.

Just after arriving at the party, I called home to give Jacob the Glenns' new phone number. They had just moved into a new house, and I wanted to be sure the kids could reach us if they needed anything. Jacob reported that everything was fine. Aaron was there, Trevor had returned, and the pizza had arrived. All was good. I poured a glass of wine and began to relax.

Shortly before dinner, the Glenns' phone rang. It was Trevor. Jerry and I gave each other a quick glance and I got up to take the call.

"Hey Trev, what's up? Everything okay?"

"We're bored. Can we ride our bikes to the Tom Thumb and rent a video?"

The Tom Thumb convenience store was about a mile from our house, and by now it was dark. "No. You have plenty of videos," I said. "Find something to do."

Trevor said, "Let me talk to Dad."

I laughed and jokingly said to Jerry, "Your son would like to speak with you." Jerry got up and took the phone, but he barely got a word out before Trevor started in.

"Dad, we're all ready to go. I've got a flashlight, Aaron is wearing a white sweatshirt, and Jacob is wearing your jogging vest. We'll go straight to the store and come straight back. Can we go?"

It was hard to counter all the safety measures they'd thought of.

"Okay," Jerry said. "But go straight to the store, and come straight home," he repeated.

He hung up, and we both returned to the living room.

Five minutes later, the phone rang again. It was Jake.

"Mom, Carmen doesn't want to go," he said. "Is it okay if Rochelle comes over to babysit while we're gone?"

"Yes, that's fine. Thanks for letting us know."

It made me feel better when I realized how responsible they were being.

I returned to the party once again, just as everyone was sitting down to eat. We'd been gone for only about an hour and a half, and already we'd talked to our kids three times.

The dinner Steve had prepared was amazing, and we were all laughing and visiting when the phone rang again. When Vicki answered and indicated it was for us again, everyone laughed.

Jerry went to the kitchen to take the call, then returned quickly and grabbed my arm.

"We have to go," he said quietly.

"What? Aren't the kids back yet?" I asked him.

"Two of them are. Someone took Jacob."

That's all I knew. Something in Jerry had changed with that phone call. I could see it in his face and could feel his sense of urgency. I grabbed my purse and we walked out without telling anyone we were leaving or why. We just left.

On the way out to the car, I angrily asked Jerry, "Who told them they could go to the store?"

"I did. So, if you want to blame me, go right ahead," he snapped back.

I knew it wasn't Jerry's fault, but I was just so shocked and confused.

"Tell me what happened."

The call came from our neighbor, Merle, Rochelle's dad. He told Jerry that on the way home from the store, the boys had been stopped by a man with a gun who took Jacob. Trevor and Aaron had run home and told Rochelle, then she called Merle. He was at our house and needed to hang up so he could call 911.

It was the longest drive of my life. It probably took only twenty-five minutes, but it felt like forever.

We didn't talk much; each of us was lost in our own terror. It was so dark out. *Where was Jacob?* What exactly were we dealing with? I couldn't take it anymore.

"Drive faster!" I screamed at Jerry.

"I'm already going seventy-five!" he said. "I don't want to get pulled over."

"Who cares!" I yelled back. "At least then we'll have a police escort!"

More silence.

I put the window down and let the warm October air blow in my face. I tried to shake myself back to reality. What was going on? Who would do this? *Why would someone take a child?* My brain raced with questions, but I couldn't sort them or say them out loud. I knew Jerry didn't have the answers, either.

More silence.

When we finally reached our road—91st Avenue, the same road the kids had taken to get to the Tom Thumb—we noticed a squad car in the parking lot of Styles and Cotton Dental Office. We saw more as we came to the top of the hill, about a half mile from our house. Already, there was police tape marking the scene, and we were stopped by police as we tried to drive past. We rolled down our windows and identified ourselves.

"Go home, and someone will be right up to the house to talk to you," the officer told us.

As we made the final turn into our cul-de-sac on that unseasonably warm October night, neither of us could have possibly known how much our lives would be forever changed.

{ Chapter 3 }

As soon as Jerry pulled into the driveway, I jumped out of the car and raced into the house. I ran up the stairs and threw my arms around Trevor, who was shaking with fear and adrenaline.

"What happened?" I asked him.

Trembling, he couldn't get the words out fast enough.

"We went to the store and on our way back, this man showed up out of nowhere and said 'Stop, I gotta gun.' He let me and Aaron go, but he took Jacob."

"Where did this happen?" I asked him. I was trying to be gentle, but couldn't disguise my desperation and panic.

"He walked up to us by Rassiers' driveway. We saw the gun. He told me and Aaron to run or he'd shoot. We thought he would let all of us go, but when we turned to look for Jacob, he was gone. He took him. Jacob never came. We ran home as fast as we could and told Rochelle to call 911."

Carmen was clinging to Jerry. For a moment, we said nothing as we just held them both tightly. As I glanced around, I saw Merle was there, but Rochelle was gone. Her mom, Scottie, had already taken her home.

Aaron sat huddled in the corner of our kitchen, biting his nails and looking like he wanted to disappear. As Jerry was talking to Bruce Bechtold, one of the sheriff's deputies, I felt like time was ticking away. It was past 10:00 PM, and according to what the boys had told us, Jacob had already been gone for over an hour. We needed to do something . . . right now.

I grabbed the phone and called my friend Judi Novak.

"You need to come over here and help us search the woods. Somebody took Jacob . . ."

Officer Bechtold cut me off.

"No," he said. "We'll do the searching. We have our officers out there. You need to stay home in case Jacob calls."

We heard someone at the front door as Sheriff Charlie Grafft and Detective Doug Pearce let themselves in. Officer Bechtold left to go join the search as Sheriff Grafft filled us in on what was happening. He assured us that all his officers were out searching the woods and doing everything they could to find Jacob. Volunteers from the St. Joseph Fire Department were also looking, as well as the Waite Park K-9 unit. According to the sheriff, at least fifty people were helping with the search.

"But just because we haven't found him yet, that doesn't mean he's not okay," he told us. "He could be tied to a tree or something."

What? *Oh my God.* My mind was racing.

"There's a helicopter in the Twin Cities with a searchlight, but it might take a while to get them up here. Should I call them?" he asked us.

"Yes! Please!" I begged him.

None of it made any sense. This couldn't really be happening.

Before coming over, Judi had made a few calls from home, and soon there were more people arriving at our house. Amy came home from her sleepover. Aaron's parents, Vic and Fran, arrived with their two younger daughters. My friend Nancy Bronson also came as soon as she heard what was happening.

Every time a car pulled up, we stared desperately out the window, hoping to see Jacob walking up the driveway. I just wanted this whole nightmare to be over. Everything felt so strange and ominous. Could this really be happening? Were we making a big deal out of nothing? I kept telling myself this couldn't be real. What exactly had happened on that dark road? Where on earth was Jacob?

Meanwhile, Sheriff Grafft and Detective Pearce sat Trevor and Aaron down at the kitchen table and began to question them again. They also tried to be gentle, but their questions were hard.

Did you see where the man took Jacob?

Did you see a vehicle?

Did you see headlights?

Did you hear a car engine start?

Did you hear a car door slam?

How big was he?

What did his voice sound like?

What was he wearing?

Did you hear anything?

Did you smell anything?

What color was his clothing?

What kind of mask was it?

What color was the gun?

What hand was he holding it in?

As the boys answered the detective's questions, they were both very clear about what had happened. They had gone to the Tom Thumb store to rent a movie. Trevor rode his bike, Jacob was riding my ten-speed, and Aaron was riding a push scooter. They decided on *The Naked Gun* and also bought some Blow Pops to eat on the way home. They were only a few blocks away and going slowly because it was so dark. There was no moon, and that stretch of road had no street lights.

When they started down the last hill to our house, a man dressed all in black suddenly came out of nowhere.

"Stop. I have a gun."

When Trevor's flashlight reflected off the shiny metal of the gun, the man told Trevor to shut off the flashlight, then told the boys to get off their bikes and lie down in the ditch or he would shoot. They quickly got off their bikes and did what they were told.

Once the boys were all lying facedown in the ditch, the man asked their ages. They all started talking at once, but the man pointed his gun at Trevor and said, "No, you!"

"I'm ten," he answered.

Next, he pointed the gun at Aaron.

"I'm eleven," he said.

Jacob answered last.

"I'm eleven years old," he said.

The man turned to Trevor again and said, "Run into the woods as fast as you can, or I'll shoot."

As Trevor took off running, the man looked at Aaron's face and repeated the same words.

"Run into the woods as fast as you can, or I'll shoot."

As he got up to run, Aaron saw the man grab Jacob's shoulder. By the time he caught up to Trevor and they stopped to look back, Jacob and the man were gone.

The two boys ran across the field as fast as they could. When they finally made it back to the house, less than a half mile away, they burst in the door and yelled, "Call 911! Someone took Jacob!" They were both out of breath and nearly hysterical as they tried to explain to Rochelle what had happened. They were making little sense, so Rochelle called her dad, who came running over from next door. Merle tried to calm the boys down so he could make sense of their story. When he realized what had happened, he called us at the Glenns' house, then immediately hung up and called 911.

The police were listening intently as the boys recounted the story, pressing for more details whenever they needed clarification. At one point, the questions got more pointed and jarring.

"Are you sure you weren't playing with a gun and Jacob got hurt and you're afraid to tell us?"

"Are you sure Jacob didn't just run away and you're covering for him?"

It hurt to listen to this, but the boys were adamant about what had happened. A man with a gun had taken Jacob.

After they finished interviewing the boys together, Detective Pearce and the sheriff met separately with Aaron and his parents. When they were finished, Detective Pearce left to go interview the employees at the Tom Thumb, and Sheriff Grafft left to return to the crime scene. Before leaving, he assured us he would keep us informed of what was happening.

"Should we call your mom?" Jerry asked me.

"No . . . I don't know. Yes."

We knew so little, but the word started to spread.

Sometime around midnight, I began to hear the helicopter searching overhead, getting progressively louder as the searchlight came closer to our house.

Thwop-thwop-thwop.

THWOP-THWOP-THWOP.

It was so loud in the still of the night, and the constant beat of the blades seemed to echo my heart as it pumped blood into my head.

One minute melted into the next. I had no concept of time. I just continued to stare out the window and pray that Jacob was safe. I couldn't bear to think of what might be happening to him. I just couldn't go there. Instead, I just kept talking to him and telling him to be strong.

Hold on, Jacob. We'll find you.

Thwop-thwop-thwop.

I continued to stare at the driveway, convinced Jacob would come walking up at any moment.

Where are you, Jacob?

Thwop-thwop-thwop.

Before long, another detective arrived at our house—Steve Mund from the Stearns County Sheriff's Office. He wanted to talk to Jerry and me.

"Is there anybody who likes Jacob 'too much'?"

"Is there anybody who always offers to take him places or buy him things?"

"Do you have any enemies or disgruntled employees?"

My head was swimming, and I couldn't think of one possible reason why someone would want to kidnap our son. The questioning continued, and each one conjured up more terrifying thoughts.

"Who is Jacob's dentist?"

"Who is his medical doctor?"

"Does he have any moles or birthmarks?"

"Does he have any scars or broken bones?"

I recalled the only other time Jacob had ridden my bike. He fell off, broke his arm, and spent most of the summer in a cast. I felt so bad for him that I somehow let him convince me to get a new puppy. Our first dog, Oliver, had recently passed away, and Jacob just knew that if he had a puppy, his arm wouldn't hurt as much. After some debate, Jerry and I conceded. We got a little black puppy from the local Humane Society. Jacob named him Marcus—after his favorite NFL player, Marcus Allen. Now, as I glanced at Marcus lying anxiously next to us, I could tell he knew something was wrong. He was missing Jacob too.

"He broke his right arm last year," I told the detective.

"How about scars?" he asked.

I remembered the time I'd taken Jacob in for stitches on his knee. Was it his right knee or left? I simply couldn't think straight. Even on a normal day, I probably wouldn't have been able to remember which knee it was, but nothing about this day was normal. Now it seemed so incredibly important. It made me feel better that Jerry couldn't remember, either.

"We're going to need a recent picture of Jacob," Detective Mund told us.

I got up and took his framed fifth-grade photo off the wall. He was wearing his favorite bright yellow sweater, which complemented his deep blue eyes.

"Will this work?" I asked. "It's from last year. They haven't gotten their new school pictures back yet."

I took the photo out of the frame and handed it to him. Removing Jacob's picture from the cluster of school pictures on the wall felt horrible. The blank space only made it more jarring and obvious that one of our children was missing.

Next, the investigators wanted to see Jacob's room. I was almost afraid to let them go in there because, suddenly, it seemed so personal—even sacred. This was where Jacob and Trevor slept, played with their friends, talked to their parakeets Polly and Petey, and got ready for school. Now it felt like a crime scene. Could Trevor even go in there anymore? Was I supposed to keep people out? How do you "crime-scene-ize" your child's bedroom?

They needed more photos . . . something more recent. I realized I probably still had film in my camera that I hadn't gotten developed yet. I told them we would look.

They wondered if we had shoes like what Jacob had been wearing. Of course, I knew we had an exact replica, because I'd just bought a pair of the same Nike high-tops for Trevor earlier that day. I quickly found them and gave them to the detective.

They also needed clothing he had recently worn for the search-and-rescue dogs that would be coming. My boys were awesome in their messiness, so Jacob's dirty clothes were strewn together on the floor with Trevor's. It took a little while for me to isolate something that was just his.

Although DNA analysis was a relatively new tool, they also wanted Jacob's toothbrush and hair samples. I had to pause and think about this. Jacob and Trevor shared combs and brushes (whenever they bothered to brush their hair at all), so that wouldn't work. They probably used each other's toothbrushes occasionally, too, so that wouldn't work either.

I dug through Jacob's hockey bag until I found his mouthguard. I knew this was definitely something he hadn't shared with anyone, but my heart paused. Suddenly, I was right there . . . putting the mouthguard into the boiling water, pulling it out and waiting for it to cool, helping Jacob fit it into his mouth, then watching as he bit down into the half-melted plastic. We'd stared at each other as we'd waited, both of us trying hard not to laugh.

Oh God, it hurt to turn that over.

Detective Pearce arrived with a sheriff's department telephone that could record calls. Detective Mund showed us how it worked and made sure we had plenty of blank tapes. He told us we needed to record every call, just in case someone called with a lead or demanded a ransom. We stared blankly at that phone, willing it to ring. Just one call. That's all it would take.

Just one simple call from Jacob telling us he was all right, or one tip that would lead us to him.

I had never felt so helpless. I was a problem solver, used to taking charge and fixing things. I wanted to search, I wanted to help, I wanted to do *anything* to help find Jacob, but there was nothing I could do but work with the police and wait.

Jerry called a friend from his Baha'i group to start a phone tree asking for prayers. A little later, several from the group stopped by the house to say prayers and be there as support for us. One friend, Vern Iverson, drove up from Elk River that night after receiving the call. He arrived around 1:30 AM and told us he'd recently seen a news story about an abducted child who had been found because his picture had been on TV.

"You have to get Jacob's picture on TV!" he kept telling us.

Vern worked as a chemist at Medtronic, and while he didn't have a professional media background, he was adamant that we needed to get Jacob's picture out to the public immediately.

But would it really come to that? Jacob's picture on TV? Already I was frustrated with the media. WJON, a local radio station, was reporting that a child had been lost in the woods in St. Joseph, and I was furious. I called WJON and said, "He isn't *lost* in the woods! He was *kidnapped!*"

"I'm sorry, ma'am," they told me. "We can only report what the police are reporting."

Later, when Sheriff Graft stopped back, I asked if we could start contacting the media to get the correct story out there so that everyone would be searching for Jacob on their way to work Monday morning. He agreed that would be a good idea, but wanted to run it by some people first.

In the meantime, we waited. I was hyperalert, stuck in a never-ending adrenaline rush. It was like seeing a car pull out in front of you, knowing you're about to crash, but never getting past that initial surge of adrenaline. I was probably in shock, unable to function.

My friend Nancy sat with Carmen at the top of our steps, holding her as she continued to stare at the front door and wait for her brother to come home. When Carmen finally fell asleep, Nancy picked her up and gently carried her off to bed.

Vic, Fran, and Aaron stayed the night. At some point, Fran lay down with Aaron and Trevor in our bedroom to try to settle them down. Eventually, they also faded off to a short and fitful sleep.

It was very late when Jerry's sister, Joan, my brother, Russ, and my mom arrived from the Twin Cities. Oddly, I remember Russ looking so very young when they first walked in. It was almost like we were both young again, just kids, with my mom there to take care of us. The power of her "mom-ness" was strong. She didn't know what we were dealing with either—what to say or what to do—but she was there for me, and she would continue to be there, as long as I needed her. This brought amazing comfort to me, just to feel her presence, hear her beautiful voice, wrap myself in her warmth, and breathe in the smell of her Merle Norman face cream.

{ Chapter 4 }

My mother brought a moment of relief, a glimmer of solace. She was very good at that. She was also a powerhouse. People often ask me where I find my strength, and without a doubt, I can say it was from her.

Eunice Potter (or Eunie as her friends called her) had a beautiful soprano voice, and when I was little, it reminded me of angels singing. To make extra money, she often sang at weddings and funerals, and my very favorite of her solos was "You'll Never Walk Alone." No matter what she faced, she always had the courage to carry on with hope in her heart.

My father was Bob Earley, a full-blooded Irishman from the Merriam Park East neighborhood of St. Paul. He and my mom were high school sweethearts and graduated together from St. Paul Central High School in 1937.

They were married in St. Paul, and soon after, my oldest sister Margaret Ellen (Peggy) was born in January 1944. She was followed by Nancy Ann in 1946 and Barbara Jean (Barbi) in 1947. My father's work as an insurance examiner took us to North Platte, Nebraska, so when I came along in 1949, my parents nicknamed me "the Nebraskan Special" since I was the only Earley girl not born in Minnesota.

On March 21, 1950, just four months after I was born, my father's car was struck by a train while he was driving through a railroad crossing near our home. He lived, but he was severely injured. For almost a year, my mother provided full-time nursing care, while my sister Peggy, only six at the time, was given the daunting responsibility of helping to care for her younger sisters.

Slowly, my father recovered, but his condition was complicated by his type 1 diabetes. Our family moved back to St. Paul in 1953 and lived with my Grandpa and Grandma Potter for a while, so my parents could get back on their feet.

Just a year later, on December 15, 1954, my father died. An infection in his shoulder (which had been wired together after his accident) got into his blood, and his body's ability to fight the infection was compromised by his advanced diabetes. He was only thirty-six.

I was in kindergarten by this time and old enough to understand my dad had been sick, but I had never before known anyone who actually died. What happened? Where did he go? Would I ever see him again?

Sensing my fear and confusion, my mom arranged a meeting with my kindergarten teacher, Miss Trchka, to try to explain death in words I could understand.

"Patty, your mom and I just wanted to talk to you about your dad and answer any questions you might have about his death."

We were sitting at one of the kids' tables, which was way too small for Mom and Miss Trchka but perfect for me. I could smell the janitor's floor polish outside in the hall as I wondered what questions to ask.

Miss Trchka smiled gently. "It's good to remember your dad and to talk about him," she said. "You can always talk to me if you get sad during school, okay? You'll be safe here in my room."

My mom reached over and placed her hand on my chest. "Your father loved you so much," she told me. "Even though he's not here, he'll always be with you in your heart."

At thirty-six, my mom was now a widow and a single mother of four young girls. Thankfully, she had a strong faith and a deep connection to her church. We attended Plymouth Congregational Church on the corner of Princeton and Prior, and my sisters and I went to Sunday School every week. We were greatly supported by our church family during this time, and though I'm sure we lived on Social Security, we never felt poor. Mom never complained, and we were happy.

When I was in first grade, my mom fell in love with Russell Farrar King. They met at church, and though it hadn't been quite a year since my dad's death, my mom knew he was perfect.

"Bud," as everyone called him, was about thirty years old, a pharmacist, and he had never been married. He and his dad owned King's Pharmacy on the corner of St. Clair and Cleveland in St. Paul.

Bud and my mom married on September 10, 1955. Shortly after, he adopted all four of us girls, promising to be our dad and to always take care of us. He was happy and funny, and we knew he loved us so completely. To us, Bud was never our stepdad. He was always just Dad.

For the wedding, my mom found four matching jumpers at Montgomery Ward for my sisters and me to wear. They were grey plaid, and we wore light yellow blouses underneath. (I vividly remember this, because once I outgrew my jumper, I received Barbi's as a hand-me-down, and then Nancy's after that. By the time I finally inherited Peggy's jumper, I refused to wear it anymore.)

Shortly after they were married, our parents informed us that Mom was "expecting." My dad was so excited. Whenever a new customer came into King's Pharmacy, he told them he and my mom were "awaiting the birth of the newborn King."

Russell John King was born on August 29, 1956. On the day my parents finally brought him home from the hospital, my oldest sister Peggy, now twelve, made us all clean the house and even picked out a special dress for me to wear so we could all look our best. I was so accustomed to Peggy's constant mothering that I didn't even think to protest when she decided to cut my shoulder-length hair.

All my sisters had dark and straight hair, but mine was blond and curly. Every Saturday night, each of us took a bath, then Mom put curlers in Peggy's, Nancy's, and Barbi's hair so it would look nice on Sunday morning. As for me, Mom washed my hair, then sat with me on the couch as she combed it and twisted it around her finger, forming ringlets. It was naturally curly, and it would stay that way when it dried.

Now, as I watched the curls fall onto the kitchen floor, I grew more and more anxious. Would Mom be mad? When Peggy was finally done, she handed me the mirror and I began to feel a huge lump swell in my throat. My hair was now chopped short with crooked bangs, the curls gone completely. Trying hard not to cry, I handed the mirror back to Peggy and hurried off to put on my dress.

The four of us waited on the couch for what seemed like forever until we finally saw the car pull up to the curb. Excited, we jumped up and ran to open the door.

As Mom walked in with the new baby in her arms, we all scrambled to see his little face sticking out of the tightly wrapped blankets. After giving us a quick peek at our new brother, she finally stood up and got her first good look at me.

"Oh my," she said. "Who cut your hair?"

"Peggy!" Barbi shouted.

Mom looked at me, her head slightly askance, seemingly trying to find an angle that lessened the damage. I held my breath as my chin started to quiver.

"You look beautiful," she told me with a smile.

Later that night, Mom tucked me into bed, kissed me on the forehead, and quietly whispered in my ear.

"Don't worry. It'll grow back."

I drifted off to sleep feeling safe, loved, and forever comforted by the smell of her Merle Norman face cream.

{ Chapter 5 }

What kind of mother was I? I couldn't believe I'd lost Jacob. It was my job to be there for him, to make sure he was safe. Now he was gone, and I couldn't bear the guilt. Or maybe it was shame. How did this happen? What did we do wrong? I berated myself for going to our friends' house that night. Logically, I knew we hadn't done anything wrong, but I couldn't stand not knowing where Jacob was and not being able to be there for him.

It had been such a warm day, with a high of 73 degrees, but as the night wore on, the temperature dropped into the mid-40s. Jacob had been wearing a light jacket when he left to go to the store, and I knew it wasn't warm enough. I worried that he was out in the cold somewhere, shivering and scared. I got up from the couch and stepped out of the chaotic house onto our deck just to think and breathe. The air was so quiet and still. There was no wind, no moon, no stars. As I stared into that dark night sky, I just kept repeating over and over, "Where are you, Jacob? Where are you?" I felt like he was so close, but we just couldn't reach him.

Jerry, on the other hand, felt just the opposite. With every passing moment, he felt Jacob was another mile away. Interstate 94 went right by St. Joseph, so by now he figured they could be in Canada, North Dakota, Wisconsin, or Iowa. It was as if Jerry could feel Jacob slipping away with every tick of the clock. Even if I had wanted to, I couldn't have calmed him down. We were both suffering in our overactive minds, thinking crazy thoughts and asking questions no one could answer. We were lost in deep, irrational, horrible thoughts that no parent should have to endure.

Where are you, Jacob? Hold on. Be strong. We'll find you.

It was around 3:00 AM when we learned the search had been called off until daylight. Intellectually, I understood, but emotionally, I was devastated. *How could they just leave him out there?*

Deputy Bruce Bechtold stayed at our house throughout the night to keep us posted of law enforcement efforts. All night long, we brainstormed about possibilities, and at some point, I remembered Jacob's buddy from the VA. North Junior High had a program that paired kids with veterans from the St. Cloud VA Hospital. The students visited the VA each Wednesday and did activities with their VA buddies, or just chatted. Jacob's buddy's name was Ed, but that's all I knew. Jacob liked Ed a lot, but now I wondered if Ed was the type of person the investigators kept asking us about—someone who liked Jacob "too much."

Officer Bechtold passed the information along to Detective Mund, and within the hour—in the middle of the night—Detective Pearce was headed to North Junior High to meet Jacob's principal (Ray Pontinen) and his sixth-grade teacher (Jeanie Wittrock) to get the rest of the information on Ed.

By 4:00 AM, the investigators were at Ed's residence, questioning him. He was five feet, two inches tall and elderly, had difficulty walking, and could no longer drive. By 5:00 AM, he was cleared of any involvement. When I heard this, I felt like such a jerk. Ed had been a good friend to Jacob, and now this poor man had been traumatized by a police visit in the middle of the night. What was I *doing?* I felt terrible, but I was also desperate.

As night faded into early morning, the house settled down a little bit, and most people found a place to crash, although no one really slept. Jerry went downstairs to meditate, pray, and just close his eyes for a while. He couldn't sleep, either, but needed to clear his head. My mom suggested I also try to rest, but I couldn't. I sat on the couch, staring out the window, praying and trying to negotiate with God.

Take me, God. Bring Jacob home. Don't let him be hurt. Please God, take me.

This was a hurt deeper than anything I had ever known. My gut ached. I was hyper-focused but couldn't think clearly. Terrible thoughts kept creeping into my head, but I refused to let my mind go there. I literally sat up and shook my head to make them go away. Thinking the worst wouldn't help. I had to stay strong and keep sending out positive energy to help Jacob.

On top of my own trauma, I didn't know what to say or do for anyone else. It was both comforting and hard to have people over. Normally, I would be the one taking care of *them* . . . playing hostess, offering coffee, making sure everyone was comfortable, initiating conversation. But I couldn't do it. I was caught between "Why are you here?" and "Thank God you are here."

Stay strong, Jake. We're here. We'll find you. We'll bring you home and we will heal. I know your spirit is strong, and no matter what's happening, we'll handle it. We'll heal together and move forward.

Please God, just give me back my son.

At 5:00 AM it was still dark and cold. The late October sun wouldn't rise for another three hours, so the never-ending night dragged on and on.

Finally, Sheriff Grafft called and told us it was okay to get the story out to the public. He had already put out a press release and done a short interview with the *St. Cloud Times,* so Vern immediately left for Jerry's chiropractic office, where he could make phone calls to the media without tying up our home phone line. He needed a photo, so I found a wallet copy of Jacob's fifth-grade school picture and sent it with him. I knew this younger photo didn't show how much Jacob's face had changed and matured over the past year, but it didn't matter. There was such urgency in getting his picture out there, we just had to go with what we had. The sheriff's press release had used it, so at least we were being consistent.

Every moment, every decision felt just like this. We didn't have time to think, process, or consider. The information just kept coming at us, rapid fire, all day and all night. It was like standing in front of an out-of-control pitching machine. The balls just kept coming, one after another after another. We were being hit from all sides. Sometimes we'd manage to catch one and hold onto it for a second, but at the same time, dozens more went flying past. All we could do was try to catch as many as we could without getting knocked out by the speed and intensity of the information.

"The search will resume at 8:00 AM . . . "

"The DNR is bringing ATVs . . . "

"We have a temporary command center set up at the Del-Win Ballroom . . . "

"They'll be searching a two-mile radius . . . "

"There's a bloodhound coming from Minneapolis . . . "

"They're making casts of the tire tracks and the footprints they found in the driveway . . . "

"There's a hotline that's been set up at Tri-County Crime Stoppers . . . "

"Thousands of 'missing' flyers are being printed and distributed . . . "

"We need to file an official Missing Persons Report . . . "

"Stranger abductions like this are rare . . . "

"Could be a hate crime . . . "

"Definitely a sex crime . . . "

"Child molesters . . . "

"Sex offenders . . . "

There was just so much information to process, and all of it sounded awful. The investigators kept referring to Jacob's abduction as a sexually motivated crime, but I didn't understand—*couldn't* understand—how someone could sexually assault a little boy. I didn't want to believe it. Even though they kept telling us this was the usual motive in these types of cases, I knew they didn't know anything for sure, so I just kept thinking that anything was possible. Maybe someone had lost a child and was so distressed by it they'd stolen Jacob as a replacement. Or, maybe Jacob had been taken for ransom. Every time the phone rang, I ran to get it, hoping and praying it was Jacob or the man who took him. If he demanded money, we would get it. We'd sell our house and everything we owned just to get Jacob back.

By early morning, we'd already received so many phone calls that the police were worried about us tying up our only phone line. We were told someone from the telephone company would be coming over that day to drop a second telephone line across our backyard.

Investigators recommended we let friends and family take over answering the phone for us. At first, I was a little annoyed that I couldn't even answer my own phone in my own house, but the reality was, my brain wasn't working. Jerry and I also kept getting pulled away for more questions and meetings, so our close friends and family took shifts. They made notes on small scraps of paper and taped them to the kitchen cupboards. Eventually, Jerry grabbed one of the kids' school notebooks, so our helpers could keep a more logical record of all the calls. We glanced at their notes frequently to see who was calling, when, and why. Many times we needed an explanation of what had been written down, but at least things were getting captured.

By daybreak, the corrected story was running on WJON and had also started to appear on local and regional TV channels.

"An eleven-year-old St. Joseph boy was abducted near his home Sunday night by a masked gunman . . . "

The broadcasts sent chills down my spine. Hearing Jacob's name on the radio and seeing his face on TV made it all so real. There was no denying it. This was really happening.

{ Chapter 6 }

Around 8:30 AM, a squad car arrived at our house to take Trevor to the St. Joseph Police Department so he could make an official statement. All hell was breaking loose at home, so Jerry stayed behind to manage the chaos. We were told a second car would be arriving to pick up Aaron and his parents and take them to the Stearns County Sheriff's Office (SCSO) in downtown St. Cloud.

Running on zero sleep, my body moved on autopilot as I followed Trevor and the two detectives down the front walk and into the squad car. As we turned onto 91st Avenue, I got my first glimpse of the crime scene in the daylight. Yellow police tape lined both sides of the road and officers looked up from what they were doing to watch us pass. On my left, I could see the bikes and the scooter still lying in the ditch. Two of the neighbors' horses looked on with quiet curiosity, and I couldn't help but wonder what they'd witnessed here the night before. If only horses could talk.

We slowed to a stop.

"Trevor, can you point to the spot you first saw the guy approaching?" Detective Doug Pearce asked.

"Right over there at the end of the driveway," Trevor answered, pointing.

As he leaned across me to get a better look out my window, I put my hand on the back of his head and could feel his neck tight with anxiety. I gently rubbed his back as the car began to move again. He didn't say anything more as he leaned back into his seat, his solemn face resembling nothing of the playful boy he'd been just a day before.

The St. Joseph Police Department was located in the 2,500-square-foot building that also housed City Hall, the city council chambers, and a kitchenette they shared with the volunteer fire department and the St. Joe senior citizens who played cards there on Tuesdays. Jerry's chiropractic office was only a block away, and though the kids and I had walked all over town when we lived there, I had never once set foot inside the St. Joseph Police Department.

As we entered the cluttered building, Detective Pearce invited us to follow him to a small office in the back. He pulled up a chair so Trevor could sit across from him while Detective Mike Theis and I sat in two chairs off to the side.

Detective Pearce turned on a tape recorder. "Okay, Trevor, you're aware of why you're here, right?" he began. "You know why we're taking a statement from you, right?"

"Yeah," Trevor replied.

"It involves an incident in which you, your brother Jacob, and a friend, Aaron, went to the Tom Thumb store by your house, and when you were coming back something happened, right?"

As Detective Pearce asked the questions, Trevor did his best to retell his story with as much detail as he could remember. He told them what time he thought they left the house, how long it took to get to the store, whether they noticed anything unusual when they got there, how many people were working, how many customers were there, what they bought, and how long they were in the store.

My heart ached for Trevor, and I was horrified by what these boys had experienced. He was trying so hard to be brave, but he looked so small and scared as he did his best to answer the detective's questions. Even though Jerry and I had repeatedly told Trevor he'd done nothing wrong, everything about this felt wrong. Police stations were for bad guys, not ten-year-old boys. Still, I could tell Trevor was determined to do whatever he could to find Jacob. His story and details were just what he'd shared the night before, almost verbatim.

"Okay," Pearce continued. "Going home, when you were riding your bike, right after you left Tom Thumb, did you notice anything suspicious or unusual?"

"No."

"Okay, Trevor, can you tell us what this person initially said when you guys were riding by him?" Detective Pearce asked.

"He said 'Stop, I have a gun, turn off the flashlight, go in the ditch and face the other way.' And then he asked us all our ages."

My eyes darted between Trevor and the two detectives, praying they might be able to help him remember something that could lead us to Jacob.

"Okay, what did you guys do when he said that?"

"We just followed his orders."

"So you stopped?"

"Yeah. Because he had a gun. We saw it."

"Can you describe the gun?"

"It was sort of shiny."

"Was it a long gun? Or was it a pistol?"

"Pistol."

My heart leaped. Did he even know what a pistol was? Besides squirt guns in the summer, my kids had never been allowed to play with toy guns.

"Do you recall what hand he was holding it in?"

"The right."

"Okay. And this person, how was he dressed?"

"All in black, he had a mask on."

"What kind of mask?"

"Looked like pantyhose."

"Was the mask completely pulled over his face? Or was it partially down?"

"All the way down."

The detective continued to press Trevor for details about the mask, the man's clothing, his shoes, hands, gloves, voice.

"His voice was rough," Trevor told him. "It sounded like he had been smoking."

"Okay," Detective Pearce continued. "After you guys laid in the ditch, as he told you, did he walk over to you?"

"Yeah."

"What happened then?"

"He asked us all our ages."

"Whose age did he ask first?"

"Aaron's. He said 'Ages! You!' Then he pointed to him. And then he said, 'You!' to me. And then he said 'You!' to Jacob."

As Trevor's voice rose with tension, I caught myself holding my breath, my heart pounding wildly.

"Okay, what happened then?" Detective Pearce asked.

"Then he looked at Aaron's face and told me to run as fast as I could to the woods."

"As he is looking at Aaron's face?" Pearce questioned.

"No," Trevor replied. "He looked at Aaron's face first."

"Okay, who did he tell to run first, you or Aaron?"

"Me."

"Okay, and as you were running, then he told Aaron to run?"

"Yeah."

"Did you see the man and Jacob after you had left, after you had started running?"

"I didn't look back."

"Okay, did you hear anything?"

"Uh-uh."

After a few minutes, Detective Pearce turned the questioning over to Detective Theis.

"Trevor, did you hear or see any vehicles?"

"No."

"Okay. Can you describe this person that you saw? How much he might have weighed, or how big he was?"

Trevor named a neighbor who was about the same size as the man with the gun.

"So, about five ten in height?"

He looked at me. I nodded.

"How about his build?" Detective Theis continued. "Was he a large person? Like a heavier type?"

"Medium," Trevor replied.

"Did you notice any jewelry? Some fellas have earrings, or some may have a watch. Did you notice anything?"

"No."

"Did you notice any patches or insignias on his clothing?"

"No."

I could tell Trevor was wishing he had more to tell.

"Did he pause?" I asked suddenly. "Did he breathe heavy?" I found myself throwing out random questions trying to trigger any small detail.

"Uh-uh."

"Mike, do you have anything else?" Detective Pearce asked.

"No," he replied.

"Patty, can you think of anything we neglected to ask?"

"No," I said, wishing there was more, but also feeling anxious and protective for Trevor. He had done well, but I could sense his fear as he was forced to relive this nightmare once again. We'd arrived at 9:09 AM. It was now 9:23 AM. Detective Pearce turned off the tape recorder, and it was time to go.

When we returned home, Connie Cross and Dave Glenn from the College of St. Benedict in downtown St. Joe stopped by. Both had been at the Millstream Arts Festival wrap-up party the night before, but because we had left so abruptly, they had to find out about Jacob's abduction on the radio while driving to work Monday morning. They came to lend their support with anything the college could offer, including meeting space, tables, chairs, or food. I was so grateful, but really, I had no idea what we might need in the future. All I could think about was what we needed right now. We needed Jacob.

We began keeping track of in-kind offers like these on the notes that our phone volunteers kept sticking to the kitchen cupboards. As I added another note to the growing collage, I was amazed at people's generosity and what they thought to offer. I simply couldn't grasp it. I was worthless at managing anything, and I felt worthless inside. I didn't know what to do.

Father Tom Gillespie, from St. Joseph Catholic Church, stopped by, along with Matthew ("Matti") Feeney, the church's youth minister. We weren't Catholic, but the church was the hub of our community. Jerry and I both appreciated the visit, along with their offer to help in any way they could. Matti gave me his business card and told me to call if there was anything he could do to help with our other children. On the back of his card, he wrote, "Fridays are movie nights, 7:00 PM," and he included his home address.

After they left, I taped the business card to the cupboards alongside everything else, knowing full well our kids would never want to attend movie night with someone they didn't even know. The gap between our current crisis and movie night was so vast, I simply had no words.

By midmorning, we were summoned to our neighbors' house to go talk to the FBI. The intention was to get us out of the chaos that had become our home, and although I was grateful for the temporary sanctuary and quiet, it was incredibly difficult to leave.

"What if Jacob calls?" I asked them. "I need to be here!"

The agents assured me it would be a short meeting, so I conceded. As we walked across the cul-de-sac to the Welters' home, it was hard to get past the fact that, just yesterday, our boys and their boys had been playing football together right here in our nice, safe little neighborhood. Twenty-four hours later, we were on our way to meet with the FBI. Unbelievable.

As we entered the house, I realized I'd never even been inside the Welters' home. We were shuffled into the living room and introduced to Jeff Jamar, special agent in charge (SAC) of the Minneapolis Bureau of the FBI; Allen Garber, a special agent with the FBI office in Minneapolis; and Al Catallo, an agent with the local FBI office in St. Cloud. Until that moment, I had no idea there even *was* an FBI office in St. Cloud.

Garber had just come up that morning after receiving a call the previous night from Catallo. He told us he would be heading up the multijurisdictional task force that had been set up to help find Jacob. I tried to listen to what they were saying, but I didn't understand any of it. There were so many different agencies involved. Besides the SCSO and the St. Joseph Police, the new task force also included the local and regional offices of the FBI, the Minnesota Bureau of Criminal Apprehension (BCA), and the Tri-County Major Crimes Unit, which included the sheriffs' offices of Stearns, Benton, and Sherburne Counties. I didn't understand the differences among these agencies or their jurisdictions. I couldn't identify the officers by their uniforms, and I didn't know the hierarchy behind their titles—chief deputy, captain, sergeant, detective, patrol officer, agent, special agent. It suddenly felt like I was in a different country and didn't know the language or any of the customs. I knew nothing about crime; I just needed to know that they were all working together to find Jacob.

As promised, it was a short meeting. The agents introduced themselves and gave us a brief update on what they were doing. They told us what would happen next with the investigation, and what they would need from us to help find Jacob. They also asked us a few questions, which we answered readily.

"I'm going to have to ask you to be patient," Al Garber said to us.

I glared at him. "You can ask me anything you want, but don't ask me to be patient! Jacob is my son!"

Garber apologized, then handed me his card.

"You can call me any time, day or night," Garber said as we stood to leave.

True to his word, he never asked me to be patient again.

{ Chapter 7 }

By the time Jerry and I returned to our house, everything felt ominous and strange. The chaos had mounted to such an excruciating level, it didn't even feel like our house anymore. I stared at the mountain of unfamiliar shoes in our entryway and suddenly became completely unhinged. I needed to see Jacob's shoes there. I wanted to see them kicked haphazardly onto the mat like always, and his hockey jacket thrown sloppily over the railing. I wanted it to be *our* house again—*our* shoes, *our* mess, *our* chaos. There were six of us who lived here, not five, and not twenty-five. If there were twenty-five pairs of shoes in our entryway, it meant we were having a party . . . not this.

Because of Vern's phone calls and connections, the media was responding in full force to Jacob's story. TV crews were already in St. Joseph, taking footage of the crime scene, talking to residents, and reporting on the community's response. We had no idea what was happening outside our own little bubble. We learned of the activities and events in bits and pieces, mostly from friends or neighbors who stopped by or called with news and information.

The sheriff's office was being flooded with calls, not only about tips and suspects, but from people offering to help.

Local print shops were donating thousands of flyers, and students from St. Ben's had volunteered to hang and distribute them around the area.

Volunteers from St. John's University were helping with the ground search.

Local businesses were setting out donation jars to help raise money for a search and reward fund.

A prayer march was being planned for later that afternoon, starting at St. Ben's and ending at the Del-Win Ballroom (which had become the search headquarters).

Every tidbit we learned about St. Joe's response to Jacob's kidnapping brought a new sense of hope, but also a harsh dose of reality. Someone had snagged a flyer from town and brought it back to the house to show us. Just seeing my beautiful son's innocent picture on a missing flyer was like someone throwing a dagger into my heart. I broke down in sobs.

Our friend Vern had worked so hard to generate media exposure for Jacob, and suddenly everyone wanted to talk to us—as soon as possible. We wanted the media's help, but that meant we would have to speak to them. What would we say? What *could* we say? We hadn't slept, eaten, or even showered, but we were so desperate to get Jacob's picture and story out there, we said yes to almost every request.

I had no idea what I was doing, but I trusted Vern's judgment. If everybody was looking for Jacob at every truck stop and rest area across the country, surely he would be found quickly. We were willing to put ourselves out there and do whatever it took to get our son back.

The reporters came from everywhere. They came for the story, but they also came because they truly cared. Many of them were parents themselves and wanted to help us find Jacob.

We had a steady stream of people around us all day long, yet I had never felt so alone. I couldn't sleep or eat, and I felt myself sinking into a dark abyss. The void in my heart was indescribable. I finally had to lock myself in the bathroom so I could fall apart in private. I heard someone laugh outside the door and it made me furious. How could they be laughing when my whole world was spinning apart? I forced myself to pull it together and splashed water on my face. As I reached for a towel and stared into the mirror, I saw a woman I barely recognized. My face was pale, gaunt, with dark circles under my eyes and new worry lines between my brows.

Eat something, Patty. You have to eat.

Six years earlier, when I was thirty-three, I was diagnosed with type 1 diabetes. I was just three years younger than my father was when he died from complications of the same disease.

The thought terrified me, but I was determined to manage my diabetes without having to be dependent on insulin or any other drug. Jerry referred me to a chiropractor he knew from college who had had good results managing diabetes through diet and exercise. Twice a week, while the kids were in school, I made the two-hour drive to Mankato for an office visit, then turned around and made the two-hour drive home. I went on the low-fat, high-fiber Pritiken diet, had regular chiropractic adjustments, and also had acupuncture treatments.

I kept this up for almost two years, and though I was conscientious, it was difficult. I reasoned that if a person could live like a monk on a mountaintop in a totally stress-free environment, meditate and exercise daily, eat only the purest of foods, and dedicate their entire life to mind, body, and spirit—well, maybe then a person might be able to manage this disease naturally. I wanted to live as actively and strongly as I could, but I had four kids and felt like I was losing the battle. I had dropped to eighty-seven pounds and was scared that, without help, I might actually die, like my father.

I finally went to an endocrinologist and was admitted to the hospital at the end of February 1986. I learned how to test my blood sugar, calibrate how much insulin I needed to take before each meal, and give myself daily shots. It was a whole new way of life for me, and one that I wasn't looking forward to starting.

I was in the hospital for almost a week, and a few days before I was released, I found myself staring at the calendar in my hospital room. It was Sunday, March 2, but the weekend dates were combined on this calendar, so the date actually read March ½ (March 1 for Saturday and March 2 for Sunday).

On that day, that's exactly how I felt . . . like one half of a person. I felt powerless, frustrated, depressed, and so scared that I might not even survive this horrible disease. I honestly felt like my quality of life had been diminished to about one half of what it had been before the diabetes.

Two days later, when I finally left the hospital, it was March 4—my favorite date of the year. Instead of viewing it as a date on a calendar, I chose to acknowledge it as a command: "March forth!"

And so I did. I embraced this date as my new personal beginning, and I marched forth.

I walked out of the bathroom, grabbed a paper plate, and forced myself to eat something from the growing collection of slow cookers that had appeared on our kitchen counter.

Later that evening, our good friends Dan and Mary Kay Carle stopped by to check on us. They were both licensed therapists, and they brought a new sense of support and calm to the chaos.

"I believe you have only one option," Dan told us that night. "You have to believe that Jacob is okay and he's coming home."

I needed to hear this. One detective had already told me, "We'll find Jacob. He's probably dead, but we'll find him." I couldn't take it. I couldn't think the worst. There was no reason for me to believe he wasn't coming home, so, instead, I chose to believe that he would.

My hope was stronger than their doubts, and for the rest of this very long journey, it was hope that would sustain and carry me.

{ Chapter 8 }

Another night came and went. Monday had been hard, but the nighttime was even worse. I was grateful for the quiet when everyone left or went to bed, but still, I couldn't sleep. How could I sleep in a warm cozy bed when Jacob was still out there somewhere, certainly *not* sleeping in a warm cozy bed. I felt guilty eating or showering, because I knew he wasn't enjoying those same comforts. Anything normal felt like a betrayal. When I tried to close my eyes, I could see his face in the shadows, but it wasn't his face. It lacked joy, and there was no smile. Again, I had to sit up and shake my head to get rid of the bad images.

By Tuesday morning, I was suffering from severe sleep deprivation. There still wasn't any news of Jacob, and I wasn't sure I had the strength or energy to face another day with more terrifying information to sort and process. All I could do was hold Amy, Trevor, and Carmen as closely as I could and reassure them we were doing everything we could to find their brother. I had no idea how to parent my kids through this tragedy and begged for help from friends and family to be there for them when I couldn't.

There were so many leads coming in, but nothing solid or specific that could lead us to Jacob or the man who took him. We knew investigators were following up on calls from neighbors about suspicious vehicles that were spotted in recent weeks, as well as reports from the public about known sex offenders who were living in the area. Al Garber also shared one solid lead with us about a nine-year-old boy from St. Joseph who had been approached by a man in a light-colored van earlier that summer and asked if he wanted a ride. They were interviewing the boy and his parents, and also sending in an artist from Washington, DC, to prepare a sketch.

Everything sounded so dark and ominous. However, some things started happening that gave us renewed hope and energy.

Ken Twit, the local pharmacist in St. Joe, quickly stepped up to help with the media. We wanted to keep getting Jacob's story out there, but the interviews became increasingly difficult and emotionally draining when we found ourselves having to repeat everything over and over. The coordinated press conferences helped, but we also knew each media outlet appreciated even one direct comment. We wanted to be able to provide that whenever we could.

Ken was able to be our spokesperson when we weren't available. He was also one of nine community members who very quickly formed the Friends of Jacob office in the basement of the local bank to help organize everything that needed to be done. He was joined by my friend Donna Blanchette (Kevin's wife) and a diverse group of people (all with full-time jobs) who pulled together to help organize volunteers and put them to work.

The Friends of Jacob found a more permanent space in the basement of Jerry Frieler's accounting office in downtown St. Joe. It had its own separate entrance, with a large open room in front and private offices in the back. The Friends group also found donors who arranged for phones and computer equipment. St. Ben's provided tables and chairs, and Jerry Frieler offered a few desks. Everything was pulled together so quickly. They set up a bank account for the "search and reward" money that started coming in, and soon, the Friends of Jacob group was helping to distribute flyers they printed, white ribbons that had been donated by 3M, and "Missing" buttons with Jacob's school picture—an idea started by a fellow student of Jacob's at North Junior High.

Another great help was the arrival of my sister Barbi, who lived in San Francisco. A major 6.9-magnitude earthquake had struck the Bay Area a week earlier, taking down part of the Bay Bridge, shutting down communications, interfering with telephone lines, and bringing transportation virtually to a standstill.

But in spite of all the challenges, Barbi was fiercely independent and managed to get a flight out on Tuesday, October 24. She arrived in St. Joe that evening, and as soon as she walked in the door, we hugged and cried. There were no words between us as we stood in the entryway with our arms wrapped around one another.

"I'm here. I won't leave you," she assured me, refusing to let go.

As I sobbed into her shoulder, all I could do was hug her tighter, so relieved she was finally here.

Our family made our first public appearance on Wednesday morning at a prayer vigil at St. Joseph Catholic Church. By now, we'd had many family discussions with our kids about what was happening, because we never wanted them to be caught off guard. When we learned about the prayer vigil, we discussed it as a family and decided to go. Two of our good friends offered to stay back to answer phones, just in case Jacob called or walked up the driveway.

That morning, Jerry and I, along with our kids and our whole extended family, piled into a few cars and drove together to the church. We held onto each other as we entered, and it was absolutely overwhelming to see so many people there—all for Jacob, and for us. We shed many tears as we tried to absorb the magnitude of what we were experiencing. I'd never seen Amy, Trevor, or Carmen cry so hard, and I worried whether being here at this service was too much for them. The vigil felt as somber as a funeral, and while we were all devastated by this sudden and confusing loss, we still carried hope in our hearts. Our emotions were all over the place.

After returning home, I was physically and emotionally spent. I'd gone three nights with very little sleep. My friend Joan Collins-Marotte finally convinced me to lie down and she put on a cassette tape to help me relax. As I closed my eyes, I became lost in memories as I realized what album it was—*Teaching Peace* by Red Grammer.

Our family had just seen Red Grammer perform for the first time about a month earlier. Seven of us had piled into the station wagon for a road trip to Green Lake, Wisconsin—Jerry, myself, Amy, Jacob, Trevor, Carmen, and our favorite babysitter, Shannon, who lived with us on and off and was more like an adopted daughter by this time. Shannon first came to live with us during her sophomore year of high school, when she was having trouble at home. All our kids loved her and thought of her more like a big sister than a babysitter. She was eventually placed in a licensed foster home, but we remained her "family" and hosted her graduation party after high school.

I was happy Shannon had agreed to join us on this family getaway. It was the Twentieth Annual Green Lake Baha'i Conference, and for three days we enjoyed classes and activities, both indoors and out, experiencing nature in all its glory. On the last evening, we were treated to a concert by singer/songwriter Red Grammer. I'd never heard of him before, but his songs of peace and compassion were contagious. We purchased three of his tapes and listened to them on the seven-hour drive home.

Now, as I listened to the music, so many memories of Green Lake floated through my brain. I could see the scenic nature trails and the blue skies and water. I could feel the fun and hear the laughter. Slowly, I began to feel the tension lessening. I had just started to doze off when the last song on the tape began to play. It started with the sound of a gentle heartbeat in the background.

Listen . . . can you hear the sound
Of hearts beating all the world around

I bolted upright in bed. "Listen." This was Jacob's favorite song. As I listened to the familiar sound of the heartbeat in the background, I was suddenly right there in the car again, watching and laughing as Jacob grabbed Carmen's foot and used it as a microphone as he sang along to the chorus.

Black or white, red or tan
It's the heart of the family of man
Whoa beating away
Whoa beating away
Whoa beating away

With each beat of the music, I could feel my own heartbeat inside my chest. I just knew if Jacob could hear this song on the radio, he'd immediately remember our family road trip and know we were searching for him—all the world around. I jumped out of bed and asked Joan if she would take it to the radio station and see if they would play it for Jacob as a message of hope from his family. Then he would know not to give up. I just knew this mattered, and for the first time in three nightmarish days, I felt a glimmer of hope, a renewed faith, and the strength of this unified heartbeat of humanity reaching Jacob.

Joan took the tape to KISS-FM at Crossroads Center mall and asked the station owner, Pat McKay, if he would play the song "Listen" and dedicate it to Jacob. Not only did he agree to play it, he played the song repeatedly . . . at the top of every hour for the rest of the week. He also started making copies of the song and contacting other radio stations all across Minnesota. He had the tapes delivered throughout the state by Greyhound bus and arranged for all the participating stations to play "Listen" at exactly 7:00 AM on Friday morning. He also invited our family to come to the mall for the live simulcast and encouraged me to make an on-air appeal to Jacob and the man who took him. Up to that point, I'd depended on Jerry to be the family spokesperson because I was just too broken. But this time, I believed with all my being that I could do it. This could work.

{ Chapter 9 }

The next day, Thursday, October 26, was incredibly busy. The search headquarters had been relocated from the Del-Win Ballroom in St. Joseph to
the Law Enforcement Center in St. Cloud, and there were now fifty officers
working on Jacob's case, including twenty FBI agents. At 11:30 AM, a volunteer posse of thirty horse riders from five different counties began searching
an area about one mile east of St. Joseph. At about the same time, the sheriff
held a press conference at the Law Enforcement Center (LEC) in St. Cloud.

While all this was happening, Governor Rudy Perpich flew up to St. Joseph to personally speak with Jerry and me. His helicopter landed in the
field right at the end of our circle, and as we watched, Governor Perpich,
Lieutenant Governor Marlene Johnson, and Transportation Commissioner
Leonard Levine all walked up the driveway to our house. It was surreal.

The governor was incredibly kind and compassionate. He took the time
to talk to our kids and asked how each of them was doing. He also shared his
commitment to finding their brother. After the family introductions, Jerry
and I led the group downstairs to talk about the search. The governor asked
how we were all holding up, especially Trevor. He wanted us to know that
we had his absolute support, and he agreed to activate the National Guard
for a ground search on Saturday. He also assured us if we needed anything
else, anything at all, to just call his office and let them know. We were so
touched by his sincerity. He had orchestrated our meeting to take place quietly, under the radar, while all the media was diverted to the sheriff's press
conference in downtown St. Cloud.

Also on Thursday, the FBI alerted us to a group of anonymous business-
men from the Twin Cities who were offering a $100,000 reward for Jacob's
safe return within seventy-two hours. With that announcement, Sheriff
Grafft assigned full-time officers to answer our phone and be stationed in
our home 24/7 for the next few weeks.

We did our first national interview with *A Current Affair* on Thursday afternoon. It was impossible to find a quiet corner in our own home, so the Jerzaks offered to let us do the interview next door at their house. Barbi helped me choose something to wear and fixed my hair because I just didn't care. She insisted that I at least try to look presentable on national television.

They taped us sitting at the Jerzaks' kitchen table, and through tears, I did my best just to string words together.

"This shouldn't happen anywhere. . . . Who would take a child away from their parents? I couldn't fathom it. . . . We taught him that people are good. We've worked for peace all our lives, and this is a real violent act. I don't understand it."

Once again, Jerry did most of the talking. Toward the end, they asked me about Jacob.

"He's bright. He's got a real clever sense of humor and a quick mind. . . . He plays goalie. He's cool under pressure. All these things give me hope that, if there's an opportunity, this boy will be home."

"Is he a survivor?" the reporter asked me.

"He's a survivor," I replied with conviction.

After the interview, they asked if we had any home video footage of Jacob. I ran home to look and found a video that had just been taken earlier that summer as we were standing in the driveway. Jacob was looking straight into the camera before he turned and ran up to Jerry and me, then jumped into Jerry's arms for a hug. I was afraid to hand over the video, but they assured me they would make a copy and return it shortly. Within hours, they had not only made a copy for their 6:30 PM broadcast, but also provided copies for all the local TV affiliates, including their competition. We were told this was unprecedented and were so grateful for their extra kindness and cooperation. I felt in my heart that all the media were working their hardest to help us find Jacob.

That night, we gathered around the TV with our family and friends to watch *A Current Affair*. It was short and dramatic, with the show's scary music in the background, but they announced the new $100,000 reward and posted the toll-free number.

Not long after the show aired, people began calling the toll-free hotline and turning in Jerry. At least fifty people called him in as a suspect because they didn't like the way he looked on TV. He was too calm. He didn't cry.

He didn't look as terrified or angry as they thought he should be. It was awful.

I asked FBI Special Agent Al Garber to call me twice a day. I didn't want to bug him all the time with my questions, but I needed some structure in my life. Al agreed to call me after the morning briefing and again after the evening briefing. In between phone calls, I would write down my thoughts or questions so I would be ready for him when he called. Sometimes, that second phone call came late at night, but I always knew he would call. That was so important to me.

The investigators couldn't tell us everything that was going on, but they shared enough to instill our confidence in the investigation and the search. Every so often, they would run names by us, but they didn't want us to get too excited over any specific lead, only to be let down.

"You'll see me excited when Jacob walks through that door," I told them. "Until then, I won't hold my breath over any particular lead. But please, just tell me what's going on. I need to know the facts."

This had already become an issue when I stumbled across Jerry and Vic Larson, Aaron's dad, having a quiet conversation about Aaron. I heard only enough to hit the ceiling.

"*What?* And you didn't tell me?"

For the first time, I learned that Aaron had been groped by the man who had taken Jacob. As the boys had been walking to go lie down in the ditch, the man had reached around and groped Aaron's crotch. Suddenly, I understood why the sheriff kept telling everyone this was a sexually motivated crime.

Aaron had shared this detail on Monday morning, when he gave his statement at the SCSO. I wasn't exactly sure when Jerry had first learned about it, but I was livid to learn he'd been keeping secrets from me. I knew he was only trying to protect me from another harsh reality, but I didn't want to be protected. *How dare he and the investigators keep this from me?* No facts could possibly be worse than the awful things I had already created in my own head.

From this point on, I begged that no one keep secrets from me, including Al Garber. I assured him I could handle the truth. What I couldn't handle was deception.

In many ways, this changed everything. Now I *knew* it was a sexually motivated crime, and what did that mean for Jacob? What kind of pervert were we dealing with? What was Jacob having to go through? A whole new set of nightmares began, and once again, I found myself having to shake more horrible images from my brain.

The one thing I absolutely couldn't deal with was the never-ending parade of psychics. They started calling almost right away, and Jerry offered to talk to them because I just couldn't. One time, a psychic came to our house and Jerry begged me to talk to her. She asked me to sit on the lower bunk in Jacob and Trevor's room, then she sat next to me and told me to hold my hand out, palm facing up. Next, she put her hand just above mine, but not touching. We sat like that for what seemed like forever, then she finally told me I could put my hand down.

"You can find him," she told me as she stared me straight in the eye. "You can find Jacob."

I just about decked her. I stood up and said, "If I could find him, he would be home!"

So many of these psychics told me they could sense how close Jacob and I were to each other, and they believed our closeness was the key to finding him. I desperately wanted to believe this, but try as I might, I couldn't.

After a while, I refused to talk to any more psychics. Their painful images and harsh premonitions did nothing to help me. Often, they would say things like, "He's getting weaker. You're running out of time." Or, once a psychic told Amy, Trevor, and Carmen that Jacob would be home by July 20. I was incensed. I knew that when that date came and went, it would be just one more unnecessary disappointment for our kids. We had enough to face without people like this fabricating any more.

On Friday morning, October 27, our whole family got up extra early and drove to Crossroads Center in St. Cloud for the radio station's live simulcast of the song "Listen." At least twenty close friends and family members gathered in the hall outside KISS-FM as I stood in front of the live mic and made a tearful appeal to the man who took Jacob.

"I just want Jacob to know that this song is for him to hear. The heartbeat of humanity is beating for him. I know it will give him strength, and if there's an ounce of compassion in the man who is holding him, he will let him go safely. Listen, Jacob. Can you hear our prayers? We love you."

My message for Jacob was simulcast live on KXSS in St. Cloud and KS95 in Minneapolis, and at exactly 7:00 AM, the song "Listen" rang out on dozens of other radio stations throughout Minnesota. I so much believed in these powerful words that were uniting the heartbeat of humanity to help us find our son, Jacob.

Listen . . . can you hear the sound
Of hearts beating all the world around
Down in the valley, out on the plain
Everywhere around the world a heartbeat sounds the same

Black or white, red or tan
It's the heart of the family of man
Whoa beating away
Whoa beating away
Whoa beating away

I was vaguely aware that we should have asked for permission to copy Red Grammer's song and broadcast it this way, but I so badly wanted Jacob to hear the heartbeat of humanity searching for him, I didn't even think about it.

A few days later, I got a call from Red. As I stammered through an apology, I tried to explain how grateful I was for him and the strength his song had given us in our search for Jacob.

"No problem," he interrupted. "What can I do to help?"

He made plans to fly to Minnesota and visit the St. Joe schools on Halloween so he could perform impromptu concerts for the kids. I was so grateful.

We began to sing this song every evening as we held hands and prayed for Jacob's safe return. For our family, Red would truly become a shining light in the devastating darkness.

{ Chapter 10 }

As the days dragged on, I worried about the emotional toll this was taking on our kids. Amy was so quiet. She didn't like having so many extra people around and spent a lot of time alone in her room. When she couldn't handle all the chaos, she would often escape to Rochelle's house next door. Rochelle was there that night, so Amy didn't have to explain anything to her. They were both going through this nightmare together.

Carmen returned to sucking her thumb and needed a lot of extra hugs and comfort. At eight years old she couldn't possibly understand what was going on. My mom, Shannon, and Nancy Bronson all gave her a lot of extra love and attention to help her navigate this scary new world.

Trevor needed constant company and never wanted to be alone. He spent his days playing basketball in the driveway, going bowling with friends, and keeping busy. He appeared to be okay on the outside, but at night, he would crawl into bed with Jerry and me and just sob. When he would finally drift off, he thrashed around all night long in fits and starts. He got very little sleep, and I worried how he would ever overcome what he had witnessed that night.

My friend Kevin called to confirm that I wouldn't be accepting the math teacher position at St. John's Prep. He figured as much, but the headmaster had asked him to check with me, just to be sure. It had been only a few weeks since the interview, but it was hard to even remember the woman I'd been then—a woman with dreams of her future. Right now, all I could do was try to survive the moment-to-moment-ness of my new reality.

New hope arrived on Saturday, October 28, when one hundred National Guard members from the 1st Battalion of the 136th Infantry in St. Cloud came to St. Joseph to help with the search. We were told there was even a waiting list for additional guard members, because so many had responded to the call. In a show of support, each one wore a white "Jacob's Hope" ribbon tied to their fatigues.

The guard members were joined by DNR agents, law enforcement officers, mounted police, and volunteers, for a total of nearly three hundred searchers. The plan was to cover every square inch of St. Joseph Township, plus another sixty square miles of surrounding area. It was a massive effort that also included helicopters from the National Guard, DNR, and State Patrol. If Jacob was still in the area, I was confident they would find him.

That morning, I watched out our window as the searchers walked shoulder-to-shoulder through our yard. It was like experiencing something from a Stephen King movie, only this was real. No one spoke as they combed our property, moving like water washing over rocks, then seeping into the next property, and then the next.

Later that afternoon, students from Saints Peter and Paul Middle School held a rally for Jacob at the municipal arena in St. Cloud. This event was especially meaningful to us because it had been organized by the kids. I had no idea what to expect, but I knew how deeply all the children in our region were hurt and scared by Jacob's abduction. Our entire family chose to attend, so once again, we piled into a few cars and drove the six miles to the arena.

As we arrived, we were shocked to see well over a thousand people gathered for the event. It was the strongest show of public support we had yet encountered.

The rally was held in the parking lot of what we had always called the West Arena. This was where Jacob had practiced hockey, played in the Squirts Hockey League, and attended Hockey Goalie Camp just one year earlier. It was a place laden with memories.

We were guided to the front of the crowd, where we all sat on the blacktop and waited. The rally started with a song by The Crayons, a musical group of boys and girls in grades three through six from the St. Cloud area Catholic schools. They all wore matching red T-shirts, and their sweet innocent voices were like a shining ray of light in what had been a very dark week.

Some of Jacob's friends shared things they'd written, and I was especially moved when our neighbor's son, Joel Welter, got up on stage. Normally, he was such a quiet kid—I couldn't imagine him being up on that stage in front of so many people, but he did it.

"The only thing I can do for Jacob is pray for him," he said. "As an eleven-year-old, I can't really search for him. I'm still thinking of *'Jacob is'* and not that he *'was.'* "

We had been missing Jacob for six days now, and even though I was still in a fog, I was deeply moved by the children's beautiful program and the sheer number of people who came to support us.

When we got home, the first thing I did was check the phone log. The pages had gotten denser as time had gone by, averaging at least one entry every five minutes, starting very early in the morning until very late at night.

On this day—October 28, 1989—there were a total of sixty-seven calls. Aside from the typical messages from reporters, investigators, and psychics, the one that stood out to us the most was from a representative for Terry Steinbach, the Oakland A's catcher.

19:59 Terry Steinbach who is playing in the world series will wear a J on the back of his helmet tonight. Media expected. Announcers have the info on Jacob!

Terry Steinbach was a native of New Ulm, Minnesota, and wanted to raise awareness of Jacob's kidnapping. This was a big deal! The World Series had been interrupted for more than a week as the Bay Area worked to recover from the earthquake. Now, millions would be watching from around the country as people tuned in for Game 4. To have a fellow Minnesotan make this heartfelt statement on such a huge national platform was absolutely amazing. News of Jacob's abduction was reaching both coasts by now.

At 11:00 PM on Sunday, October 29, the $100,000 reward for Jacob's safe return expired. It had been a full week since he was kidnapped, and I so desperately wanted to believe this reward money was the ticket to finding him. But the one call we needed never came.

On top of that disappointment, the National Guard's search had yielded no new information. Their very noticeable presence on Saturday had been so encouraging, and on Sunday, another hundred troops had joined the search. Now, after two full days of searching, they'd found nothing.

The constant THWOP-THWOP-THWOP from the overhead helicopters had finally stopped, but the new silence was almost more terrifying. For a week, we had watched as all these people and resources showed up to help us find Jacob—law enforcement, DNR, military personnel, search and rescue dogs, a posse of horseback riders, ham radio operators, and even small aircraft flying clubs that had all come together to aid in the search. I didn't even know most of these things existed in Minnesota. But as we watched the searchers pack up and go home, we were left with a horribly empty feeling. *Now what?*

Thankfully, more hope arrived the very next day. David Collins was the father of ten-year-old Kevin Collins, who had been abducted from the Haight-Ashbury area of San Francisco just five years earlier. Kevin had last been seen talking to a tall, blond-haired man while waiting for a bus home after basketball practice. After a lengthy and well-publicized investigation, Kevin was never seen or heard from again.

When David Collins learned about Jacob's kidnapping, he assured us he knew what we were going through and offered to help. He and his wife, Ann, had started the Kevin Collins Foundation in 1984, and they had put together a nationwide mailing list of law enforcement agencies and other places where missing kids are commonly found, like truck stops, hospitals, and social service agencies. He coordinated volunteers to help with mass mailings to these places and worked diligently to keep Kevin's face in the media. Because of his efforts, Kevin's story had been featured on national broadcasts, magazine covers, billboards, and milk cartons.

Although I was grateful for the energy, ideas, and powerful exposure David Collins could bring to us, I grappled with almost everything he was proposing. I didn't want to think long term. How could I? The Collins family had been searching for *five years!* I could barely face this agony for one more minute, let alone days, months, or years. Part of me just wanted David Collins to go away.

However, with David's help, Jerry worked with our volunteers at the Friends of Jacob office for the next three days to coordinate a mass mailing that took place at Kennedy Elementary School the evening of November 2. They were hoping to attract a hundred volunteers that night, but close to a thousand people showed up to stamp, address, stuff, and sort 35,000 flyers. Many even brought their own stamps. Even David Collins (who had helped coordinate several other mass mailings for missing kids) had never seen such an outpouring of community support.

Before heading back to San Francisco, David left us with a packet of information from the Kevin Collins Foundation for Missing Children. In it were facts and statistics about stranger abduction, prevention advice for parents and kids, tips for recognizing an abducted child, and information on how to help. As I read, one paragraph really stuck with me:

> The problem in assessing the magnitude of the stranger abduction issue is, in large part, one of bookkeeping. To this day, there is still no effective national clearinghouse of cases involving child abduction. Most cases are handled at the local and state level. It is not required by law that local authorities share information about either the child or abductor with the National Center for Missing and Exploited Children, or any other central office. So they don't.

I set the packet aside, hoping I would never have to look at it again. But this packet from David Collins would soon set my life on a whole new trajectory as I found myself coming back to it again and again for the next two and a half decades.

Over the eight days Jacob had been missing, I'd been talking to him regularly. I kept telling him to hold on and stay strong, but I needed him to know more. I wanted him to know how hard we were working to bring him home. I wrote him this letter, hoping to share it with him. As time went on, I learned that talking to him directly in this way helped me to calm down and stay focused on everything we were doing to find him. Some of the letters were published in our local newspapers.

October 30, 1989

Dear Jacob,

Each morning I wake up, I feel drugged, weighed-down, troubled. The bad nightmare is still here.

My heart hurts as days pass by without you. I wrestle over the details again and again. Who could have done this? Where are you, Jacob?

It is absolutely crazy here. Our house is so busy with people coming and going. Officers are now permanently stationed here,

24/7. Sheriff Grafft is having his officers work their regular shifts during the day, then put in another eight-hour shift here at the house. I know they've been watching us, too, noting anything suspicious about our behavior. I realize they don't know us and they need to make sure we're not involved, but it's all so hard.

The media has been amazing. The way you were stolen from us is so unusual, it's drawing national attention. Your dad has been doing most of the talking and is doing his best to answer all the reporters' questions. I just beg for someone to come forward and tell us where you are. We've been told it must be someone from here, or someone who knows the area. If that's the case, this person must work or eat or shop or buy gas nearby. Is he curious? Is he showing up at events like an arsonist who shows up to watch the fire he set? Does he live alone? Surely a roommate, friend, or family member would notice a change in this man's behavior since you were kidnapped. Does he have an obsession with the news? Does he shut off the TV every time they talk about your abduction? Does he make any smart-aleck comments about your abduction at home or at work?

No one has slept much. Psychics started calling almost right away. Your dad talks to them. I can't.

Amy, Trevor, and Carmen are surrounding themselves with friends. No one wants to be alone. One night there were twenty-four people who slept here . . . on the floors, hide-a-beds, couches, and sometimes three or four to a double bed.

The Baha'is set up volunteers to come to the house and answer phones. It's just too crazy for us. One time I answered the phone and a quiet woman asked if I was Jacob's mother. When I said yes, she started screaming at me. "Give your heart to JESUS and he will return your son! It's Jesus who can find him, but you have to give yourself up. Pray! Shout your loyalty from the mountaintops . . . Jesus, Jesus . . ."

I didn't know how to respond. I *was* praying. I *am* a Christian. I couldn't take the yelling and the blame she was placing on me. I know it wasn't God or Jesus who took you away from us, Jacob. It was some really bad guy wearing a mask and holding a gun. Trevor and Aaron saw him, and now they have to live with the nightmare.

Most people are kind. Neighbors have been bringing flowers,

food, Kleenex, toilet paper, cards . . . you name it. Yesterday, the guy who pumps our septic tank came and did it for free, without even being asked. He said he figured we'd need it, with all the extra people we had staying at the house. Can you believe that? And our veterinarian, Dr. Nielsen, stopped by to check on Marcus and Shannon's dog, Cinnamon, to make sure they were doing okay. Isn't that amazing? Marcus knows something is wrong. He hasn't been eating much, and I can tell he misses you horribly. Mostly he just follows me around the house all day long like a shadow. He needs you back, Jacob.

People I barely know are helping to clean, do laundry, or open the mail. You wouldn't believe all the mail! In the beginning, I desperately tore open every letter, looking for a lead or a ransom demand from the man who took you. Eventually, there was so much, we had to get help from volunteers. They mark on the cards if money was sent so we can keep track and turn it over to the search and reward fund. People have been so generous, and everyone wants to help. The whole world is desperate to find you.

So much has been donated. Printing for all the flyers, computers, telephones, tables, and everything we need to set up our Friends of Jacob office. Jacob, you now have more friends than any human being could ever have. I want so badly for you to meet all of them. I don't go to the office much. It's too overwhelming seeing all the boxes of your "Missing" flyers, and all the volunteers helping to send them all over Minnesota. There's even a map, so we can see where they're going. The goal is to cover the whole state.

I'm struggling with trying to find anything that I can do. Some days, I feel like I can't even get out of bed, but I force myself. That might be all I accomplish in a day, just getting up. Normal things are impossible. I feel guilty crawling into a cozy bed at night. I think about you not being able to crawl into your own cozy bunk bed downstairs with Trevor. I'm afraid to close my eyes at night. The dark is so dark and ominous. All the scariest thoughts that I manage to overcome during the daylight hours come back as the sunlight fades, and I feel smothered by this thing that feels like a cold blanket of the darkest dark. I see your face, but as I drift off to sleep, it sometimes gets distorted and I jerk wide awake again. I see your eyes closed and I will them open. I need to see you, hear you, feel your skinny little body snuggled up next to me in your favorite rocking chair. I can smell your sweaty hair. You are so close but so very far away. I don't know how to make you appear for real. I dream about it. I visualize you running up the driveway screaming, "Mom, I'm home!" I can feel your warm hug, and eventually, I sleep.

Now it's morning again. I took a shower, but I feel like it's a luxury I don't deserve. I don't want to eat, sleep, comb my hair, or put on clean clothes because I know you can't. I try to be there for Amy, Trevor, and Carmen, but it's so hard. This morning, I couldn't get up. I pulled the covers over my head and told myself I was never getting out of bed again. It's too hard. It hurts too much. "I can't do this anymore," I said to myself. But, Jacob, then I saw you, curled up in a ball and saying the same thing. "I can't do this anymore. It's too hard, it hurts too much. They're never going to find me." I bolted up screaming, in that place between wake and sleep. "Hang on Jacob! We'll find you, but you have to stay strong!"

I got up. How could I expect you to stay strong if I couldn't? I love you, Jacob, and I promise I will never stop searching for you.

Love,
Mom

{ Chapter 11 }

It had been over a week since Jacob's abduction, and there were no firm leads. Now we were being told the FBI wanted to interview Jerry and me separately. On Tuesday, October 31, at 4:30 PM, a car arrived at our house and we were driven to the Comfort Inn in St. Cloud—which is perhaps the biggest oxymoron I've encountered in my lifetime.

Jerry and I were escorted to separate rooms. Special Agents Steve Gilkerson and Craig Welken led me to a small suite, and I was seated at a table. The agents sat down directly across from me.

"Okay, Mrs. Wetterling," Agent Gilkerson began. "We need to ask you some questions. Some of these might get rather personal and be difficult to answer, but we need to ask so we can narrow our investigation and find Jacob. Are you ready?"

"Yes."

My hand shook as I reached for the glass of ice water in front of me.

"To get started, why don't you tell us a little about Jacob. What kind of kid is he? Does he like sports? Does he have a lot of friends? Does he do well in school? That kind of thing."

"Jacob is eleven. He's in sixth grade. He's a good kid—really smart and clever. He has a lot of great friends, he gets good grades at school, and his teachers always have nice things to say at conferences."

I paused a moment as my eyes welled up with tears. I reached for a Kleenex and continued. "He's really good at sports. Loves them all, especially hockey and football. He's really kind and . . ."

I had to pause so I didn't break down. "He hates it when things aren't fair."

I closed my eyes and shook my head at the irony. How unfair was *this*? The agents gave me a moment as I tried to pull myself together. When I could finally speak again, I continued.

"Sometimes he'd come home from school and tell me about some random kid who got in trouble that day over something that wasn't their fault—like getting caught for passing a note when they didn't even write it. Stuff like that really bothered him."

As I spoke, Agent Welken scribbled notes onto a yellow notepad while Agent Gilkerson continued with more questions.

"So, Mrs. Wetterling, . . . "

"Call me Patty."

"Okay, Patty. Tell us a little about yourself, any activities you're involved in, what your typical day looks like."

I figured these were the easy questions, so I rattled off my answers fairly quickly. Most of what I did revolved around my kids. When I wasn't grocery shopping, planning meals, or doing laundry, I was chauffeuring them around to their friends' houses, school activities, sports practices, dance, or Brownies. Besides being entertainment coordinator for the Millstream Arts Festival, my only other official title was PTA president.

They wanted to know who my closest friends were, as well as Jacob's and Jerry's closest friends. They asked about our financial background, where we shopped for groceries, where we shopped for clothes, what were Jacob's favorite stores, who delivered our newspaper and our mail. Did we have any disputes or disagreements with neighbors, employees, or family members? Was there anyone who might enjoy or gain something from Jacob's abduction?

Next, they asked me about Jerry's activities, which required longer answers and many more follow-up questions. He had formerly been president of the St. Joseph Chamber of Commerce, was currently president of the St. Cloud chapter of the National Association for the Advancement of Colored People (NAACP), and was an active member of the Baha'i Faith.

The agent taking notes asked us to pause a moment so he could catch up. Then, the questions continued.

"Okay. Patty. These next few questions are going to get a little more personal. Can you tell us about your marriage? How long have you been married?"

"Sixteen years last April."

"Have either you or your husband been married before?"

"No."

"Have you ever had an affair? Keep in mind, we're just trying to build a list of potential suspects here. Someone who might have taken Jacob to get back at one or both of you."

"No. I've never had an affair."

"And you're happily married?"

"Yes. But it's not like we haven't had our challenges like every other married couple," I added after a short pause.

"Can you explain?"

I took a deep breath. Two years ago, we'd gone through marriage counseling after a particularly rough patch. Jerry had been concerned about my growing friendship with one of his Baha'i friends, and I'd been concerned about his tendency to constantly reach out to people he perceived to be in need, many of them women. After providing resources and encouraging them to get help for their depression, alcoholism, or domestic abuse, Jerry sometimes extended an invitation to join his Baha'i group. Consequently, he ended up spending a lot of his free time with them. I never honestly believed he was having an affair with any of these women, but some seemed overly grateful and somewhat dependent. I felt he was naive about some of their intentions.

"We eventually sorted it all out, but it was hard," I said, concluding my lengthy explanation.

The agent taking notes was scribbling rapidly now, which completely unnerved me. Was I being too open? Was I sharing too much? What would Jerry think about my answers? I knew we didn't have anything to hide, but what if I said something wrong and only made things worse?

The other agent continued with his questions.

"Can you tell us a little more about the Baha'i church? Are you a member?"

"It's not a church. And, no, I'm not a member."

"Can you explain?"

I sighed and took another deep breath.

This was always so difficult.

Jerry joined the Baha'i Faith in 1973, six months after we were married. We had recently moved to Davenport, Iowa, so he could attend school at Palmer College of Chiropractic, and we were just starting to settle into our new life together. We found an apartment above a laundromat downtown, made some new friends, and were having fun getting together with them on weekends for drinks, dinner, and live music at the local bars.

The one thing we hadn't settled on yet was a new church home. Jerry had been raised Missouri Synod Lutheran and I had been raised in a Congregational church, so we compromised and attended an Episcopal church for a while to see if that might suit our spiritual needs.

One day, we were walking in downtown Davenport when somebody handed Jerry a brochure about the Baha'i Faith. He was intrigued, so I agreed to go with him that evening to attend an informal fireside gathering at the home of a young couple who were members of the faith.

When we arrived, the couple thanked us for coming and invited us to join them in the living room where about a dozen people were gathered in a circle. Everyone was encouraged to introduce themselves and give a little background about our families, our jobs, and any knowledge we had about the Baha'i Faith.

While I was tense and guarded with little to say, Jerry seemed right at home. He explained that we were newlyweds and had recently moved to Davenport from our home in Arlington, Virginia, where we had both worked as math teachers.

"Patty's a math teacher at Bettendorf Middle School, and I'm in my first year at Palmer College of Chiropractic," he added. He went on to share about our new apartment, our new puppy, Oliver, and our different Christian upbringings.

"That about sums it up," he finally concluded.

Our hosts told us a little more about themselves and the role the Baha'i Faith played in making their lives meaningful. One of the first things we learned was that Baha'is don't have local churches, and that most spiritual gatherings are held in local members' homes.

They shared that Baha'is believe that God periodically sends divine messengers to encourage moral and spiritual development throughout mankind. They believe that Moses, Jesus, Muhammad, and, most recently, Baha'u'llah are some of the messengers of God who have revealed spiritual guidance to humanity. The Baha'is also strive for world peace and specifically advocate for racial unity, gender equality, universal education, and harmony of science and religion.

It all hit Jerry to the core. He began studying more about the faith and attending informal gatherings. The next thing I knew, he'd become a Baha'i.

Over the next few months, I wrestled with everything spiritual. I challenged my own beliefs and wondered if we should even stay together. If we had children, what would they grow up believing? Part of me wanted to be supportive, so I read some of the books Jerry brought home and began attending the open Baha'i gatherings with him, but every nineteen days, when they celebrated Feast (their religious service), non-Baha'is weren't allowed to attend. This only strengthened the mystery and confusion of his faith—and my feelings of being left behind.

This was, by far, the hardest and most challenging thing we ever faced as a new couple. We were just starting our new life together when, all of a sudden, everything changed. Jerry gave up drinking because the Baha'is forbid the use of alcohol or drugs, so suddenly we stopped going out to the bars to listen to bands and we no longer hung out with the same friends. Over and over, I just kept thinking, where was the *we* in this decision?

We continued to have many heavy discussions, trying to figure out our shared core beliefs. I learned about other religions and looked for common values and teachings among all of them. Over time, that strengthened my own beliefs, and I felt less threatened. I knew in my heart we both wanted to make this marriage work, and I didn't want to give up on Jerry and me. I was confident we'd figure it out.

After three long hours of questioning by the FBI, I returned home from the Comfort Inn exhausted and alone. The agents who were interviewing Jerry weren't done by the time the others had finished with me, so I gladly accepted their offer of a sandwich and a ride home. I was physically, mentally, and emotionally drained.

I was filled with gut-wrenching thoughts. The Baha'i discussion had only been the beginning. I had been asked to provide details about my side of the family, the Kings, including all my siblings and their spouses. Next, they asked me about the Wetterling side, including Jerry's siblings, their spouses, and other family members.

They wanted to know about our friends, our social life, our community involvement, our marriage, our religious beliefs, our personal challenges. At one point, they even asked me if I thought Jerry might be gay.

I stared at them, incredulous.

"No," I answered tersely.

Where was this going? Could they possibly think Jerry was a *suspect*?

Now, I was worried. During my interview, I was completely open with the FBI agents because that's just the way I am. I wear my heart on my sleeve and am not afraid to share whatever's on my mind. I didn't have any hidden secrets or dark closets I hadn't already dealt with.

But Jerry was very different from me. He analyzed everything. Throughout our marriage, this had always driven me crazy. Whenever I asked Jerry a question, he often replied, "Why are you asking?" or "When do you need an answer?" or "I'll have to think about that for a minute." He always seemed to weigh his answers before replying, so I could only imagine how his FBI interview was going.

It was another three hours before Jerry finally returned home. I had no idea what to say to him. I wanted to know what they'd asked him, but I could tell he was completely burnt out.

Still, I couldn't resist.

"Did they ask you if we have any gay friends?"

He didn't answer.

"Did they tell you that your brother-in-law looks like one of the composite sketches?"

Still no answer.

"Did they ask you about being Baha'i?"

"Who wants to know?" he finally snapped, defensively.

"Me," I said softly. "Your wife."

Jerry was well aware the investigators were looking at him as a suspect. We both knew he was completely innocent, but it was still absolutely devastating. It was also ridiculous and maddening: all the time and resources they were wasting on Jerry could have been focused on the real kidnapper, who, we both felt, was slipping further and further away.

With all the new questions and added scrutiny, it felt like the investigators were trying to divide us. To deal with the trauma, we slowly began to revert to our core selves. I was the realist, focusing on solid leads and facts; Jerry was the idealist, focusing on principles, prayers, and spiritual energy. While I turned to the cops, he turned to his faith.

I worried we might never find our way back.

{ Chapter 12 }

I met Jerry during winter quarter of my senior year at Mankato State College. After waffling between majors for three years, I finally decided on math and picked up minors in education and psychology to go with it. The last requirements for my diploma were a quarter of student teaching and then a final spring quarter in Mankato.

I signed up to teach at an American school in Mexico. It was an exchange program that our college set up, and I was looking forward to traveling and seeing more of the world.

After Christmas break my parents drove me back to Mankato, where our group boarded three large buses to begin the long ride to Mexico. I found a seat in the middle and introduced myself to some of the other women. I recognized a few familiar faces from campus, but I really didn't know anyone well.

A chaperone introduced himself and set out some basic rules regarding behavior on the bus, then went over the stops along the way. Our first night's stay would be in Emporia, Kansas. They'd booked us four to a room, so I asked the three girls sitting nearest to me if I could join them. I was relieved when they all said yes.

Word spread quickly, and against all the rules laid out so carefully by our chaperone, it was decided that this would be a great night for a party—in our room. That's the night I officially met Jerry.

We had a college geometry class together fall quarter but never really spoke. I later learned he called me a "brown-nose" because I was always the first one in the room and sat in the front row. He, on the other hand, usually slunk into class late, seemingly hungover, and he always sat in the back. I was unimpressed.

After getting checked in to our hotel in Emporia, my roommates and I had barely started to unpack before people began pouring into our room.

A few of the guys had scored some beer, and before long, it was standing room only.

Soon, a tall, lanky guy with wavy brown hair and glasses sauntered over to me. It was the guy from my geometry class.

"Hi. I'm Jerry."

I learned he was from Mason City, Iowa, and had three older sisters, just like me. Other than that, the list of things we had in common was pretty short. When he learned I was a member of a sorority, he just laughed at me.

"Oh, so you're one of *those*," he said with a smirk.

"And what does *that* mean?" I answered, playing along.

"Nothing. Just interesting."

As we bantered back and forth, I suddenly found myself wanting to know more about this mystery guy. I was amazed we had no friends in common, and I'd barely ever seen him on campus. Who was this Jerry, and what was it about him I found so intriguing?

The following morning, we scrambled back on the bus, and this time I found a seat closer to the back. A group of guys had started playing a card game called 500, and I begged in, even though I'd never played before.

As the dealer dealt the cards and explained the basics, I quickly arranged my hand in suits. I loved cards and figured I'd be able to pick it up, but had no idea how to bid. I stared at my hand blankly, wondering what to do, then turned to Jerry, who was sitting in the row across from me.

"What would you bid?" I asked, leaning back.

As he leaned over my shoulder to look at my hand, my heart skipped a beat.

"Seven hearts," he whispered.

Soon, the card game melted away and the moves became mindless as Jerry continued to coach me. I was acutely aware of the closeness of him, his hand on my shoulder, his whispers in my ear. I'd dated other guys, but I'd never felt this mysterious chemistry before. I had had my first conversation with him only the night before, and suddenly I was more curious about him than I'd ever been about anyone I'd ever dated. Who *was* this guy?

When we reached Monterrey, a small group of us got off the bus to meet our host families, while the rest—including Jerry—continued on to Mexico City. I wouldn't see Jerry again for three months as I became completely engulfed in my new job teaching math to seventh, eighth, and ninth graders at the School of the Americas in Monterrey.

Toward the end of our quarter of student teaching, our group in Monterrey was allowed a full week off to tour more of the country. We arranged to meet with some of the other student teachers in Mexico City, and I couldn't wait to see Jerry again.

We met at a hotel bar in the heart of the city and had fun catching up with everyone as we compared stories. Later, Jerry walked me back to my hotel room and I mentioned that our Monterrey group was continuing on to Acapulco for the weekend.

"Would you like to join us?" I asked him.

He managed to find a bus ride with the locals who were taking their chickens to market. After his long and exhausting journey, I surprised him by announcing I'd booked us on a sunset cruise the following evening. I'd been watching this small cruise ship launch each evening and couldn't think of a more perfect first date.

The next evening, we had trouble hailing a cab and arrived at the dock just as the boat crew was pulling up the boarding ramp. When we finally caught our breath and grabbed complimentary margaritas, Jerry and I toasted the beauty of the evening, the magic of Mexico, and this newfound freedom of being twenty-one and twenty-two and on the verge of the rest of our lives.

We continued our conversation after the cruise, walking along the white sandy beach. Jerry was a rebel. He challenged everything I said and pushed me to think outside the box. He was fun, smart, unpredictable—and he made me laugh. After a while, we found a spot on the sand to stargaze and snuggled together, listening to the ocean. I had no idea where any of this would lead, but I wished I could stay in that moment forever.

When we returned to Mankato State that spring, Jerry and I both had some thinking to do. Two years earlier, Jerry had learned his draft number was 125 out of 366 and had been told those whose birth dates fell within the first third of the drawing were the most likely to go to Vietnam. That put him right on the borderline, and with graduation looming, he needed to figure out what to do. His four-year college deferment was about to expire.

That previous spring, we'd lived through the horror of the Kent State shooting, which was followed by riots and protests across the nation, including right on our own campus. Though we didn't know each other at the time, we'd both gone through a lot of soul searching about the war and wanted to see it end without any further bloodshed or loss of life.

Jerry knew he would never be able to fight. At his very core he was a man of peace, so he decided to file for conscientious objector status. He was willing to serve our country, but it just wasn't in him to fight. After graduation, he planned to return to Mason City for the summer, get a job, and wait to hear from the draft board.

Meanwhile, I began searching for my first teaching position, and I ran across an intriguing job listing on the bulletin board of our college placement office. They were looking for a secondary math teacher to teach aboard a ship in Piney Point, Maryland—about an hour and a half drive from Washington, DC. The salary was slightly higher than what I was expecting, and it included housing, which was a plus. I wasn't entirely sure what a merchant marine was, but I was confident I could teach math and was ready for an adventure. I filled out the application and was offered the job.

It was a twelve-month contract, so from June 1971 through May 1972, I taught high school math aboard the *Charles S. Zimmerman* at the Harry Lundeberg School of Seamanship. My students were young men who had dropped out of school and wanted to pick up their GED (General Education Diploma).

By then, Jerry had received the good news that his conscientious objector status had been approved. After working all summer as a bartender and saving his money, he came out to visit me in Maryland and ended up staying. He found a job in Washington, DC, with the National Jogging Association that fulfilled his two-year alternative service obligation, qualifying under the category of "promoting the nation's health." Jerry began to study the benefits of preventive medicine through exercise, and with his college minor in physical education, this turned out to be a really great fit for him.

Jerry lived in a home in Arlington, Virginia, with three other roommates. On the outside, the place looked like the *Leave It to Beaver* house—a white two-story corner home in a nice neighborhood with a small yard and a white picket fence out front. However, on the inside, these guys were definitely not the Cleavers. I visited there on weekends while teaching at Piney Point, and pretty soon Jerry's four roommates and their girlfriends became our best friends.

While working for the National Jogging Association, Jerry became all about health and fitness, and I admired his commitment to living a healthy lifestyle. We became vegetarians, started running together, and biked all over from Arlington to parts of Maryland and into the District. We also continued to reflect on the war and found ourselves swept up in the free-spirited, peace-loving hippie movement. We were all about "Make Love Not War" and regularly donned our Virginia Is For Lovers T-shirts.

When the school year started again in the fall of 1972, Jerry and I were both hired as junior high teachers, but at different schools. He taught math and phys ed at a wealthy school district out in the Virginia suburbs; I taught math at Kent Junior High in Palmer Park, Maryland.

Kent Junior High was part of the Prince George's County School District and located in a predominantly Black neighborhood about a half mile from the Washington, DC, city line. During the previous school year, a lawsuit had been filed in federal district court alleging that Prince George's County was fostering a system of illegal segregation by not taking enough steps to integrate the schools. The judge ruled in favor of the plaintiffs and set a deadline of December 4, 1972, for the district to produce a desegregation plan that would require the transfer of almost 33,000 students to neighborhood schools that had never even seen a school bus before.

It was shaping up to be a tumultuous year, and I was only a few weeks into my new teaching job at Kent Junior High when I received a devastating phone call from my sister Nancy. It was October 4, 1972.

"You need to come home," she managed to choke out between tears. "Dad died today. He had a heart attack at the store."

My legs turned to rubber and I fell to the floor, breathless and unable to respond.

"Russ was working with him when it happened," she said through tears. "The other pharmacist called for help, and the ambulance came right away. They tried to save him, but he was already gone."

Our brother Russ, only sixteen, had witnessed the whole thing. "He's really having a hard time," Nancy told me. "We need you home."

I couldn't even imagine the nightmare poor Russ was living through. He and Dad had always been so close. "I'll be there as soon as I can," I promised.

When I told Jerry what had happened, he offered to fly home and be with me for the funeral, but I said no. "The school year just started and you don't have any extra money," I rationalized. "You stay. I'll be fine."

But the truth was, I wasn't fine.

All the way home, I told myself I had to pull it together and be strong for my family, but I fell apart the minute I saw my sisters waiting for me when I got off the plane. They were all there, and I melted into their arms as soon as I made it out of the gate. Bud had loved all of us so completely. He'd adopted my sisters and me when we were just little girls and loved us like we were his own. I couldn't believe he was gone.

We were all worried about Mom, but she was so strong, as always. At fifty-three, she had just lost her second husband, and we realized it probably hadn't fully sunk in for her as we watched her keep busy with all the practical matters of planning a funeral. There were decisions to be made, people to be contacted, Bible verses to choose, food to plan. I had intended to come home and be strong for her, to sweep in and take away some of her burden. But, as always, she was the one who provided strength for the rest of us. She was our rock. In the midst of chaos, she could always stay calm and carry on.

My dad was buried in the bow tie I'd sewn him for Christmas. On the day of the funeral, the church was packed with friends and family, and toward the end of the service, we sang my dad's favorite hymn—"How Great Thou Art." I didn't even make it past the first two lines before the tears started streaming down my face.

Oh Lord my God
When I in awesome wonder...

We all cried as we remembered Dad belting out this beautiful hymn so many times over the years. I cried harder as I listened to the people singing all around me, and the memories came flooding back.

One of Dad's favorite tricks was to line up all five of us kids and ask people, "Which one do you think looks most like me?" I was still the only one in the family with blond hair and blue eyes, so people would always pick me because Bud's eyes were also blue. He would laugh and laugh over that trick, and it always made me feel so special.

Bud loved limericks and Burma Shave poems. He loved taking us out for dinner and on family vacations. He lived his life so fully, every single day, and always found great joy in everything he did. He was the strongest male role model I'd ever known, and now, he was gone. He was only forty-nine.

I was suddenly overcome with emotion and so mad at myself. Whenever I dated someone, Dad always asked me, "Is this the one? Is this the love of your life?" I just laughed and told him, "When I find him, you'll be the first to know!" But I hadn't had a chance yet to tell him that Jerry was the one.

Jerry was so different from anyone I had ever known or dated before. He could be quirky and impulsive, maybe even a little eccentric. But he was also deep, thoughtful, and kind. He was an introverted idealist who loved pushing the envelope and getting to know people one-on-one. On the other side of the spectrum, I was the extroverted realist who loved meeting new people everywhere I went. He was six-foot-one; I was five-foot-one. He was small-town; I was big-city. We were as yin and yang as they come, but none of that mattered. We were both ready to be *us*.

{ Chapter 13 }

On Thursday, November 2, 1989, I received a bouquet of flowers from the FBI. The card read, "Our prayers are with you and your family."

It was my fortieth birthday.

Prior to October 22, my days were so busy with the kids and their activities, I hadn't even had time to *think* about turning forty, let alone dwell in the angst that typically accompanies it. If anything, I'd been looking forward to starting my next chapter as a part-time math teacher at St. John's Prep.

Now, eleven days later, none of it mattered.

I woke up on November 2 faced with yet *another* day of searching. Our family was in shambles. Carmen was on antibiotics, recuperating from an ear infection. Trevor was sick with chills and a fever. Amy looked pale as a ghost. She still couldn't handle the throngs of people in our house, and she especially resented the media. Rochelle and some of her closest eighth-grade friends surrounded her with love and unwavering support, and I was grateful they could provide her with some sense of normalcy.

Every day, I tried hard just to survive. Whenever I broke down and thought I couldn't cope one minute longer, the world presented us with yet another act of kindness that renewed my strength and spirit.

On November 1, we briefly attended a benefit dance and auction at the Del-Win Ballroom to thank the six hundred supporters who had shown up and raised over $20,000 for the Friends of Jacob Fund.

On November 2, my birthday, we attended a balloon launch at Amy's school—Apollo High School in St. Cloud. We were asked to write our own message of hope on a card and then tie it to one of the red and blue balloons (Apollo's school colors). Our kids, along with all their friends, joined us at this event to help launch a thousand balloons out into the universe to help spread awareness and hope. Later that same night, the Minnesota North Stars, our professional hockey team, wore the letters "JW" on the back of their helmets to help generate more national awareness of Jacob's kidnapping.

Two sophomore girls from Cathedral High School came up with the idea of "Hands for Jacob," held on November 4—a four-mile chain of people holding hands all the way from St. Joseph to St. Cloud, while KXSS-FM simulcast the song "Listen" over the radio.

In a game against the Los Angeles Rams on Sunday, November 5, the Minnesota Vikings wore special baseball caps along the sideline that said "Jacob's Hope" and "Listen."

Local singer-songwriter Douglas Wood had been so moved after volunteering at our mass mailing event that he went home that night and wrote the song "Jacob's Hope." It quickly became another anthem for our search.

Jacob's Hope

There's a child all alone in the world tonight
He was stolen away and we cry for his plight
But he's not really gone, cuz we won't let him go.
We are Jacob's Hope.

Jacob, can you hear us
We send you our prayers
We send you all our strength and our love
And we're not giving up 'til we bring you back home
For we are Jacob's hope.

There's a dream that we dream, how the world should be
Where the children are safe, where the children are free
But we know if it's to happen, we must make it so
For we are Jacob's hope.

On Wednesday, November 8, Jerry, Trevor, Aaron, and I were invited to watch our brand-new NBA expansion team, the Minnesota Timberwolves, play their inaugural game against the Chicago Bulls at the Metrodome. As we took center court before the game, more than 60,000 fans rose to their feet and clapped for a full minute as we looked on in amazement and tried to hold it together. We knew this game would be especially meaningful for Jacob, not only because it was the first-ever Timberwolves game and he loved basketball, but also because he shared a birthday with Chicago Bulls superstar Michael Jordan.

Jerry and I tried to attend as many of these events as we could, determined to do everything to get the word out, but it was often difficult—especially for the kids. They didn't want all this extra attention; they just wanted their brother back so everything could go back to normal. We did our best to shield them from the chaos, but it wasn't easy. Jacob's name and face were everywhere.

People were hosting fundraisers, rallies, and prayer vigils. They were wearing "Jacob's Hope" buttons, displaying signs of support in their yards, and tying white ribbons—to symbolize innocence and hope—to road signs, mailboxes, lamp posts, and car antennas. Also, at the suggestion of other parents who had missing children, Minnesotans began to leave their porch lights on for Jacob so he could find his way home. This, in particular, caught on like wildfire.

Truly, it felt like the whole world was holding us up and supporting our search. It was absolutely beyond anything we could have possibly imagined.

On Saturday, November 11—Veterans Day—we were invited to attend the inaugural launch of a POW/MIA hot-air balloon purchased by a local nonprofit that raised awareness for military personnel who were prisoners of war or missing in action. Freedom Flight, Inc. planned to release forty-two black helium-filled balloons, one for every Minnesota soldier who was currently a POW or MIA in Vietnam. With those, they were also planning to release one white balloon for Jacob.

On the day of the event, Jim Tuorila, president of Freedom Flight, greeted us warmly. "Welcome! Thank you for coming. I'd like to introduce you to some of our veterans and families who have photos to share of their missing loved ones."

As Jerry and I shook their hands and listened to their stories, we could feel the strength of their hope. Many had been searching for a long time, and they carried an intense, powerful commitment to never forget their fathers, brothers, friends, and sons who had not returned from war.

After a short prayer and a few words of support for the families, my heart swelled with hope as the Freedom Flight group released their forty-two black balloons and I let go of my one white balloon. I continued to watch as Jacob's balloon lifted skyward among all those soldiers' balloons, and I knew right then we would never give up. Jacob was indeed missing in action, and these veterans knew more than anyone else our absolute need to continue to hope until we could finally bring him home.

A few days after the POW/MIA event, Sheriff Frank Wippler from Benton County (and a member of the Tri-County Major Crimes Unit) brought me a videotape that told the stories of several POWs who had been missing for a very long time. The families of these POWs had been warned not to expect much, and not to get their hopes too high for their loved one's safe return. They were told that prison conditions were awful, prisoners were often held in isolation, and sometimes they were even tortured. But the soldiers on this tape *had* returned home, and when they did, they far surpassed anyone's wildest expectations. One became a CEO of a major corporation, one a motivational speaker, and one a scientist. I was so grateful for the positive messages these soldiers had shared. The fact that they found the inner strength to persevere, make their way home, and then embrace life upon their return exemplified the hope we were currently living. Our hope was powerful, and it was real.

Sheriff Wippler was an incredible source of strength for me in those early days. A few weeks into the investigation, he began calling our house just to check on me.

"How ya doin', kid?"

Frank was my age, but he always called me "kid."

"I'm tired," I told him honestly. "I haven't slept much."

"What do you mean you're tired?" he snapped back. "Who the hell is going to find Jacob if you quit? Get up. I'll meet you at the Law Enforcement Center in an hour."

He was right. I could never quit, but sometimes I just needed a kick in the butt to get started. And for me, seeing at least thirty officers on any given day answering phones and scrambling in their efforts to find Jacob was always strengthening.

I can do this, I told myself. *I have to do this.*

I got up and went to meet Frank.

Slowly, I began to get my bearings. Aside from the daily updates with our local newspapers and TV affiliates, Jerry and I had now done interviews with *Inside Edition, A Current Affair, ABC World News Tonight, CBS Evening News, Good Morning America, People Magazine,* and *Time Magazine.* By this time, I wanted the whole world to know about Jacob so they could watch for him. I really never thought about the millions of viewers I was speaking to when I did these interviews. I simply spoke to the reporter in front of me, one-on-one. All were kind and caring, and I knew they could help. Soon, this became my daily mission—to talk to anyone and everyone who could help us find Jacob. My confidence grew with each interview, and finally, I had found something I could do. I could be our family spokesperson.

{ Chapter 14 }

I was just starting to gain some footing in my new role with the media—and then came *Geraldo*.

We'd been contacted by the people at Geraldo Rivera's show because they wanted to do a show on Jacob's kidnapping and the huge community response. It would be a live interview with Jerry and me, but we were also told to make sure we had the sheriff and the FBI supervisor on hand, as well as other close friends and family. They wanted to tell the story of the huge volunteer effort and the community's outpouring of support; our goal was to get Jacob's picture out to a large national audience and help spread awareness about his kidnapping.

Four or five members of Geraldo Rivera's production crew showed up at 7:00 AM on Thursday, November 9, for a taping in the afternoon. After taking a quick look around, they decided to set up in the lower level of our split-entry home.

"Is it okay if we move the furniture?" one of the crew members asked me. "We need to figure out the best angle to make more room for more people."

"Sure," I said.

They went straight to work picking up the heavy hide-a-bed couch as they rearranged the family room. I cringed in embarrassment when I saw the popcorn, dog hair, and other random junk underneath. Logically, I knew it didn't matter, but I still bent quickly to pick up the mess, embarrassed and self-conscious about everything.

For hours, we tried to keep people, kids, and pets out of the crew's way as they set up a makeshift soundstage. They had cameras, monitors, audio equipment, light stands, umbrella diffusers, headsets, and microphones. It all connected to a million cords that ran up our stairs, into the garage, and out to a satellite truck that was parked in our driveway.

When they were finally ready for us, they clipped small microphones to our clothes and gave us earpieces. There was no TV monitor for us to watch, which was somewhat startling for me. We knew Geraldo was taping in front of a live studio audience in New York City, but without a monitor we had no idea what was happening on his end. We could only hear the audio side of the broadcast:

> A heart-rending story is unfolding right now in America's heartland. His name is Jacob. The eleven-year-old snatched at gunpoint from the town of St. Joseph, Minnesota. It happened on October 22.
> Since then, Dr. Jerry and Patty Wetterling, Jacob's parents, have been holding a vigil . . . hoping, and praying, and working for a break in this case. They join us today via satellite from their home in St. Joe.

The sound of clapping filled our earpieces, and after a few moments, Geraldo began speaking again.

> Every time it happens, it puts an entire community into a state of shock. It's like a giant punch in the gut, because all we can do, all the police can do really, is to speculate as to the intentions of the kidnapper. And the options are horrifying.

By now, I was getting really nervous. I didn't want to hear about horrifying options. I had no idea where this was headed.
He continued.

> Before we meet the Wetterlings, let me also introduce John Walsh, who joins us via satellite from Washington, DC. John is, of course, best known as the host of the successful FOX television program *America's Most Wanted*, but he's also the founder of the Adam Walsh Outreach Center for Missing Children, which was founded after his son Adam, age six, was abducted and later found murdered.

Now I was officially freaked out. Yes, I knew about John Walsh and his son, Adam, but this wasn't what I wanted to talk about. We were less than three weeks into our search and still had very high hopes of finding Jacob alive and bringing him home. That's why I had agreed to do this show. Where were we headed? I couldn't even look at the cameras. I stared at my hands and forced myself to concentrate on what Geraldo was saying.

GERALDO: What must your day and nights be like as you wait, Dr. Wetterling?

Jerry did a good job of describing the chaos we were currently living. Then, Geraldo directed his questions to me.

GERALDO: Patty, for you, is there that tension when the telephone rings or when you see the FBI agent for the first time in the day, or maybe one of the sheriff's deputies . . . what's it like for the mom?

I had only an instant to think about my responses, but tried my best to steer the conversation in a positive, hopeful direction.

ME: We still believe that Jacob is going to come home. And yes, I look forward to the phone calls from the FBI, the sheriff, and they've been wonderful about keeping in touch with us. And they are still encouraged.

GERALDO: As the days, Patty, turn to weeks, does hope fade? Or are you determined not to let that happen?

ME: I think I've changed in my emotions. I was very scared, very petrified, and now I'm driven. We're going to bring him home.

GERALDO: Is it something that causes you nightmares? Do you try to pursue a reason? Why? Why your boy? Why that night?

ME: I can't answer those questions. A very wise man, a friend of ours, told me that, as he saw it, we have one option, and that's to believe that Jacob is fine and he will come home. And I choose not to think about all the horrible options you've made mention of at the beginning. I just won't allow those into my mind at this point. I just want to believe that he's fine, and we're going to get him home.

That was the most I said in the entire hour. They never even talked to our volunteers from the Friends of Jacob office about the huge community response—which we had been led to believe was the focus of the program.

Next, Geraldo directed his questions to John Walsh in Washington, DC.

GERALDO: There are so many grim similarities between what is happening now to Jerry and Patty Wetterling, and what happened to you and your wife with Adam those years ago. What can they, the Wetterlings, do? Are they, in a sense, powerless now to the whim, the whimsy, the awful capriciousness of this mad man?

JOHN WALSH: I've learned a lot in the last eight years, and I know that the serial pedophiles that roam this country are getting better and better at it, and it's a game to them. Jacob needs your strength because, unfortunately, if he's not found—and I hope he will be found alive—but if he's not found, he will be just another missing child.

I know what these families are going through. They're going through the nightmare of not knowing. They're hoping, as the Wetterlings are, that sometimes, in a rare instance, a child comes back after being gone for a long time. But all the people sitting there today know the harsh reality . . . that lots of kids that are taken—particularly when they're that age—and they're not taken by some caring person who brings them to Disneyland. They're taken by someone who is into sexually assaulting children, and if you're lucky, you'll find the body in a field.

What?

I wasn't ready to hear John's harsh reality, and I was furious with Geraldo for his sensationalistic coverage of our search. We were new to all of this, and I was still very much focused on hope. As a mom, I couldn't be expected to just pull a switch like that. I still vividly remembered the birth of this beautiful child, and all the years of his nurturing and caring. I had been there when he learned how to crawl and walk. I'd watched him grow and become the Jacob we all knew and loved—making friends, telling jokes, playing sports, doing homework, practicing trombone, dreaming big dreams, and looking forward to his future. I longed to hold my son again and had constant visions of him running up the driveway and jumping into my arms.

Jacob was *alive*. He wasn't just a body in a field.

When the show was finally over, I tore off my microphone and ran upstairs, vowing to write a horrible letter to Geraldo telling him how awful I thought the show was.

My sister Barbi followed me up the stairs and, very calmly, suggested I write him a thank-you note, instead.

"You never know. You might need to talk to him again someday."

I hated to admit she was right, but the next day, I sent a thank-you note to Geraldo and his entire team.

It had been eighteen days, but I still had so much to learn.

{ Chapter 15 }

The Geraldo show was a turning point for me. After nearly three weeks of feeling absolutely helpless, I finally moved to a new place of hope and conviction. From my earlier struggles with diabetes, I'd learned that helplessness was incredibly wearing and could slowly erode the spirit. I couldn't let that happen to me again. I needed to stay positive to help find Jacob.

Three weeks had gone by and Jacob was still missing. No matter how hard we'd tried, none of the tears, prayers, songs, hugs, or media interviews had brought him back. I felt defeated and discouraged, and yet, I remembered what Frank Wippler had told me.

"Who the hell is going to find Jacob if you quit?"

His words echoed through my head every morning as I forced myself to get up and get dressed. I knew the task force was also feeling discouraged . . . the constant ups and downs, the big leads that went nowhere, the passing of time with still no answers. It had been hard on all of us.

With my mom and my sisters still there for support, I decided we should bring some encouragement to the task force working at the Law Enforcement Center in St. Cloud. All I could think of was to bake some chocolate chip cookies to offer in gratitude.

I hadn't spent a lot of time at the LEC, but whenever I came in, I sensed that some of the officers were uncomfortable having me there. I was Jacob's mom, and my presence put a human face to their investigation. They were working hard and wanted to have answers for me, but they just didn't have them. A few would even get up and leave the room whenever I came.

Cookies softened it for all of us. As an added plus, it gave me something to do. I welcomed the opportunity to get out of my head for a while and just concentrate on the physical act of mixing the ingredients and dropping dough onto the cookie sheet. The smell of the cookies baking provided familiar comfort and aromatherapy for my whole family. I also enjoyed the sense of accomplishment I felt when the cookies were finally sitting on the cooling rack. I felt like saying, "Look at that! I actually accomplished something today!"

Before long, chocolate chip cookies became my trademark. This one small thing made me feel purposeful, useful, and helpful. I also theorized it was impossible to be mean, angry, vindictive, or cynical while making chocolate chip cookies. Some days were double batch days, but baking the cookies always helped ease some of the darkness and helplessness. I think the kids appreciated them too.

On November 20, the scale of the investigation was pulled back, and they started taking officers off the case. Nearly a month had passed, and the SCSO was going bankrupt over the extra hours. Meanwhile, other crimes were still being committed, so officers were being reassigned to their usual law enforcement duties.

Regardless of the personnel cuts, the investigation intensified. Although the team didn't share a lot of details with us, detectives were following up on all kinds of leads. They were interviewing patients of Jerry's, including their husbands, ex-spouses, and ex-boyfriends. They were also talking to former neighbors of ours, teachers, coaches, priests, and even Boy Scout leaders. Jacob had never even been in Boy Scouts, but detectives were leaving no stone unturned. It was overwhelming to everyone in the community, but especially draining for those who were directly affected.

Along with the questioning, rumors had started to circulate. One day, we received a horrific letter stating that Jacob had been taken by a satanic cult and would be sacrificed on Halloween. We were told there was no evidence to support this.

There was also a rumor that Jerry wasn't Jacob's real dad at all, and a long-lost boyfriend of mine who was actually his biological father had taken him. I had no idea where that came from.

Probably the most hurtful rumor we ever heard came just after Jerry had gone back to work. One day, two of his coworkers pulled him into the back office and asked, "Is it true that Baha'is kill their first-born sons?" This was stupefyingly outrageous and deeply insulting. It was painful for both of us, but especially for Jerry.

Thanksgiving was approaching. It was usually my favorite holiday, but this year, I just couldn't do it. I was in no mood to celebrate and didn't feel very thankful for anything. I didn't want to celebrate Thanksgiving without Jacob, so I suggested we grill hamburgers instead. I was overruled.

"We'll all come up," Peg and Nancy said. "Barbi and John can help with the turkey, and we'll bring everything else."

Reluctantly, I agreed.

When we woke up on Thursday, November 23—Thanksgiving morning— it was brutally cold outside, even by Minnesota standards. It was the coldest weather of the season so far, with a daytime high of only 16 degrees and temperatures expected to fall below zero by evening.

For weeks, I'd been dreading the thought of Thanksgiving without Jacob. But as the house started to come alive with the arrival of family and the comforting smell of turkey in the oven, I was able to refocus my thoughts and feel true gratitude for all those who were helping us.

By midmorning, our whole extended family had arrived with slow cookers, roasters, foil-covered baking dishes, and Tupperware containers. We unanimously agreed to make a second Thanksgiving meal for all the investigators who were still on duty that day, so we roasted a second turkey on the grill and doubled all the fixings. After dinner, we packed the car and delivered it to all the dedicated people at the Law Enforcement Center in St. Cloud who were working around the clock to find Jacob. It was then I realized we really *did* have much to be thankful for.

"Jacob's My Son"
By Patty Wetterling
November 24, 1989
St. Joseph Newsleader

It's 4:00 AM. Our 24-hour police watch, coverage, help, and support ended at 11:00 PM last night. I shed a few tears as we entered another phase in this very long search.

There are people who take children and keep them for whatever reasons for long periods of time. That's sad, and yet in many ways these children are "taken care of," and I want that very badly. Food and warmth and sleep and possibly even conversation. I pray that

Jacob has found this, too, so that his days are less fearful, less frantic, less painful.

I find myself functioning with less emotion. There's a numbing process we all go through in order to survive—a temporary callousness.

We are all driven. We believe in love, we believe in prayer. We have drawn strength from all of the people in this community. Thank you.

We also believe in laughter. It's very healing. Families to surround ourselves in love. Songs to freshen our spirit. Dance to lighten our steps. Hugs to hold us together. Hands to reach out to one another, and hearts beating together as one.

Apollo High School has planted "Jacob's Tree of Hope," and Cold Spring Granite has donated a plaque. More days than I care to count have passed and still we are very hopeful Jacob will return safely soon. In my heart, and at Apollo High School, Jacob's Hope is carved in granite.

Let's continue to work together to make the world a better place.

The weekend after Thanksgiving, Jerry and I sat everyone down for a family meeting.

"On Monday," Jerry began, "I'm going to start seeing patients two days a week. And your mom and I think it's important for all of you to go back to school too."

I watched their faces carefully, gauging their reactions.

"Jacob's investigation is still going on and we're doing everything we can to help the police find him," I assured them. "But the best thing we can do for our family right now is to try and get back on a regular schedule."

I knew Carmen actually *wanted* to go back and looked forward to her normal routine. Her teacher had already helped tremendously in calming the students' fears and had been counseling them on how to be supportive of Carmen when she returned.

Amy was willing to give it a try, but was a little more apprehensive about returning. She was in eighth grade, the youngest class at Apollo High School, and she worried what other kids might say or how they would react to her.

Over the past few weeks, she'd realized that most kids had no *idea* what to say to her, which often made her feel sad and alone. To cope, she just kept studying hard and staying busy with homework.

As for Trevor, he wanted nothing to do with school. His teacher hadn't helped the situation by sending home notes saying how far behind he was getting. ("Trevor has already missed three spelling tests, two science tests, and is getting very behind on reading.") He hated reading on a *good* day, and realizing that he wasn't sleeping and couldn't concentrate on anything, I knew this was going to be an uphill battle. I tried to use my adult reasoning on him.

"Trevor, you can't just live on a fourth-grade education," I told him. "You need to go back to school so you can advance to fifth grade with your friends."

He just stared at me blankly.

"Not only that," I continued. "It's a law. All children have to go to school."

"Even when your brother is missing?" he asked me.

I had no reply. My adult reasoning had failed me miserably.

Eventually, the kids all returned to school, my mom returned to St. Paul, my sister returned to San Francisco, and Jerry returned to work. Investigators still called every day with questions about our activities, people we knew, and any potential suspects, so Jerry's initial days back in the office were often interrupted. But, the reality was, he was our sole source of income, so if Jerry wasn't at the office treating patients, we would have no income at all.

Fortunately, Jerry welcomed the distraction of his work, and it helped him to focus on what he was good at. He received a lot of support from his patients and staff who were all glad to see him back. He was a good doctor.

It seemed everyone was better off on a regular routine. That is, everyone except me.

While Jerry and the kids were all back at work and school, I had nowhere to go. Every day, I just sat home alone trying not to tear my hair out. I made lists of things to do or try. I visited the Friends of Jacob office and started working with the volunteers a bit more. I also asked a lot of questions and studied the packet David Collins had left me from the Kevin Collins Foundation. Slowly, I started to learn more about child abductions and the kinds of people who commit crimes against children. I felt an unbelievable need to share this information with other parents, but I wasn't really sure how to do that. Instead, I just kept reading, learning, and asking more questions.

{ Chapter 16 }

Shortly after Jerry was back at work, a young man named Kris Bertelsen came into his chiropractic office, accompanied by his dad. Kris was a sophomore at Apollo High School and had been living in the St. Cloud area for only a few months. Prior to that, he lived in the town of Paynesville, about thirty miles away.

Kris told Jerry that for a period of about two years, several juvenile boys in Paynesville had been randomly attacked after dark and sexually molested. He knew of at least seven or eight incidents and had been involved in two of them, himself. He told Jerry about someone named Duane (Dewey) Hart, a man in his early forties who had been arrested for molesting kids in the Paynesville area a few years earlier, but never went to jail for it. Most people were afraid of Hart and strongly believed he was the one responsible for the random stranger assaults in Paynesville. Kris said he had already gone to the task force with this information on October 24—two days after Jacob's kidnapping—but hadn't heard anything back.

We were familiar with Duane Hart. His name had been turned in by at least six people during the first week of the investigation, including the sheriff of a neighboring county. We knew he was a strong suspect, but investigators told us that his MO was very different. Hart was a "groomer" who enticed his young victims with drugs, alcohol, gifts, and attention. The man who took Jacob did so by force, presumably because he didn't have the kind of personality to entice his victims. The investigators also told us Hart didn't have a car, which seemed to move him down the suspect list.

As Kris and his father left the chiropractic office that day, Jerry thanked them for coming in to speak with him and assured Kris he would be heard this time.

Not long after Kris's visit, we also learned about Jared, a thirteen-year-old boy who had been abducted and sexually assaulted in the nearby town of

Cold Spring just nine months before Jacob's kidnapping. On November 30, investigators interviewed Jared and his parents and confirmed that the details of the two abductions were strikingly similar.

On January 13, 1989, Jared (who was twelve years old at the time) had been walking home after dark when he was stopped by a man in a car who asked him for directions. As Jared was giving the directions, the man got out of the car, grabbed him, told him he had a gun, and shoved him into the back seat. He drove Jared to a remote location and sexually assaulted him. Afterward, the man drove Jared back toward Cold Spring and let him go a few miles out of town. He told him to get out of the car and "run as fast as he could or he would shoot."

Because of the similarities between the two cases, the FBI believed the two abductions were connected. Jared had already produced a composite sketch, selecting eyes, ears, and mouths from a book of samples. On December 13, the FBI flew in a professional sketch artist from Washington, DC, and had him work closely with Jared to produce a much more detailed sketch.

The following day, FBI Supervisory Agent Jeff Jamar and Sheriff Charlie Grafft held a press conference to release Jared's new sketch and announce the likelihood that the two cases were linked. This information brought in a flurry of new leads, including names of men who looked like the sketch and others who were believed to have victimized boys. We didn't know Jared's last name, but were so grateful to this very brave thirteen-year-old—who had already been through so much—for stepping up to help us find Jacob.

Two days later, they brought Jared back. They had developed another suspect: Danny Heinrich, a Paynesville man in his late twenties who had been an early suspect in Jared's assault. The FBI had tracked down a car Heinrich had previously owned that fit the description of the car Jared described. They asked Jared to sit in the back seat and, on a scale of one to ten, tell them how closely he felt it resembled the car that had been used during his assault. He ranked it a nine out of ten.

Later that same day, the FBI also asked us whether we had ever heard of Danny Heinrich from Paynesville. We didn't recognize the name or the photo they showed us, but we found it strange that, in just a matter of days, there were now two strong suspects from Paynesville, a town less than thirty miles away from St. Joseph.

As the weeks went on, we would often hear these names together—Hart and Heinrich—often in the same sentence. Yet, at the same time, Hart and

Heinrich were just two more names among the dozens of others we'd already been asked about. They were both strangers to us, and from everything we were told, these types of crimes were almost always committed by someone who was known to the family.

We moved on.

Christmas was just weeks away, and I dreaded the thought of spending another holiday without Jacob. Thanksgiving had been hard enough, but Christmas was all about the kids—decorating the house, picking out the tree, visiting Santa, baking cookies, singing carols, shopping for gifts. I couldn't face any of it.

I coped by trying to ignore the impending holiday and, instead, turned my focus to reading the mail.

The letters and cards were magical when they first arrived, and for the next twenty-seven years, I held onto every single one. At first, I didn't have an option. The mail we received after Jacob's disappearance became part of the investigation, and I was afraid to let anything slip through the cracks. Who knew what might become potential evidence?

Many people sent donations or words of encouragement.

"Our son died recently, and we wanted his memorials to go toward helping find missing children. What could be more important?"

"I saw you on television the other night, and you have no idea how often I've had you in my heart and in my prayers. My daughter is Jacob's age and we will continue our prayers for Jacob's safe return to his loving family." —Ohio

Other letters were more intense and personal.

"Back in 1988, our sixteen-year-old daughter ran away along with three others from here. They headed to Texas. After six days, they were located, and police helped us make arrangements to fly her home. Hearing of Jacob's disappearance is like a knife in my stomach and I just hurt so much for you. I pray that God is giving you strength."

The letters and pictures from kids were especially heartwarming and always made me smile.

"Don't ever give up looking for Jacob. If I knew my parents gave up hoping for me, I wouldn't want to come back."

"This song is to Jacob. It's called 'I Love You.' I love you, Jacob, but I can't come give you a hug. But one thing I can do is find you in my heart and love you." —Molly, second grade

Every day, I continued to read through the piles of letters and drew on them for strength. When I was exhausted from the tears and lack of sleep, I'd read another card.

"Keep going. Jacob needs you."

"You're not alone. We're all praying for you and your family."

In addition to the letters, we also continued to be carried by the goodwill of our community. To make sure public hope didn't diminish over the holidays, Police Chief Bill Lorentz installed an eleven-foot-high candle that said "Jacob's Hope" in black letters on the roof of City Hall. The flame stayed lit every night and could be seen throughout downtown.

The sights and sounds of the season were everywhere, and like it or not, Christmas was still coming, with or without Jacob. Putting up our own Christmas decorations was the furthest thing from my mind, so we were incredibly grateful when the president of First American Bank stopped by with a decorated Christmas tree from the annual Holly Ball in St. Cloud. We were also grateful to friends and family who brought over cookies, handmade ornaments, cards, and gifts. Although I didn't want to abandon Amy, Trevor, and Carmen, I just couldn't muster the energy for Christmas shopping and gift wrapping that year. To me, Christmas was just one more day without Jacob.

On December 23, two days before Christmas Eve, one of my friends was shopping at Crossroads Center in St. Cloud when an announcement came over the building's public address system.

"Jacob Wetterling has been found!"

The crowd instantly erupted into cheers of joy. It was the Christmas miracle everyone had hoped and prayed for.

Almost instantly, our phones began ringing off the hook with people calling to confirm whether Jacob had been found in Texas. We had no idea what was happening and couldn't confirm anything. The sheriff's department called and told us they were trying to track down the source of the rumor. Their office had also been flooded with calls, along with all the local newspapers and TV and radio stations. Everyone was desperate to know if the report of Jacob's recovery was true.

Sadly, it was not.

Although Jerry and I both wanted to believe it more than anything, we had learned by now not to get too excited about any news reports until we could confirm them with the task force. It wasn't long before we were disappointed once again. It wasn't Jacob. Apparently, there was a nineteen-year-old soldier who had been wounded in Panama and was now safe in a Texas hospital. Radio stations had reported that this young man named Jason had called his mother in Minnesota to tell her he was okay. Somebody mistook "Jason" for "Jacob," and word spread like wildfire. Even though it wasn't Jacob, we were genuinely grateful this soldier had been found safe and could celebrate Christmas with his family. At the same time, something else had stirred in me. I was so inspired by the public's amazing reaction, I became filled with the possibility of what *could* happen. I got choked up just thinking about what an incredible celebration it would be when Jacob finally came home for real.

On Christmas morning, a man named Mike Clark and a group of twelve veterans from the Anoka branch of Vietnam Veterans of America arrived at our house after walking sixty-five miles from Anoka to St. Joe. They had left two days earlier, on December 23, and used the walk to raise money for the Friends of Jacob Fund. They didn't stay long, as they had their own family gatherings to get to, but it meant the world to us to feel their commitment, strength, and support. Truly, Jacob had become "everybody's child," and Jacob's Freedom Walk would be continued for many years to come.

Somehow, we made it through the day. Our house was relatively quiet, since most of our family members had already been up to visit over the weekend, then returned home to celebrate with their own families on Christmas Day.

As night fell that evening and everyone finally drifted off to sleep, I stayed in the living room and stared at the stocking I had made for Jacob years earlier. It was red and had a toy soldier on the front. It hung in its usual place, in front of the fireplace, along with Amy's, Trevor's, and Carmen's. Four stockings for four kids. No matter how long it took to find him, we would always be a family of six. As I stared at the stocking, I prayed that wherever Jacob was on that cold Christmas night, he would remember our happy family celebrations from years past and know that we would never give up looking for him.

Hang on, Jacob. Wherever you are, we'll find you.

{ Chapter 17 }

We weren't clueless to the possibility that our son was no longer alive, but we chose to believe otherwise. We felt strongly that if Jacob had been murdered, the searchers would have surely found him by now, or there would have been some kind of sign that Jacob was no longer with us. But that wasn't the case. There was no evidence to support the fact that Jacob was gone, so instead... we hoped. Every day, we actively and consciously chose hope.

It wasn't always easy, especially given the disturbing nature of some of the calls and leads that came in.

Within a short time of Jacob's disappearance, a man from the Pleasant Acres neighborhood in St. Joseph got into a standoff with police and barricaded himself inside his house. The man in the house had a gun and was talking about Jacob, so it was thought perhaps Jacob was inside the house with him. Police surrounded the home and evacuated a few others nearby. When they learned this person was a former patient of Jerry's, that only added to the drama. After a few hours, the man surrendered and was taken to the St. Cloud Hospital for mental evaluation. Sadly, Jacob was not found inside the house.

Also, within weeks of Jacob's abduction, a young man in his late twenties was picked up near the railroad tracks in Little Falls. He was suicidal, screaming that he wanted to die because he had done terrible things and didn't want to spend the rest of his life in jail. He was from St. Joseph and currently living with his brother in Little Falls. After officers arrived and talked him down from his suicide attempt, he was transported to the Brainerd hospital for evaluation. This man was investigated for many years.

One day, we received a phone call from the Jacob Javits Federal Building in New York City. It was from a pay phone in a secure part of the building that was typically not open to the public. The caller said he was Jacob, but nothing ever came from this lead. They couldn't find the caller.

Another time, some young boys called us from Utah saying they were friends with Jacob. They put their friend on the phone and after telling us he was Jacob, he said he just wanted to let us know he was okay. Local police figured out who had made the call, and not long after, we received a phone call from the boys with an apology.

There were also endless calls from people who claimed to have spotted Jacob—a flight to Amsterdam, a homeless shelter in the Twin Cities, a convenience store in Reno, a gun show in Phoenix, a flea market in New Mexico. Many of the leads came to us directly, either by phone or letter, and when investigators didn't feel the leads were credible, we often followed up on our own.

My favorite success story came from a couple from Minnesota who thought they had seen Jacob in Florida. The boy had looked very thin and scared, and the man he was with was holding on to him with a very firm grip. The couple was traveling and didn't really know who to call, so they called the FBI in Minneapolis. When they described the boy, it sounded like it could be Jacob. And when they described the man, Al Garber recognized him as someone who had kidnapped boys before. They caught up with the man and the boy in Flagstaff, Arizona, and although it wasn't Jacob, one twelve-year-old boy got to go home to his family in California because this couple had seen one of Jacob's flyers. They noticed a suspicious situation, they called it in, and law enforcement responded. From everything I was learning, this is *exactly* how kids get found.

Most leads were quickly vetted and went nowhere, but fewer days brought more terror to our family than February 13, 1990.

It was just four days before Jacob's twelfth birthday. Around 3:00 PM, FBI Special Agent Al Garber called and told me they had sent an officer to Jerry's office in Albany to tell him to come home. They needed to talk to us.

At 11:30 AM, a worker had found a body near the Ford Dam on the Mississippi River in St. Paul. It looked to be a young boy about Jacob's age, but they were unable to make a positive identification because the boy's head, hands, and feet had been cut off. Divers were searching the river for the missing parts, and Al promised to keep us posted as things evolved. We were also warned there were already media teams at the site, so something might show up on the news sooner rather than later.

I broke out into a sweat. This can't be the ending. It just can't.

Please God. No.

For the next few hours, we waited by the phone as we continued to receive calls from friends, media contacts, and, of course, the psychics, but we just let them go straight to the answering machine. Thankfully, the story hadn't hit the news yet.

Then it did.

Suddenly, the calls started coming in one after another. Many of these media contacts had become like close friends, and they were worried for us. Darryl Savage from WCCO-TV, Pat Doyle from the Minneapolis *Star Tribune,* Bruce Hagevik from WCCO radio, Dennis Stauffer from KARE-11, Bob Metoxen from the Minnesota News Network, Scott Rapoport from *Inside Edition,* Angela Cushman from KSTP, Ralph Jon Fritz from WCCO . . . I wrote them all down in our phone log.

We received other calls, too, from friends and media contacts who hadn't yet heard what was happening. Each time, I had to take a deep breath from way down deep and pretend nothing special was going on. We were determined not to feed this fire, but it was grueling. The phone calls just kept coming, all day and into the evening.

That night our house was filled with about thirty of our closest friends and relatives who had heard the news and wanted to be there for us. Everyone seemed sure this was it, the end. Surely the boy in the river had to be Jacob. Who else could it be? The only people who didn't seem to believe it were Jerry and me.

Throughout the evening, divers continued their search. They eventually found one of the child's feet, along with another body they would later have to identify. (It turned out to be a woman who had committed suicide months earlier by jumping off a bridge.)

By 11:00 PM—after eight hours of angst and not knowing—Al Garber finally called and said the words we were aching to hear.

"It's not Jacob."

They had compared the child's footprint to Jacob's baby footprint. It wasn't a match.

"We still don't know who it is, though," Al told us. "So, if you could just wait on telling anyone, that would be helpful."

It was impossible. For about ten seconds, I tried not to show any emotion as Jerry and I walked back into the living room, but I couldn't disguise the relief on my face. I burst into a smile and was immediately grabbed up into hugs, tears, and smiles.

When I could finally think and breathe again, a new and horrible thought overwhelmed me.

Who was it?

Who was this other child who had been killed, dismembered, and thrown into the river? I was overcome by anguish and horrible guilt. How could I feel so happy when some other poor mom would be devastated to hear it was her son? The gut ache deepened.

Later, we learned that someone had broken into a crypt at a Minneapolis cemetery, stolen the body of this recently deceased boy, cut off his head, hands, and feet, then thrown him into the river. It was a tiny bit of a relief to know this child had already been dead when this horrible act occurred, but it was so hard for us to wrap our heads around this disgusting act of desecration. Who could do this? And how could we survive in this dark new world where things like grave robbing and dismemberment existed?

{ Chapter 18 }

We all struggled over how to acknowledge Jacob's birthday that first year. Several weeks earlier, Scott Meyer of the public relations firm Mona, Meyer, McGrath and Gavin in the Twin Cities had offered to help us set up a nonprofit organization (NPO) in Jacob's name. He and fellow staffer Nancy Groen helped us draft bylaws, a vision statement, and an organizational structure. Finally, we received our official NPO status, and we decided to mark the occasion by announcing the founding of the Jacob Wetterling Foundation (JWF) on February 17, 1990—Jacob's twelfth birthday.

We made the announcement at a special event at Lake George in St. Cloud. Over two hundred people attended, and afterward, we released yellow, blue, and white balloons. Each carried a card with the foundation's name and address and a message that read, "Hope is seeing success where others see failure, seeing sunshine where others see shadows and storm."

It was a perfect message that fit the mood of the day. Outside, the weather may have been cold, dark, and gray, but we chose to see sunshine instead.

February 17, 1990
St. Cloud Times

Dear Jacob,
Happy Birthday. It's your special day, and my heart breaks that this year you didn't get to choose what you wanted to do. I want you to know always how special you are and how much I love you. Please remember the many wonderful times we have had together. Think about the O.D. game you play with Dad and Trevor. Think about the Vikings games, the fishing trips, video games, and friends

sleeping over. Think about all the things we're going to do when you are finally free.

I believe in you and all the great things that the future holds. Please hold on to your dreams as I hold on to you every minute of every day. I love you. We're going to find you and life will be good again.

May you feel the warmth of the love and prayers and hope sent to you from all around the world. Hang on, Jake.

All my love,
Mom

As days turned to weeks, and weeks turned to months, we maintained our hope that Jacob would come home. The kids were back in school, Jerry was back at work, and I was back to cooking, cleaning, doing laundry, and shuttling the kids to their activities. My days became more routine, but with Jerry working full time, I became the one who met with investigators and talked to our case manager at the National Center for Missing and Exploited Children (NCMEC). I also began reaching out to other missing children organizations and reading everything I could find about missing children.

When David Collins from the Kevin Collins Foundation had visited a few months earlier, he'd shared stories about other long-term missing children who had survived and returned home. I studied those stories, clung to them, and literally carried them with me wherever I went. The most well known was the story of Steven Stayner.

Seven-year-old Steven Stayner had been abducted from his hometown of Merced, California, on December 4, 1972. He was walking home from school when two men approached him in a car and told him they were collecting donations for the church. He agreed to show them the way to his house, so he got in their car and was kidnapped. For the next seven years, Steven grew up as an abducted, sexually abused child. He was brainwashed into believing his parents no longer wanted him and that he'd been legally adopted by his abductor. Even though he attended school and was often left home alone, he never tried to escape or ask for help because he was terrified of what his abductor might do. Over time, he learned to live with the lie and accepted his new reality.

When Steven was fourteen years old, his abductor kidnapped another little boy—five-year-old Timmy White from Ukiah, California. Steven didn't want to see Timmy suffer the same abuse he had endured for the past seven years, so after a few weeks, he snuck Timmy out of the house and hitchhiked forty miles back to Ukiah. Once there, he took Timmy to the police station, and both boys were recovered. Steven later spoke about how he could have been found if people had just been paying attention.

> I believe the single most important thing you can do to help find
> abducted children is to be aware of the problem and keep an eye out
> for suspicious "family situations" around you. While it may be hard
> for you to tell an abducted child from an abused child, it's not hard
> to tell a child in trouble. And it's not hard to do something about it.

I learned so much from Steven and was strengthened by his story of survival. At the same time, it pained me to learn there had been so many signs and opportunities along the way to save him from his abductor. People needed to learn these signs and be more aware of the problem of missing children. Clearly, there was work to do.

I began to develop a razor-sharp focus. I read everything I could about missing children and spoke to Ron Jones, our case manager at NCMEC. I kept asking him about the success stories.

"How do missing kids come home? How do they get there? What has to happen? What do we need to do next? How can we engage people? What is our message?"

In just a few short months, I had learned a lot about missing children, including common lures that were used to abduct them, the kinds of people who take them, and tips for parents to keep their children safe. I wanted to share what I'd been learning, and by early spring I felt I was ready. By this time, we had used some of the search and reward donations to hire our friend Ron Marotte to run the office of the Jacob Wetterling Foundation. With his help, I began lining up safety talks at schools, churches, and any other group or organization that was willing to listen. Word began to spread, and soon we were getting several calls into the JWF office from other parents and community members who wanted to hear my message.

Almost every time I spoke, someone asked how in the world I would ever be able to let my other kids go anywhere on their own. Didn't I just want to keep them locked up forever?

It wasn't like that. Our kids were so scared already—not only by the horrors of what had happened to Jacob, but also by the way our home life had completely changed. Nothing was the same. They often saw me crying, and police officers were in and out of our home almost every day for the first few months. Psychics were coming into our home, asking to see Jake's bedroom, touching his things, and making scary predictions. The media was constantly trying to get in our faces, and everything about our family had become public. Our kids knew I was willing to do whatever it took to help find Jacob, but this also terrified them because they were afraid something might happen to *me*.

It was important for me to try to take away the fear. I wanted people to know that scaring kids does not make them safer. Helping them to be confident and to stay connected to their parents (or other trusted adults) is what makes kids safer.

As I worked to help my kids feel less scared, I was finding my own way to rebuild our world. It felt like everything that had ever been meaningful to me—every gift, every cherished moment—had been tossed up into the air and was swirling around me like money in a wind machine. Day by day, I pictured myself reaching out and grasping for one thing at a time, clinging to it, then desperately reaching for another one as the storm raged all around me.

I cherished the world we had previously known, the world Jacob knew. Soon, that wish became a big part of my message and my fight. I believed in a loving, caring world, and although I'd become aware of a much darker place, I didn't want to live in it. I couldn't survive there. I needed to find some glimmer of hope just to get up in the morning, and because of the public's endless outpouring of support, I knew firsthand there were more good people in the world than bad. I firmly believed that if all those really good people could just pull together, we could be so much stronger than one really bad man. I wanted our children to believe in good people and to not be afraid of the world. It took a tremendous amount of effort to try to rebuild the world we once knew, but we kept at it and persevered. I had reached a point where I refused to let the man who took Jacob take anything more.

As I continued to speak, I always gathered more stories. Very soon, I realized the richness was in the stories. Nobody cared about the statistics.

They remembered the hope. Over time, I developed a message that was very simple and covered four key points.

1. *You are special.*

Early on, a reporter stuck a microphone in my face and asked, "So what makes Jacob so special? Kids have been taken before Jacob and they've been taken since, but we've never seen a response like this. So what makes Jacob so special?" I was stunned into silence and it took me a moment to respond. When I finally gathered my composure, I said, "He's my son. There's nobody in the world like him. He loves peanut butter. He sneezes when he looks at the sun. He's a great brother to his sisters and younger brother. He's a good friend. I love him. I could go on forever. Yes, Jacob is special. Every child is special and they need to hear that from caring adults."

I learned that the number-one lure that gets children into dangerous situations is not candy or money. It's attention and love—kids want to be loved and want to feel special. Pete Banks, who was in charge of law enforcement trainings at NCMEC, always told the officers to give their own children a hug. "Tell them you love them. Tell them how special they are, and that you're proud of them, because if you don't, someone else will. There are bad people out there who prey on children. They look for vulnerabilities and will offer them that love and attention. Don't give them the opportunity."

2. *Nobody has the right to hurt you, physically or sexually.*

This was something that was seldom talked about before Jacob was taken. Although there had been a few horrific high-profile cases of child sexual abuse, there was little discussion about it in the mainstream. Few schools had comprehensive sex education, and even fewer had sexual abuse prevention messages. Jacob gave us an opportunity to talk to children and open up the discussion.

3. *If someone does touch you or hurt you sexually—or even says something that makes you feel yucky—it is not your fault.*

Kids have a tendency to blame themselves for anything that goes wrong. They blame themselves when their parents get divorced or when their family is having financial difficulties, so it's not hard to imagine how much guilt and confusion they feel when someone does something to them that feels so wrong. They don't want anyone to know about it, and many times they're even told by the victimizer that it is *their* fault. We need to let kids know it's *never* their fault if someone touches them in ways that make them feel uncomfortable, and we need to tell them in advance. When I spoke to kids, I always told them, "It's never your fault, just like it wasn't Jacob's fault that he got kidnapped."

4. Don't keep it a secret.

When sexual abuse does happen, kids need to know they should tell an adult they trust. If that person doesn't do anything, they need to keep telling until someone helps them. We need to listen to kids when they *do* tell. I have a dear friend whose boys told her that her friend's son was mean and bad. She wrote it off and told them he was just a teenager and was going through a tough time. Years later, my friend found out this young man had been sexually assaulting all three of her boys.

I was often caught off guard with the openness and honesty of the kids' questions. Once I said, "If an adult shows you pictures of people without any clothes on and that makes you feel uncomfortable, tell a trusted adult." One child raised his hand and asked me, "Does that include all the naked lady pictures my dad has in the garage?"

Another time, I was sharing how Jacob had been abducted by a masked man with a gun, and a girl shared that her mom's boyfriend had threatened her with a knife.

Clearly, these kids needed some private follow-up with their teacher or guidance counselor. Whenever possible, I made a point of talking to the kids' teachers beforehand. I was a teacher myself, and I knew that they could be watchful of anyone acting out or asking tough questions. My message often took time to process, so I encouraged the kids and their teachers to continue the discussion when they returned to their smaller classrooms.

The education I got from kids was life changing for me. They wanted to talk. One girl wrote me a note about her best friend who always hung out with an older neighbor, a man who bought her things and took her places. One day he asked her and her friend to sleep over, but her dad said no. She wrote, "I was lucky because the police came and arrested him for sexually molesting kids. He molested my friend too."

Often, kids had questions but were afraid to ask because they didn't want to feel stupid. I learned about one girl just entering high school whose dad was still giving her baths.

The more talks I did, the more I began to realize this was a much bigger problem than I'd even realized. We needed to move beyond "don't talk to strangers." Kids needed better tools, and parents needed to open the discussion.

One little kindergartener said it best.

"Why didn't people make a big deal about this *before* Jacob was kidnapped? Why does it always take another kid?"

Exactly.

As my message began to spread, so did the work of the Jacob Wetterling Foundation. In addition to the safety talks I was giving, JWF was also busy coordinating media interviews and public service announcements, organizing community awareness events, and hosting fundraisers. Missing and exploited children had clearly become a hot topic in our state, and people were starting to pay attention.

On April 5, 1990, Jerry and I were invited to the Minnesota State Capitol to address the house and senate on Jacob's abduction and the issue of missing children. Representative Jeff Bertram of Paynesville arranged the appearance for us, and we used the opportunity to thank our legislators for all the support they had shown us during the five and a half months since Jacob had been kidnapped. Jerry gave the invocation that began the floor sessions, and all the lawmakers wore white "Jacob's Hope" ribbons that day.

Afterward, we met with Governor Rudy Perpich, who told us he was planning to establish a commission on child abduction that would make recommendations to the 1991 legislature for changes in child safety laws.

I told him to count me in.

October 21, 1990
St. Cloud Times

Dear Jacob,

It's been almost a year since you were taken from us and I still miss you so very much. Some things have changed. Cinnamon is no longer a puppy—she's as big as Marcus. Carmen is growing up so fast. There are so many things she can do now . . . she says you'll hardly recognize her. Amy, I think, is compiling lists of things to tell you about—you two always got along so well. Trevor misses you terribly. He's so often looking for someone to play with and he lost a lot of his enthusiasm for sports. Aaron is quietly waiting for his friend to come home. Shannon's at St. Ben's now—a dream she always had.

Some things haven't changed. We left your room just as messy. Remember how frustrated you were last fall because after wearing goalie skates for so long you thought you couldn't skate on regular skates? I found out last winter that those skates hadn't been sharpened right and it wasn't your fault you couldn't skate on them. I wanted you to know that, for the same reason that whatever has happened to you and whatever you've been forced to do—it's not your fault. It's survival. Please don't believe that we don't want you back—that's one of the many lies you've probably been told. If pictures were taken, don't believe that they'd show the pictures everywhere if you left. If they do, they'd get arrested.

You've done nothing wrong and we love you. Remember how I always believed in you? Whatever you wanted to do, whatever dream you had—you could do it? I still do, Jake. I believe you have your whole life in front of you and you can still reach for all the good that life has to offer. You are so special and we can get through this. Just grab onto the first opportunity you get to get away. You can do it, Jake.

We'll never stop looking for you and we'll never stop aching until we can throw our arms around you and cry and laugh and plan and strive for a better life for all of us.

Hang on, Jake.

Love,
Mom

{ Chapter 19 }

In July 1990, I was one of twenty-seven Minnesotans appointed to the new Governor's Task Force on Missing Children. The group was formed in direct response to Jacob's kidnapping but was intended to serve and benefit all missing children. Our task was to get a better picture of the problem of missing children in Minnesota, and then to come up with some recommendations that we could present back to Governor Perpich by February 15, 1991.

We were a diverse group that represented a wide variety of perspectives. Our members included people from human service agencies, education, law enforcement, social service agencies, missing children organizations, criminal justice, the arts, the religious community, parents of missing children, and concerned citizens. Because the issues surrounding missing children were also so diverse, the task force was divided into five subcommittees: Non-Family Abduction, Parental Abduction, Runaways and Thrownaways (kids who are thrown out of their homes by their parents or guardians), Public Education/Information, and System Needs.

I was elected chair of the Non-Family Abduction Subcommittee and dug into the research right away. The first thing I did was ask law enforcement officers, "What would have helped you in the search for Jacob?" Neil Neddermeyer, a detective with the Hennepin County Sheriff's Office in Minneapolis, was very clear. He told me, "Two things. First, a central repository of information. And second, sex offender registration."

The central repository of information would allow all Minnesota law enforcement to coordinate information so it could be better shared between agencies. At the time Jacob was kidnapped, each local law enforcement department was keeping its own records of offenders who committed crimes within their own jurisdictions. This resulted in silos of information that were inaccessible to other departments, and there was no way to search all the data at once, quickly. Minnesota's BCA was aware of the problem and had already begun creating a central repository for the data, but they needed funding to complete the task.

Sex offender registration was a newer thought. California had been registering sex offenders since the early 1970s, but in 1990, they were one of only six states that had any type of registration.

In investigating Jacob's kidnapping, Stearns County had identified over five thousand sexual offenders in Minnesota during the first few months alone. Other law enforcement agencies were calling the SCSO just to check this list of names for other cases they were investigating. This made me wonder: if Jacob was found, what would happen to that list? The way I understood it, once our case was closed, that meant none of this information would be available to other agencies.

By now, I'd learned a lot about the types of people who committed sexual crimes against children, and in most cases, the offender had many victims— sometimes over a hundred. I'd been told that treatment was ineffective at best, and sometimes even detrimental since the offenders learned how *not* to get caught while being treated for their crimes.

I became convinced we needed some type of registry in Minnesota to help investigators solve these types of crimes and lock up the criminals who committed them. I brought this idea to the task force and began investigating the laws of other states so we could use the language as a reference in creating similar sex offender registration in Minnesota.

That summer, Carmen begged me to let her attend Girl Scout camp with a friend. Part of me wanted to say no, but she had spent nearly a year being afraid to do anything outside of our home, and I was proud of her for wanting to go. It was only for three nights and was less than an hour away, so we agreed.

The next day, my heart leaped when I received a call from the camp nurse. Carmen didn't feel well and wanted to come home. She was complaining of a stomachache, but the nurse suspected it may have been brought on by something that really upset her.

When I arrived at the camp, Carmen was waiting outside on a bench with one of the camp counselors. She didn't look well, and I could tell she'd been crying. On the way home, she finally told me what happened. She was wearing her "Jacob's Hope" button when another little girl asked her about it. When Carmen explained that Jacob was her brother, the little girl replied, "My mom says he's dead."

I had to pull over while we both hugged and sobbed. I was so heartbroken, but also mad at myself for allowing Carmen to be so vulnerable and alone. I couldn't take away her pain or stop her little brain from seeing that horrible vision in her head. Somehow, I needed to fix this.

A week later, Jerry and I sat the kids down for another family meeting. School was about to start, and I wanted to make sure none of them would be caught off guard like that again. We sat in a circle in the living room and talked about Carmen's experience at camp, and what the kids could do if they ever found themselves in a situation like that. Amy and Trevor both repeated what we'd been saying for such a long time. There was no proof that Jacob wasn't alive. They offered suggestions like, "I've gotta go," or "That's not we believe." I also suggested, "You don't have all the information," and "We choose to hope." Amy said that one of her good friends always met her between classes, so she never had to walk the halls alone. Trevor shared how he stuck with his friends . . . the ones he knew he could trust.

I explained how our friends were so important, like a cocoon that made us feel safe and protected. I also reminded them that this space, our family circle, was a safe place where they could talk about whatever was going on in their worlds.

Jerry shared how he missed Jake every single day and thought about him whenever he went biking or running. He explained that this was his own special time to offer up prayers for Jake to stay strong.

"We all need to stay strong," he added.

As parents, Jerry and I were very familiar with our own pain, but we hadn't imagined some of the things our children were having to face. I felt better knowing we had built this safe space to talk, share, and listen.

We all agreed it was important to keep doing the things that made us happy. Carmen and Amy continued with dance, Trevor continued playing Sega with his friends, and all three of our kids continued playing soccer. The neighborhood O.D. games dwindled off without Jake, but we still enjoyed inviting friends over to watch the Minnesota Vikings on Sunday afternoons. As a family, we looked forward to this "regular stuff" in our lives to keep us going.

As October 22, 1990, loomed closer, we were forced to face the horrible reality that Jacob had been missing for a full year. The number of investigators working on his case had dropped from seventy-five to eight. There were four investigators on the case from Stearns County, two from the state's BCA office, and two from the FBI. Tens of thousands of leads had been reported, but still, there was no sign of Jacob.

We had no idea how to commemorate such a sad and somber anniversary. I had spent the past year just trying to survive, and even in my new role as a child safety advocate, I was still just a mom who was desperately searching for her son. I didn't want to think about a first "anniversary." I hated to even call it that. Weren't anniversaries supposed to be happy occasions?

The kids had just started another school year, and I lost it completely on the day they came home with their new school photos. It was often the ordinary things that sent me to tears. Normally, I'd look forward to this annual trip down memory lane—taking the frames off the wall, seeing how much the kids had changed over the years, then putting their new school photos on top of the previous ones. But in the fall of 1990, there was a new and noticeable sadness in each of my kids' faces. Gone was the sparkle of absolute innocence. Instead, their eyes seemed to hold a questioning expression that was hard to define. It tore my heart apart to see it and to know all that these kids had lived through, especially Trevor.

After almost a year, Jacob and Trevor's room still looked the same. Everything remained the way they had left it, but no one used it anymore. Trevor continued to keep his clothes in his room, but he never played in there or slept in his bunkbed ever again. It was too ominous and scary. Instead, he slept in a sleeping bag on the floor of our bedroom or on a fold-out bed in Carmen's room. Nighttime was like musical chairs. We never really knew where anyone would end up. But it definitely wasn't in Jake and Trevor's old bedroom.

Family, friends, and our close-knit community of St. Joseph once again held us up and got us through that first anniversary. There were several events planned, including a prayer service at the College of St. Benedict, a tree-planting ceremony at Centennial Park, a walk/run for Jacob, and a Sunday-evening prayer service with candlelight vigil at the St. Joseph Catholic Church.

At the tree-planting ceremony, we released twelve homing pigeons that my sister Barbi sent from California, along with a note: "Since I can't be there

with you, I am sending to you a symbol of hope, of freedom, of flight. . . .
With their release from their cage they will take with them some of the rage
and horror of the past year and show us a freedom which we await so impatiently. As the homing pigeon circles the skies to find his way back to his
roost, so will Jacob one day be free to find his way back home again."

It was a powerful, memorable moment.

Following the anniversary, I tried to move forward once again. I refocused
my energy on getting a bill passed that would mandate sex offender registration in Minnesota. Our task force had been working hard on gathering research and would soon be prepared to share our findings with the governor.
However, less than two weeks later, Governor Rudy Perpich lost his bid for
reelection. This meant we would need to present our recommendations to
the new governor, Arne Carlson. We could only hope this governor would
be as supportive of our efforts as Governor Perpich had been.

It didn't go well.

On the day we presented our report, we brought along several victims who
had stories to tell. They included a former runaway who would share her
experiences of homelessness and exploitation, a father whose children had
been kidnapped by his estranged wife, and me, a mom whose son had been
kidnapped by a complete stranger.

However, before we even got started, Governor Carlson leaned back in
his chair, put his feet on his desk, and seemed completely unreceptive to our
cause. After listening to two victim stories, he leaned forward and asked,
"Am I going to have to listen to more of these?" He clearly wasn't engaged in
what we had to say.

When it was my turn, I shared my story, then spoke on behalf of our subcommittee to present our recommendations. They included:

- Registration of convicted sex offenders
- Establishment of a Violent Crime Center
- A time limit of four hours for law enforcement agencies to submit
  reports of new incidents to the Violent Crime Center
- BCA training about the use of the Violent Crime Center to appro-
  priate agencies

- Updated sentencing guidelines that recommended imprisonment after two convictions for second degree sexual assault, rather than three
- Mandatory treatment for sex offenders

When I finished, Governor Carlson simply looked at me and said, "A sex offender registry? You can't do that. These people have rights."

I was sitting next to our sheriff, Charlie Grafft, who suddenly rose to his feet—angry and glaring—ready for a confrontation. I had to put my hand on his arm and encourage him to settle down.

"We can do this," I assured the governor.

The process was long, and at times grueling, but I was convinced that having a registry of people who commit sexual offenses against children would help to solve these violent crimes. Every day, I studied the issue, reviewed other state's laws, and was in regular contact with Detective Bob Schilling from the King County Sheriff's Department in Washington state who could cite cases and instances where the registry had helped.

Finally, the Minnesota Sex Offender Registration Act passed with near-unanimous support in both the house and senate and was scheduled to go into effect on August 1, 1991. With the law's passage, Minnesota would become the fifteenth state in the nation to require mandatory registration of sex offenders.

October 11, 1991
St. Joseph Newsleader

Dear Jacob,

The pain goes deeper every day I miss you. My prayer is that you're not suffering. I want so badly to hold you.

Remember how we used to rock in that big old rocking chair—even when you were big? We've all changed so much, and yet through each phase we carry you with us in our thoughts, in our hearts and in our plans.

Please feel our love and live on the memories of all we shared and the dreams of what life can be. We'll hold you in our hearts until that glorious day when we can hold you in our arms.

We'll never stop looking for you.

Love,
Mom

{ Chapter 20 }

Before Jacob was kidnapped, I knew absolutely nothing about crimes against children, especially *sexual* crimes against children. Now I had a vast knowledge of the topic and was proud of my contributions to this important legislation. So, when US senator Dave Durenberger called to congratulate me and ask for my help in putting together a similar bill at the federal level, I eagerly accepted.

Senator Durenberger was from our neck of the woods and had a strong attachment to Jacob's case. He grew up and attended school in Collegeville, just five miles west of St. Joseph, and had been paying close attention to our local legislative efforts while speaking to congressional leaders about introducing legislation for a national sex offender registry.

The idea of expanding sex offender registration to every state made a lot of sense to me. Ernie Allen, president of NCMEC, told me the center had been receiving calls on their hotline asking which states did *not* have registration laws. It seemed that offenders were choosing where to live after they were released from prison based on which states didn't have mandatory sex offender registration.

I thought, "We can fix that."

On May 22, 1991, I joined Senator Durenberger in Washington, DC, to show my support for the new sex offender registry bill before Congress. Once again, I shared our story and explained that Jacob had likely been taken by a sex offender who had a previous history of similar crimes. I cited studies that showed most child molesters continue to offend, both before and after their convictions. I also gave an example from our own case, sharing that it had taken Minnesota authorities a year and a half to discover there was a convicted sex offender living just a half mile from the very spot Jacob had been taken. This man was eventually cleared, but I told lawmakers how incredibly important it was for investigators to have immediate access to this kind of information in the first few critical hours after a child goes missing.

One month later, on June 26, 1991, the US Senate unanimously approved Senator Durenberger's amendment to President Bill Clinton's crime bill, requiring child molesters to register their addresses with police for ten years after their release from prison. In his address to the Senate, Durenberger cited much of the research we did for the Minnesota legislation:

> Sexual crimes against children are widespread. The people who commit these offenses repeat their crimes again, and again, and again. And local law enforcement officials need access to an interstate system of information to prevent and respond to these horrible crimes against our children.

The amendment was named the Jacob Wetterling Act, and similar legislation was introduced in the House by Minnesota representative Jim Ramstad. Now, we just needed that to pass before the bill would be introduced before the full committee.

On August 1, 1991—the very day our Sex Offender Registration Act went into effect in Minnesota—I was once again in Washington, working with Jim Ramstad to lobby other members of the House for passage of the national bill. In his address to the US House of Representatives, Representative Ramstad thanked me graciously, noting that my presence "personified the situation and brought home the need for this legislation."

The amendment was approved and passed on to the full committee, but it didn't jump all the hurdles that session. There were years of work ahead of us before the bill would become law, but the Jacob Wetterling Act was gaining momentum in Washington, and Congress was finally paying attention to the public's mounting concerns over child safety.

During the fall of 1991, Jerry and I were really struggling. We had faced so much and come so far, but between his work, my travel, and our tag-team parenting system, we were finding very little time to spend with each other. When we did find time to talk, it was usually about Jacob's case or foundation business. We had lost so much of what we used to have in common. Certainly, and understandably, much of the joy had left our marriage.

It had been over a year and a half since we started the Jacob Wetterling Foundation. With the staff and structure we had in place, we could keep Jacob's search alive, while at the same time providing hope and resources to other searching families. However, the added stress was taking its toll. When David Collins had encouraged us to start the foundation so soon after Jacob's kidnapping, it made sense. But I wished he had also told us how hard it would be trying to start a new business during the most chaotic and traumatic time of our lives.

At home, Jerry and I were still operating in survival mode. We both kept busy with our own schedules, and we had very little time for each other at the end of the day. That was okay with me. I found him hard to talk to, and Jerry preferred to avoid any deep discussions that might result in an argument.

We found our own sources of support, but there was one thing no one could help me with: the loss of intimacy in our relationship. My world was now dominated by pedophiles, sex offenders, and victims of sexual assault. Every day I struggled to push away disturbing thoughts of all the horrible things that might be happening to Jacob. The trauma was more than I could handle, and I couldn't even imagine feeling desire or pleasure from sexual intimacy again. I often wondered how victims of sexual violence ever found their way back to normal relationships.

I knew I'd married a good man, but I missed our closeness. Every day was still a struggle. Since our son's disappearance, Jerry and I had been interrogated, polygraphed, pitted against each other, and made targets of lies and scandal. We were even extorted.

In November 1990, a prisoner from Buffalo, New York, mailed us a letter threatening to tell people we had arranged our own son's abduction in order to raise money. The letter said if we didn't send him a check for $100,000 by November 27, he would "sing like a canary" and expose us. Seven months later we received some justice when this man was indicted on extortion charges and eventually convicted, but still, it unnerved us.

Jerry and I did seek marriage counseling—which helped. After each session, we made it a point to go out to dinner, just the two of us, and talk about whatever had come up. It felt good to revisit some of our favorite restaurants, especially after not doing this for so long. I didn't like taking more time away from the kids, but the bottom line was . . . we needed to do this to hold our marriage together. It was the one time we could really hear what the other was feeling, without interruption, and we both looked forward to these special "date nights."

Still, sometimes all we could do was cope. We focused on what was practical. Are you going to be home tonight? Who's picking up Trevor? Who's taking Amy to dance? It wasn't always an ideal marriage, and I'll admit there were times I didn't think we would make it, but we were determined to figure it out and survive.

As if the emotional struggle wasn't enough, there was also the financial part. I had no income and received no money for my speaking appearances, but with all my traveling and lobbying, I was incurring a lot of expenses. Even though the foundation offered to reimburse me for my travel expenses, I refused to take any money from them because I was afraid people might accuse me of making money from Jacob's disappearance.

In reality, the financial side of Jacob's abduction was devastating. Of course, no searching parent wants to talk about the expenses involved in looking for their missing child, but because we are all so willing to do *anything* to find them, money is a huge added stress. Many victim's families end up going broke because they try to personally support the ongoing expenses of their loved one's investigation. Parents lose their jobs because of absenteeism or distractions at work, and still others are exploited by unscrupulous private investigators who run up huge bills. Up to this point, we had been *managing* the extra expenses, but just barely. Many other families weren't so fortunate.

One day, Jerry sat me down and told me he had withdrawn over $30,000 from our retirement fund to pay for expenses related to Jacob's investigation.

"What?!" I said in shock and anger. "How?"

"It just keeps adding up—the travel expenses, cell phone bills, pizza for the volunteers . . . "

"And psychics," I added bitterly.

He took a deep breath before continuing.

"We can't keep spending like this. Something has to change."

I knew he was right, but I was still angry. How could he have withdrawn that much money without even telling me about it? Was I really that hard to talk to? The reality was, we had only Jerry's income to rely on. He was working so hard and was the only one totally carrying us. This was a big wake-up call for me. I would have to figure out a way to continue my prevention and advocacy work without doing everything at no charge.

The foundation also bore the brunt of the increasing financial burden. Because of the large number of toll-free calls coming in to the Tri-County Crime Stoppers' tip line about Jacob's case, we were informed there wasn't enough funding for its ongoing support. It was Benton County sheriff Frank Wippler who called to tell me they were going to have to take down the tip line. By this time, that national toll-free number had been printed on millions of posters that had been distributed all across the country, so taking it down was simply not an option. Instead, the Jacob Wetterling Foundation agreed to start paying a portion of the bill. With three full-time staff members and monthly expenses now at $20,000, Jerry and I both worried the foundation was on shaky ground.

It had been almost two years since Jacob's disappearance, and life had become so fast and complicated. Jerry and I were wrestling with the demands of raising a family, running a chiropractic practice, serving on JWF's board of directors, educating children about personal safety, supporting other parents in the search for their missing children, advocating for stronger sex offender laws in Washington—all while trying to keep our own marriage intact. I had spoken at three hundred events over the past year and was on the road so often that Jerry finally had to ask me to start scheduling one day off per week.

It didn't help matters that I'd become so highly recognizable throughout our state. Gone were the days when I could just run to the mall or our family could go out for a quick bite to eat without being interrupted by people offering hugs, condolences, encouragement, and well-wishes. I still wasn't used to being a public face, and it drove my family crazy, especially the kids.

"I miss all the normal things we used to do as a family," I said to my good friend Judi one day.

"Well, Patty, I hate to tell you this," she said, throwing her arm over my shoulder. "But 'normal' is just a setting on the washing machine."

In the fall of 1991, NCMEC released a computerized, age-enhanced photo of what Jacob might look like at age fifteen.

I knew it was coming. Several months earlier, NCMEC had called and requested photos of Jerry and me at age fifteen, as well as of Amy, who was fifteen by now. I'd pushed to get this age-enhancement done, but as I stood holding the unopened manila envelope in my hand, I wasn't so sure I actually wanted to see it. I took a deep breath, carefully opened the envelope, and was completely unprepared for the wave of emotions that hit me. There was no cover letter, no explanation or context—nothing to soften the blow. Instead, I simply found a photo of someone who sort of looked like my son . . . but wasn't.

NCMEC forensic artists work hard to capture the spirit of missing children and utilize science to generate what a child might look like as they age. In this photo, Jacob's hair was darker, thick, buzzed and spiked—not the soft, sandy brown hair that got sweaty and wavy whenever he played hard with his friends. This haircut might have been the "in" style for boys his age, but I knew Jacob would never have worn his hair like that. I also knew he would never wear a collared shirt like the person in this photo. I'm sure I was in denial and being overly critical, but it was just so hard to see the more mature facial features and realize how much we had missed.

I put the age-enhanced photo on the coffee table and tried to get used to it by taking a sideways glance every time I walked by, but that didn't help. I still couldn't look at it. Eventually, we gave NCMEC the go-ahead to distribute the photo. Logically, I knew this was an important tool for investigators to use in their search, but for me, it was just another painful reminder of all we had lost.

{ Chapter 21 }

In the spring of 1992, the Jacob Wetterling Foundation was struggling with a host of internal problems, including miscommunication about our focus and vision. We had formed the foundation out of urgency and desperation to help find Jacob and other missing kids. We expanded our scope to provide safety education for kids and parents, and to serve as a resource for other searching families, but every case was different. In addition to working for missing kids, we were now faced with cases of missing adults, child exploitation, parental abductions, and international abductions. Interaction between searching parents, law enforcement, and media varied from case to case, and it became obvious we needed more clarity of vision and action.

We also found ourselves taking in leads and tips and had to ask ourselves a whole new set of questions. Are we a resource center or an investigative agency? What do we do with this information? What if a tipster wants to remain anonymous? How do we forward the information to law enforcement? Are we supposed to share the information with the victim's family? We had experienced at least one act of vigilantism after passing along a tip, and we didn't want to make that mistake again.

Compounding these "vision" problems, we were also operating from an ineffective set of bylaws that essentially allowed our executive director to make decisions and take on projects without the board's knowledge or approval. This was especially frustrating for me as board chair and spokesperson, because I often felt like I didn't know what was happening within our own organization, or which families we were even helping.

Clearly, we needed to take a timeout and address some of these issues. At that time, the JWF board consisted of nineteen members (including Jerry and myself) who met monthly. There was also a five-person executive committee that included the president, vice president, treasurer, secretary, and the foundation's executive director (neither Jerry nor I served on the executive committee). Following an emergency meeting to discuss these problems, the executive committee decided to take a three-month hiatus, so the organization could refocus and reorganize. Although the office would remain open during this time, programming would be scaled back. Fortunately, one of our board members volunteered to send us his agency's intern to help answer the phone and take care of standard office duties.

As part of the restructuring, the executive committee also made the grim decision to dismiss all three paid staff members, including executive director Ron Marotte. Although Jerry and I were in agreement with the need for change, this was especially difficult for us. Ron was a dear friend of ours, and we'd become close to the other two staff members as well, so the decision to let them go was more than painful.

News of our staff dismissals came as a great shock to the entire community. I worried people might think we had mismanaged finances or were closing for good. Would we survive this? Was this the right thing to do?

Following the dismissals, several board members resigned, and many of our longtime volunteers were upset. Some left for good. Sandi Laski, one of our JWF board members, offered to step in as interim director while we searched for someone with nonprofit experience.

Sandi worked hard to keep us afloat and functioning during this incredibly challenging time. She also hired an office coordinator who became one of my dearest confidantes—Alma Hansen. Alma took over most of the victim assistance work while we began the search for a new executive director. After eight months, we hired Bob Lee, who had served the past nine years as executive director of a nonprofit group that worked to create affordable housing in the Twin Cities. Bob was exactly what we needed. He had twenty years of experience with nonprofit work, an incredibly effective leadership style, and a quick sense of humor that always made our difficult work more pleasant. Slowly, we began to rebuild. Within months, JWF began charging a regular speaker fee for most of my appearances, and I was finally able to get reimbursed for my travel expenses. This greatly helped with our family finances, as well as with the solvency of the organization. Much of the worry and work that Jerry and I had taken on since the founding of JWF began to ease, and we began to find our way back to each other. Bob made us laugh and helped us enjoy life again.

⤛

In November 1992, I was invited to join the board of directors of the National Center for Missing and Exploited Children. After learning they covered all travel and lodging expenses for board meetings, I gladly accepted.

I was appointed to the program committee, and for the next two years, I continued to work with NCMEC to get legislation for a national sex offender registry passed. I learned so much from Ernie Allen, president and CEO of NCMEC, as well as from a fellow board member, Robbie Callaway, who was the assistant national director for the Boys and Girls Clubs of America. They knew who would be supportive of the bill in Congress and how to get me in front of them.

On Wednesday, April 13, 1994, I attended my first White House briefing, one that outlined the president's crime bill. I was one of about two hundred attendees—including police officers, politicians, and crime victims—who were invited to attend. There were nine of us from Minnesota who met in Representative Jim Ramstad's office, then were driven to the Old Executive Office Building for the meeting.

Attorney General Janet Reno started the briefing by giving an overview of the three main elements of the crime bill (punishment, policing, and prevention), then fielded questions. She spoke candidly about her experiences working as an attorney with police and walking the beats with street cops to learn more about crime.

Next, we heard from Lee Brown, director of the Office of National Drug Control Policy, Chief of Staff Mack McLarty (who was filling in for Vice President Al Gore), and Madeleine Kunin, deputy secretary of the Department of Education. The briefing ended with the statement, "This administration wants to hear from you."

After the briefing, we met once again with Representative Ramstad, to debrief. Our group was all in agreement that in order to properly address the issues surrounding child safety in the president's crime bill, three acts needed to be passed.

First, the Morgan P. Hardiman Task Force on Missing and Exploited Children would increase the resources available to local law enforcement for difficult kidnapping cases by having specially trained investigators who would be able to work on these cases full time.

Second, the DNA Identification Act would provide funding to improve the quality and availability of DNA analysis to law enforcement.

And finally, the Jacob Wetterling Crimes Against Children and Sexually

Violent Offender Registration Act would require sex offenders who victimized children to register their addresses with law enforcement.

I shared how sex offender registration had been shown to be an effective
tool by states that already had it, but it broke down when offenders simply
moved to a different state that didn't have the requirement. This new federal
law would require any person convicted of a sexually violent crime to register their address with law enforcement for ten years after their release.

On September 13, 1994, the Jacob Wetterling Crimes Against Children
and Sexually Violent Offender Registration Act was passed and signed into
law by President Clinton as part of the federal crime bill. Jerry, my mom,
and I flew out to DC for the signing of the bill, which was held in the White
House Rose Garden. Senator Durenberger and Representative Ramstad
were amazingly supportive, offering tours around the area and graciously
introducing us to many of our country's leaders.

Over the years, people have often asked me how it feels to have a federal
law named after your son. To be honest, in many ways it was awful. Jacob
had been missing almost five years, and it was difficult to hear his name being tied to sex offenders and crime. On the other hand, it was such an honor
and a tribute to Jacob, his sense of fairness, and the very world he knew and
believed in. My journey had been one of desperation, and I truly hoped that
our efforts would make a difference for other families of missing children.

October 22, 1994
Fifth anniversary

Dear Jacob,

Jacob, you know how much we love you. Don't let anyone tell
you differently. We hope that happy memories have helped carry
you through. They have helped us. Don't give up your dreams. We
know we can all heal through this . . . but we need you home.

We love you, Jake. We'll never give up on our search to find you
and to bring you home.

Hugs and kisses,
Mom

{ Chapter 22 }

Even though none of us wanted to face the reality of a fifth anniversary, our family had finally come to realize that the pain of Jacob's loss was not just our own. This was never more apparent than at Jacob's school, where plans for a memorial were already underway. Two of his classmates, Alison Feigh and Kelli Mullen, were planning a courtyard ceremony at Apollo High School to honor Jacob, and they invited us to join them. They were also raising money for the Jacob Wetterling Foundation by selling "Jacob's Hope" T-shirts at the school, and all the athletic teams would be wearing "JH" on their uniforms during homecoming week.

Once again, it was the kids who showed us the way.

Someone came up with the idea of a time capsule, so we chose to host a public get-together at La Playette Restaurant and Lounge in downtown St. Joe. It was held on the anniversary, Saturday, October 22. We encouraged people to bring something special to put inside the time capsule so we could share these items with Jacob when he returned home. It could be anything—a letter, a favorite poem, a wish, or something else that was reflective of the past five years.

The time capsule was handmade by a thirty-four-year-old industrial arts teacher at Holdingford High School who had passed away earlier that year. The items we received included an autographed football from the Apollo Eagles football team, a "Class of 1996" keychain, a hockey puck, and several letters from kids, parents, and community members, all addressed to Jacob.

We had a great turnout, and when I stepped up to the microphone to thank everyone for coming, I tried to share some of what I was feeling after five years of searching.

"Five years ago, I knew nothing about child abduction or really anything about crimes against children."

I had learned so much. I shared how I continued to study success stories of kids who came home and kept those stories in a three-ring binder that I carried with me whenever I traveled. My hope sustained me, along with the support of countless people who continued to hold us up. I ended with one of my favorite quotes by Pablo Casals: "We must all work to make the world worthy of its children."

When I finished speaking, we allowed some time at the open microphone for people to share their thoughts and feelings. It was emotional, and many people, young and old, shared how much their lives had changed since Jacob had been taken.

Jerry and I were surprised to find Al Catallo from our local FBI office at the event. We'd seen so little of him over the past few years that I had begun to develop a sense of abandonment, as if he'd just moved on to other cases and forgotten all about us. Thankfully, I discovered that wasn't true. When Al pulled out his wallet to make a donation to the foundation, I noticed he still carried a photo of Jacob with him. It was placed right alongside the photos of his own kids, and my heart swelled in gratitude.

"Thanks, Al," I said. "And thanks for coming."

"How does your schedule look in the next week or so?" he asked us. "We've been reviewing the case, and we have a new theory we'd like to discuss with both of you."

A few weeks later, I found myself driving through downtown St. Cloud for a 6:30 PM meeting with Al Catallo and another FBI agent from Minneapolis whom I had never met before. Because Jerry was often late arriving to things because of last minute drop-ins at the chiropractic office, I decided to drive separately.

The St. Cloud field office of the FBI was inconspicuously located on the fourth floor of the Wells Fargo Building. I'd never been there, and I was curious to see it. There was nothing showy or glamorous about the place. I followed the receptionist back to a meeting room, and we passed several messy cubicles cluttered with stacks of papers and boxes. There were no family photos on any of the desks, no crayon-drawn pictures on the cube walls. It was all just cold, lifeless, and depressing.

Before long, Jerry arrived and the meeting began.

The new guy started out. "We just have a few questions. In studying cases of abduction, we tend to look for anything unique about the circumstances. In Jacob's case, there are two things that stand out."

He looked at Jerry.

"The first one is your position as president of the local NAACP. Can you tell me more about this? When did you first become president? Have you ever had any individuals upset with the agency or you?"

Once again, Jerry explained there had been a few minor requests for assistance but no big lawsuits or excessively angry people. The agent acknowledged they had searched for any other instances where an NAACP member or branch president had been targeted in a similar manner but had found none.

Once again, the agent focused his gaze on Jerry.

"The second unique factor in this case, Jerry, is your involvement with the Baha'i Faith. We appreciate your agreeing to the polygraph last week and helping us work through this possibility."

It was Jerry's third polygraph.

"Can you tell me a bit more about the Baha'i Faith? Where is the headquarters and who is the top person running the organization?"

"The Baha'is don't have clergy," Jerry patiently explained. "When there are enough members in a community, they elect a nine-member Local Spiritual Assembly, or LSA, which guides the community and manages administrative duties."

"Are you on the LSA?" Agent Catallo asked.

"No. I'm not."

"Where are the headquarters?" the new agent continued. "There must be someplace where faith decisions are made. Who is in charge?"

Jerry sat back in his seat. He had answered these questions many times before.

"National Spiritual Assemblies are elected to handle the affairs of the country. They elect members to the Universal House of Justice, which is our supreme governing body. It's located in Haifa, Israel."

"And the faith started in Iran?" the agent asked.

"Yes," Jerry answered. "Baha'is believe God has sent messengers at different times to deliver his messages to the world."

By now, both of us were curious to know what any of this had to do with Jacob's kidnapping. Where were they going with this?

The new agent leaned forward and got straight to the point.

"Our theory is that Jacob was kidnapped by the Baha'is and taken out of the country to be groomed as a future leader."

Jerry was usually very measured with his words, but not this time.

"That's ridiculous," he responded testily.

The air was thick as I watched this tense stare-down between Jerry and the agent. I shook my head. So now they were back to us again . . . as if there was something we had done to cause our son to be taken from us, as if Baha'is were into kidnapping. This whole line of thinking was preposterous. They were grasping at straws.

Jerry finally broke the silence.

"The Baha'is did not take Jacob to groom him for leadership. But as long as we're sharing crazy theories, I had a lead from a psychic last week from Texas. Do you want to hear about that? She sent me a sketch of a house where Jacob was supposedly taken, and it looks just like that big weird house near the quarries."

I stared at Jerry. I knew the house, but had no idea where he was going with this. The mysterious house he was talking about sat high on a hill and looked like a makeshift castle. It had towers and turrets made out of old farm silos, and huge windows that overlooked the surrounding area.

Jerry continued.

"One of the family members has come to a few Baha'i events. Maybe they should be checked out."

"Okay. I'll see what we have on them," Agent Catallo said.

The new agent then turned to me and said confidently, "We think Jacob knew the person who took him. There's only one set of footprints on that dirt road—Jacob's. That would mean the person who took him was walking a significant distance away, not dragging him or carrying him. It appears Jacob went willingly."

I just stared at him, fuming.

"Can I borrow your gun?" I asked.

He didn't say a word.

"No, seriously. Give me your gun, and I'd like you to walk 'willingly' down the hall with me. Let's go."

"Okay, calm down," Agent Catallo chimed in. "There *may* have been a gun."

"Are you kidding me?" I yelled. "Don't change the facts! There was a gun. The boys *saw a gun* and they've both said that from the very beginning. You *know* it!"

I couldn't believe it had come to this. My whole body shook with fury. They were never going to find Jacob.

After we left the meeting, Jerry and I started arguing in the parking lot. I didn't believe the Baha'is had anything to do with abducting Jacob, but I challenged him on being so open and for bringing so many strangers into our home over the years. I was also mad he hadn't backed me up about the gun. While I had been battling it out, he had just sat there, silent.

I watched as Jerry angrily got into his car and pulled away, assuming I would follow. I didn't. Instead, I got into my own car and called Benton County sheriff Frank Wippler on the car phone I'd been given by our sheriff. It came in a black carrying bag, was connected to a giant battery that plugged into the cigarette lighter, and had a magnet antenna that I had to place on top of the car whenever I wanted to use it.

"Hi Frank, it's Patty."

Back in the beginning, Frank Wippler was the one to tell me, "What do you mean, you're tired? Who the hell is going to find Jacob if you quit?" I knew I could trust him to be straight with me.

"I have a question. Were there two sets of footprints in Rassiers' drive-way? These FBI guys are telling me there was only one set and that Jacob went willingly."

He scoffed.

"Maybe there was only one set when the abductor was walking on the grass, but there were definitely two sets of footprints. Steve Mund took a mold of what we believe are the abductor's footprints. They were right next to Jacob's."

Frank agreed to meet me for a drink downtown. When he arrived, I an-grily shared the gist of our meeting and how, once again, it felt like they were trying to pit Jerry and me against each other. It took more than one drink, but he finally managed to calm me down.

The next day, Sheriff Wippler called to see how I was doing.

"How ya doin', kid?"

I smiled in spite of myself.

"I'm okay," I said unconvincingly. "Thanks for helping. I made it home."

"I know," he confirmed. "I followed you, just to make sure."

{ Chapter 23 }

In the fall of 1995, Amy was nineteen and in her second year at the University of Minnesota, Twin Cities. When she had first chosen the U, I'd been worried she would feel lost, because it was so incredibly big. But as it turned out, that's exactly what she wanted. She wanted to go to a big university where nobody knew her and she could blend in. For the past six years, our family had lived in a fishbowl. Now, Amy enjoyed living in Minneapolis, where she had started over, met new friends, and could continue redefining herself and her future.

Trevor and Carmen were also growing up, and both were busy with school activities and sports. Trevor, age sixteen, was a sophomore at Apollo and a member of the junior varsity football team. When Amy moved out, he took over her room and enjoyed having his own space. He had also recently passed his driver's test and was now able to drive himself to his job at the Parkwood movie theater in St. Cloud. Carmen, age fourteen, also stayed incredibly busy with friends, dance, basketball, and soccer. Neither of them liked to sleep alone in their own bedrooms, so nearly every night they still fell asleep playing video games or watching TV in the downstairs family room, each claiming a leg of the L-shaped sectional.

After six years, I decided it was finally time to clean out the boys' room downstairs. Though none of our kids wanted to stay in there, I figured we could at least use it as a guest room. I started by packing up all Jacob's things and putting them in plastic totes out in the garage. Next, I bought a gallon of paint, hoping to breathe some fresh life into this space. I felt good about my decision. Heaven knows I had put it off long enough.

As I was painting the inside of the closet, I suddenly stopped in mid-stroke. There, on the back wall, Jacob had written his name in cursive, "*J-a-c-o-b.*" I placed my hand on his signature and could almost feel his pulse beating right through me.

"Hey Jake," I said as tears slid down my cheeks. He was right *here*. After taking a moment to say a short prayer, I wiped my tears, picked up my roller, and carefully painted around it.

It was now Jacob's senior year of high school, and both Jerry and I felt the void of what should have been. The Apollo Eagles football team put his picture on the back of their team program with the words, "Jacob's friends and teammates dedicate their season's efforts to Jacob. There will always be a place for him on the team and in our hearts."

Aaron Larson, who had been with Jacob and Trevor that night, was a standout on Apollo's football team and remained close to our family. We regularly attended the home games to watch him play and continued to be good friends with his parents, Vic and Fran. Although Aaron rarely talked about the night Jacob was kidnapped, I knew from his mom that he still struggled. He wrestled with the same questions over and over. Why Jacob? Why not him? What happened that night? What could he have done differently to save his friend? They were questions no one could answer, and—as we did with our own kids—we wished so badly we could take this pain away from him.

Travel was my escape, and I was driven by a never-ending need to make continued changes. On September 14, 1995, I once again found myself in Washington, DC, this time testifying with John Walsh before the Subcommittee on Crime for the House Judiciary Committee.

Both John and I felt strongly that the federal government needed to be more involved with child abduction cases. We urged Congress to expand the FBI's role by providing immediate assistance to local police departments to deal with the urgency and magnitude of a child abduction. John was also pushing to make killing a child a capital crime, even in states that didn't have the death penalty. I didn't support the death penalty, so John and I often clashed on how best to tackle the problem of child abduction. Still, we made a good team—each with very different delivery styles, but always with the same end goal in mind.

I was also busy lobbying Minnesota lawmakers who were uneasy with the idea of public notification. Many of them were arguing that it infringed on a person's right to privacy. This made me crazy. I was so sick of convicted sex offenders having all the rights while the children they killed or abused had none.

Two years earlier, in June 1993, Jeanna North had gone missing from West Fargo, North Dakota. Almost immediately, her parents reached out to JWF to help with her search. I met with Jeanna's father, Scott, just days after her disappearance. This case was especially troubling to me because the details hit so close to home. Like Jacob, Jeanna was only eleven, and Fargo was only two hours away from our house in St. Joe.

A year and a half later, in January 1995, Kyle Bell, a convicted child molester, confessed to killing Jeanna and dumping her body in the Sheyenne River. He was a neighbor of the North family, and at the time Jeanna went missing, he was living across the street from them. It was absolutely heartbreaking to hear Scott share his belief that Jeanna might still be alive if only he'd known his neighbor was a convicted child molester. He would never have extended her curfew that summer evening when she begged to go rollerblading with her friends.

Even after repeated plunges into the icy Sheyenne River, divers never found Jeanna's body. Her family held a memorial service for her on Tuesday, February 28, 1995, and I was asked to speak. With every bit of strength and fortitude I could muster, I vowed to honor Jeanna's memory by making changes that would help protect other children.

One year later, on May 17, 1996, I was in Washington, DC, when President Bill Clinton signed the federal community notification bill into law. Megan's Law, an addendum to the Jacob Wetterling Act, required law enforcement to notify the public of a sex offender's presence in their community. The law was named after Megan Kanka, a seven-year-old girl from New Jersey who, in 1994, had been raped and murdered by her neighbor ... another convicted child molester.

When President Clinton signed the bill into law that day, I stood right beside him at his desk in the Oval Office, along with Megan's parents, Rich and Maureen Kanka; John Walsh; and Marc Klaas—the father of twelve-year-old Polly Klaas from Petaluma, California, who had been murdered after being kidnapped at knifepoint during a slumber party at her own home.

At the press conference afterward, some of the reporters questioned the constitutionality of the law. John Walsh pushed his way toward the microphones and said in a raised voice, "This is letting parents know that the fox is in the henhouse. Believe me, I've hunted these people for nine years now.

They're predators, they prey upon children—that's their business. We deserve to know these people are in our neighborhoods!"

Once again, while I agreed with John's sentiment and understood his passion, I didn't like how he was defining the problem. In speaking to the public, he constantly used inflammatory language like *predators* and *monsters* to define pedophiles, but in reality, most of them don't look like predators or monsters at all. Typically, they're not strangers, and they live right in our own communities—in our families, our churches, and our schools. We may think of a child molester as a stereotypical dirty old man, but the truth is, they're more likely to be a coach, a teacher, an uncle, or even a brother.

With respect to John and all that he had done, I stepped up to the microphone and tried to clarify our message. "It's like warning children about a dog in the neighborhood that's known to bite. We would tell our kids to stay away from that dog," I said. "It's not about revenge. It's just one piece of a large puzzle that brings us closer to our goal of a safe society. I do think it will have a positive effect."

It wasn't the first time John and I clashed, and it wasn't the last, but the signing of Megan's law was an important milestone for both of us, and on that, we could both agree.

A month later, while I was in Washington, DC, for a NCMEC board meeting, I was asked to attend President Clinton's weekly radio address. He had been working to connect all the state registries to form one national database, which would prevent sex offenders from moving from one state to another without being detected.

I was honored to have been asked, so I switched my return flight to a later one that evening and was at the White House by 6:00 PM, ready for the thirty-minute taping.

President Clinton was notoriously late, and I grew more and more anxious as the minutes ticked by. Eventually, I alerted an aide that I had an 8:00 PM flight and wouldn't be able to stay.

"Wait right here," he told me.

A few minutes later, the aide returned.

"I'm so sorry. We're not able to get to the radio taping before you have to leave, but if you have just a few minutes, President Clinton would like to meet with you."

As I stood there in shock, the aide left again and returned minutes later.

"Follow me," he directed, then escorted me into the Oval Office.

I had been in this room just weeks earlier for the signing of Megan's Law, but this time, I was all alone. I looked around and tried to take it all in.

The Oval Office really is oval, with a fireplace on one side and the president's desk on the other. As I waited, I stared at the old Resolute desk and imagined little John-John peeking out from behind the secret panel while his dad, President John F. Kennedy, worked above him. The beautiful, wood-carved desk sat in front of three tall, colonial-style windows that were covered in heavy, gold drapes. The blue trim on the drapes complemented the bright blue carpet that was embedded with the presidential seal immediately in front of the desk. I eyed the red-and-white striped couches that faced each other in the middle of the room and wondered if I should sit down. How many world leaders had sat on these very couches, collaborating on decisions that could alter history?

Before I could decide whether to sit or stand, President Clinton came rushing in and apologized for being behind schedule.

"Thank you for all the work you're doing work to help protect kids," he said as he shook my hand.

I had my opportunity to say something significant in that moment . . . something brilliant so he would remember me. Instead, I blurted out the first thing that came to my mind.

"I'm sorry I can't stay—my youngest daughter Carmen is starting high school this year and she has a soccer game tomorrow morning."

President Clinton just smiled and nodded.

"I understand, you have to go. Kids are what it's all about. You have to be there for them."

A photographer took our picture as we chatted a few more minutes. Before leaving, I had one more brilliant comment to share with him.

"You know I'll be back," I said with a grin. "I don't go away easily, and we're not done yet."

"Good," he laughed. "We don't want you to go away. You're doing great work."

{ Chapter 24 }

It was the spring of 1996, and I was facing the sad reality that Jacob's class would be graduating from high school in just a few short weeks. Jerry and I both wanted to go to the ceremony, but we were torn. Should we or shouldn't we? We had kept in touch with many of Jacob's friends and wanted to be there to cheer them on, but we knew our presence would make it hard. On the other hand, neither of us really wanted to stay home and wallow in sorrow either.

Thankfully, I had one more thing on my calendar to help keep my mind off it for a little while longer. In mid-April, I received a letter telling me I had been nominated to be a torchbearer in the 1996 Olympic Torch Relay. On June 1, I would be carrying the Olympic torch for one kilometer on its way to the Summer Olympics in Atlanta, Georgia.

Few experiences in my lifetime have been as spirit-lifting for me as this. The flame was officially lit on March 30, 1996, in Olympia, Greece, and was passed torch-to-torch until it made its way to Athens. From there, it was flown to Los Angeles, then continued its eighty-four-day, forty-two-state journey to Atlanta.

I began training, even though the relay route was short—about a half mile. I was probably more nervous at the thought of having to wear shorts in public. On behalf of Champion and Hanes, I had been given an official torchbearer uniform, which included a T-shirt, a pair of shorts, and a pair of socks. There was no getting out of it. I had to wear the shorts.

To show her "support" from California, my sister Barbi bought me a new sports bra and somehow managed to get my whole family—including all my siblings—to sign it with words of encouragement, using sparkly fabric markers. They presented this special article of clothing to me just days before my torch-carrying experience. My kids wrote, "Go for the Gold!" "I love you Mom," and "Did you ever know that you're my hero?" My siblings were a little more outrageous with "Hope and SUPPORT," "Atlanta or BUST," "Hurrah for an UPLIFTED torchbearer," and, from my brother, "Wear this and no one will notice your shorts!" As usual, my sister Barbi was there for me, even if she couldn't be there in person.

As I trained along my rural road—always having to pass the site where Jacob was taken—I often cried whenever I thought about the run. I was so proud and honored to have this experience, yet in my mind, I was still "just a mom." I was Amy, Jacob, Trevor, and Carmen's mom. A wife. A housewife. Who was I to be carrying the Olympic flame?

On the day of the Olympic relay, I got dressed in my official Olympic Torchbearer uniform and pinned my "Jacob's Hope" button to my T-shirt. At 7:00 PM, Jerry, Amy, Trevor, Carmen, and I drove to the parking lot of a Minneapolis church, where we were joined by my sisters, their husbands, Jerry's sisters, and, of course, my biggest fan, my mom. We posed for a group photo and I spoke briefly to the media before boarding a bus with my fellow runners. We were each given our torches, and before getting dropped off at our individual starting points, each of us had the opportunity to introduce ourselves and explain how we'd been selected to run. We had one former Olympian on the bus, Doug Peterson, who had competed in Nordic skiing during the 1976 and 1980 Olympics. When he talked about his experience representing the United States and all it stood for, there were many tears and goosebumps.

When it was my turn, I explained that I was carrying the torch for my son, Jacob.

"On October 22, 1989, my son Jacob was kidnapped by a stranger less than a mile from our home in St. Joseph. This powerful Olympic flame reminds me of the hope we carry in our hearts every single day. It never goes out, and I can feel Jacob's spirit here with each of us as we continue to spread the hope and move the flame along on its journey to Atlanta."

At each drop-off site, our leader jumped off the bus and introduced the runner to a cheering crowd. When my turn finally came, it was comforting to see all my family and friends gathered on the corner of Calhoun Parkway and Lake Street.

I had about ten minutes to mingle and let other people hold the torch so we could pose for pictures. Then Irene Schmitt—a community hero from Mora, Minnesota—arrived with her burning torch, passed the flame to me, and it was my turn to carry this important part of history.

Suddenly the three-and-a-half-pound torch no longer had any weight ... it actually felt like it was carrying *me*. Words can't explain the power of this flame—the shared spirit of humanity, the very long journey it had already covered, and the awesome responsibility of making sure the flame never went out. As I ran, I felt so connected to that flame. It suddenly felt like my life's purpose: to carry this message of child safety, to protect it from the elements, and finally, after my leg of the journey was over, to transfer it to the next amazing human being to carry, preserve, and pass on.

Five days after my torchbearer experience, I found myself standing in front of 370 of Jacob's classmates as I prepared to begin my commencement address at their high school graduation.

Just a few weeks earlier, I had received a call from the Apollo High School principal, Jim Sharpe. He began by explaining how the Class of 1996 had suffered so much tragedy over the years. It began with Jacob's kidnapping, when they were only sixth graders. Five years later, in 1994, two popular fourteen-year-olds from St. Joseph, Daniel Schlauderaff and Lisa Case, had been struck and killed by a car one Sunday morning while in-line skating. Later that same year another fourteen-year-old, Tia Cobb, was killed in a car accident. Then, in January of their senior year, Brian Klinefelter, a St. Joseph police officer, had been shot and killed in the line of duty. He was the brother-in-law of Trevor's good friend, Jeff Schneider. Finally, just two months before their high school graduation, one of their own classmates, Jon Janzen, was killed in a car accident. Jon was popular, a good student, and one of Apollo's star hockey goalies.

"These kids need to feel good about their accomplishment and be given permission to laugh and enjoy graduation," he told me. "Things are so difficult at school right now—it's like walking through a morgue. There are no smiles, no chatter about future plans, just tears and sad faces. Can you help?" He asked if Jerry and I would be willing to give a commencement address for Jacob's class, along with Jon Janzen's parents.

"Yes, of course," we told him without any hesitation.

On June 6, 1996, Jerry and I arrived at Halenbeck Hall on the campus of St. Cloud State University for the Apollo High School Class of '96 graduation ceremony. I choked back tears as the band began playing "Pomp and Circumstance" and the kids all walked in wearing their caps and gowns.

They looked so grown up . . . and somber. I thought of the fear they had lived through, all the loss and sadness, and how they had braved it together. They had finally made it to this landmark day, and I was so incredibly proud of them.

Each of them wore a white ribbon pinned to their gown in honor of Jacob, and as tears rolled down my face, the senior choir sang "Jacob's Hope" to begin the ceremony. Afterward, Principal Sharpe shared a few words, and then it was our turn.

Jon Janzen's parents spoke first and tearfully shared about their son's love of life and how much he would want all of them to succeed and go after their dreams. It was a beautiful and moving tribute, and I was so thankful to Jerry for taking the podium next while I tried to pull myself together. He congratulated all of Jacob's classmates and thanked them for letting us be part of their lives as we'd watched them grow. Then, he turned it over to me.

I'd thought a lot about what I wanted to say, yet my words seemed so feeble compared to everything these kids had lived through already.

> We've watched you grow up very closely, because we couldn't watch Jacob. We've watched you weave your way through the dark and into the sunshine. You've carried Jacob with you along the way, and you've allowed us to be there. Now, we want you to feel happy, hopeful, and proud. You deserve to feel proud. We want you to dream big, and to follow your dreams.
>
> I love that the mascot for Apollo is the eagle. When Jacob was in fifth grade, he made an eagle out of papier-mâché and used construction paper for feathers. It was really beautiful and very detailed. After he was abducted, I thought of him every time I spotted an eagle soaring above, and it always made me smile. I searched for eagles, hoping they would send Jacob encouragement and let him know we were still here . . . still looking, still searching, and desperately hoping.
>
> Thank you all for carrying Jacob in your hearts for so long, and today, please let your hearts be happy. You deserve it. Jacob and Jon would want that for you. Let your Apollo Eagle spirits soar.

After we finished speaking, I could feel a definite release. These kids had held so much pent-up sorrow and empathy for us, as well as for Jon Janzen's parents. It was as if they needed to hear from all of us in order to get past the horrible guilt they felt for feeling happy or proud of their accomplishments. When it finally came time to throw their caps in the air, the smiles were big and genuine.

After the ceremony, we stayed for a few pictures with Aaron's family, then quietly made our retreat. It was their day, their milestone to celebrate— and while we were happy for Aaron and all the rest of Jacob's classmates, we couldn't help but feel a bit of jealousy for all that had been stolen from us. What position would Jacob have played on the football team? What girl would he have asked to prom? What college would he have selected? In some ways, it felt like the six and a half years had flown by in the blink of an eye, yet in others, it felt like time was a slow-moving enemy that kept dragging us forward from one agonizing milestone to the next.

How much longer would we have to do this? How many more milestones would we have to endure?

{ Chapter 25 }

When Jacob went missing in 1989, there were over a hundred other organizations across the country that advocated for missing children. All had sprung up after tragedies like ours, but there was no universal process to get Jacob's name and face out to them quickly. It was impossible to validate which ones were most critical and which had faded away after a child had been located. The internet was barely in existence at that point, so our only option was to contact each group individually, fill out the required paperwork, then mail it back with photos.

To make matters worse, many of these organizations didn't get along with each other. Personality clashes and competition over funding strained relationships and added further confusion for victim's families.

An amazing man by the name of Ron Laney set out to put more order to the process. In 1990, he invited eight of us who were involved with missing children's organizations to travel to Washington, DC, and take part in a roundtable discussion so we could hash it out and brainstorm possibilities.

Throughout my life, I've tended to gravitate toward people who emanate positive energy, and for me, Ron Laney was one of them. At a much younger age, he had done his share of hell raising, but he straightened out when he joined the Marines. He was sent to Vietnam, where a landmine took one of his eyes and the use of one arm. He was told to go home and collect disability, but nothing could destroy this man's spirit. He went to college, got his degree, and eventually became director of Children's Programs for the US Office of Juvenile Justice and Delinquency Prevention (OJJDP).

Ron began the discussion by asking, "Besides funding, what can we do for you?"

After we shared challenges and brainstormed possibilities, Ron suggested that, of all the ideas we had generated, annual trainings would probably be the most efficient use of the limited OJJDP funds he had to work with. Since every state already had a missing children's clearinghouse, he could efficiently tie our trainings into the annual clearinghouse trainings. He offered to provide specific breakout sessions for nonprofits like ours that would cover topics such as investigation dos and don'ts, victim support, victim testimonies, and insights into the different categories of missing children (stranger abduction, parental abduction, runaways, etc.). At our suggestion, Ron also agreed to cover other more universal topics for nonprofits, including fundraising, grant writing, and budget management.

We also began to explore the possibility of forming our own professional association of missing children organizations. Under Ron's continued guidance, we worked hard to establish membership criteria and a code of ethics, and on July 30, 1994, the Association of Missing and Exploited Children's Organizations (AMECO, pronounced UH-ME-CO) was incorporated.

In 1998, I was elected board president of AMECO, on top of my regular travel and speaking engagements. It was a busy year. In January, I was invited to speak at a law enforcement training on Oahu, so Jerry and I decided to make the trip into an early celebration of our twenty-fifth wedding anniversary on April 21.

Jerry and I both love to travel, and this was our first visit to Hawaii. As soon as my work commitments were over, we went into full-on tourist mode. We visited Pearl Harbor and the USS *Arizona*; we attended a traditional luau and ate our fill of pork, poi, and pineapple; we relaxed on the beautiful sand beaches; we walked hand in hand at sunset and reconnected with the "us" we used to be. The tropical air and crashing ocean waves brought both of us back to those magical nights in Acapulco when we had first fallen in love. We did it. Twenty-five years.

Trevor graduated from high school in the spring after a remarkable senior year. He was nominated for homecoming king, played wide receiver for Apollo's varsity football team, assisted in a second-grade classroom, and graduated with honors to top it all off. We knew he still missed Jacob terribly, especially when he saw the close relationships many of his friends had with their older brothers. But he had survived and was looking forward to starting college at St. Cloud State University in the fall.

By the end of 1998, I'd spent 105 days traveling, making presentations in sixteen states, twenty-nine different cities, and two countries. Many of my local speaking engagements were coordinated by the Jacob Wetterling Foundation, but by now I'd also been hired as a speaker/trainer for Fox Valley Technical

College in Appleton, Wisconsin. The college received grants from the National Criminal Justice Training Center and coordinated trainings at local and regional law enforcement sites around the country, focusing on missing persons. This included AMBER Alerts, long-term missing investigations, and the critical role of first responders. My role at these trainings was to present a victim impact segment, where I shared our family's story and provided helpful suggestions for officers on how to work with victim's families.

I was joined at these trainings by Colleen Nick, mother of six-year-old Morgan Nick, who had been abducted from a Little League baseball game in Alma, Arkansas, on June 9, 1995. Colleen and I first met when she reached out to JWF looking for support. We connected immediately, and not long after, Colleen was also added as a Fox Valley speaker. We began presenting together across the country and soon struck up a deep and powerful friendship.

Because our presentation schedules overlapped, Colleen and I often went out for dinner, where we could solve the world's problems as we ate. One night, Ron Laney joined us, and we presented him with another challenge.

"We need a handbook," Colleen said. "Something to tell us what to do when your child goes missing."

"Our lives get completely turned upside down," I added. "There's so much to do, but nobody knows how to start."

We pitched the idea as a much-needed tool, and Ron agreed. He set the wheels in motion, and with the help of an amazing woman named Helen Connelly (senior program consultant with Fox Valley Technical College), he pulled together five families to help us write and publish this incredible publication in only nine short months.

When Your Child Is Missing: A Family Survival Guide features instructions, resources, and heartfelt advice from real families like ours. Since its publication in May 1998, the book has been revised and updated several times, including a Spanish translation. It continues to be a great resource for all searching families.

That same year, Colleen and I convinced Ron we needed something else: a support system for parents of missing children. The new friendships we formed while working on the family survival guide taught us how important it was to talk to other parents who could understand what we were going through.

"Why not help us support one another?" we asked him.

Once again, Ron acted. In 1998, OJJDP offered a grant to start a support organization for parents of missing children. We called it Team HOPE—Help Offering Parents Empowerment. I became the project coordinator for the grant, and our goals were to offer parent-to-parent mentoring and support services to parents whose children were missing—including runaways, those abducted by strangers, and victims of domestic or international parental abductions.

In November 1998, twenty-two of us gathered at NCMEC in Arlington, Virginia, for our first mentor training, and Team HOPE was born.

It worked like this. Victims seeking assistance—usually parents or grandparents—called a toll-free number that rang through to a pager. The on-call team captain responded to the number displayed on the pager, answering questions, suggesting resources, and taking information. The caller was then paired with a volunteer (preferably someone who had experienced a similar situation) for parent-to-parent mentoring and compassionate support. The calls came in twenty-four hours a day, and we never knew what kind of crisis we might have to respond to. To cope, we had to learn how to separate ourselves from the situation and set aside our own challenges in order to assist others. This was a big challenge for these parent volunteers, but every one of them rose to the occasion.

Finally, I felt I'd come to a place where my efforts were making a difference and my life felt purposeful. I was proud of the work I was doing with Team HOPE and AMECO, I was an active board member for both the National Center for Missing and Exploited Children and the Jacob Wetterling Foundation. Still, no matter how hard I worked or what I'd managed to accomplish, nothing could replace the void Jacob's disappearance had left in my heart.

On October 22, 1998, the ninth anniversary of Jacob's kidnapping, I decided to write a public letter to Jacob's abductor, pleading with him to talk to me.

I sent the letter out to our local media, and soon it got picked up by the Associated Press and was widely distributed across Minnesota and the region.

October 22, 1998

To the man who took Jacob:

I often wonder, does October 22 mean anything to you? Do you remember the young boy you took from us? Do you still have him with you? He's an adult now, but just as loved and still dearly missed. Do you know the person you took?

Jacob was born February 17, 1978. He has his grandpa's middle name, Erwin. He loved sports and was incredibly competitive, especially with his younger brother, Trevor. They played, and they'd fight, and then they'd fall asleep, each with one arm wrapped around the other. He fished with his dad, and he had lots of friends. He was most known for his sense of fairness. Even if it had nothing to do with him, it always bothered him when things weren't fair.

He tried hard at whatever he did. He was goalie for his hockey team. I remember asking if it ever bothered him when somebody scored on him. He said, "Not really. If I stopped it, it was a great save. If it went in, it was a great shot!"

You took away a wonderful person. Someone who probably would have stood up for you if things weren't fair. Did no one do nice things for you?

I have found some comfort picturing you not as a mean old ugly bad guy, but at one time, you were an eleven-year-old boy. Someone's son . . . possibly someone's brother, needing and hopefully sharing the love an eleven-year-old boy deserves. If this love wasn't shared in your family, I'm sorry. Every child is entitled to the love and caring that family and friends provide.

If you still have Jacob, I wish for something good to happen to you, like catching a really big fish or winning the lottery. Hopefully then, you will treat him well. I hope you have peaceful moments where you can walk in the woods or on a beach, content, not miserable and vindictive.

I have a hard time getting through anniversary dates. Still not knowing where Jacob is, I continue to talk to him. Birthdays, holidays, but especially now. Where are you, Jacob? What next? I talk to God, praying for Jacob, and even struggling with trying to pray for you.

If only I could talk to you.

I'm not sure what I would say, although after so much time, surprisingly, I don't hate you. I know nothing about you. I wonder, were you ever like Jacob? Did you also love peanut butter? Did you sneeze when you looked at the sun? Did you play jokes on April Fool's Day? Jacob is not just a kid on a poster. His mom and dad, Amy, Carmen, and Trevor miss him daily. He has dreams and hopes and potential.

I still have positive dreams. For my own survival, I have had to let go of a lot of anger or I would be swallowed up in it. But the questions persist. I pray that God will smile down on us all this year and bring us some peace. All I'm asking for is your response; a call to allow me and all the people whose lives Jacob touched to find peace and a sense of calm that disappeared that night in 1989. The peace that can't return until the questions surrounding Jacob's disappearance are answered. You have held the answers for so long. You also hold the pain. Please talk to me.

With hope,
Patty Wetterling
Jacob's mom

I was so hopeful this man might call that I actually kept a notebook by the phone with a list of questions I wanted to ask him. Days went by, then weeks. The letter generated a flurry of new tips, but there was no response from the one person I wanted to hear from most—the man who had taken Jacob. At the very least, I hoped that by knowing Jacob better, he might somehow be willing to treat him better or be kinder to him. Or, if Jacob was no longer alive, I prayed I could touch this man's conscience and persuade him to talk to me and give us some peace.

Once again, my prayers went unanswered, and my questions continued. Where are you, Jacob? What more can we do? What are we missing?

{ Chapter 26 }

In 2001, I was still serving as board president of AMECO when I was also appointed as program director of Team HOPE. It was a full-time job with huge responsibilities that included filling out quarterly activity and expense reports for the grant, publishing a quarterly newsletter for volunteers, and training parents who were referred to us through NCMEC's Family Advocacy Division. Thankfully, I'd worked closely with the first director right from the start, so I knew the job well.

That same year, the Office of Juvenile Justice and Delinquency Prevention made the decision to move Team HOPE under AMECO. It sounded good on paper, but Team HOPE was now stronger, better organized, and more united than AMECO, so it felt a bit backward, like putting the parent under the child's direction.

Jerry and I had been empty nesters for over a year. In August 2000, Trevor left Minnesota to attend college in Colorado. After a year at St. Cloud State University, he was ready for a change, so when one of his good friends decided to transfer to Colorado State University in Fort Collins, Trevor decided to go with him. He didn't know what he wanted to study, but I was just glad he was still interested in college. It was hard to think about him being so far away, but both Jerry and I knew this would be a good move for him.

One month later, in September 2000, Carmen also left home, to attend the University of Wisconsin in Madison. During her senior year of high school, she had visited the campus with some of her close friends and fallen in love with it. That fall, as I made the five-hour drive to drop her off at college, I made her promise me one thing.

"I'm okay with you cheering for your UW Badgers," I told her. "But you have to promise you'll never become a Packer fan!"

Three years earlier, Amy had graduated from the University of Minnesota with a degree in criminal justice and a minor in psychology. During her senior year at the U of M, she earned enough credits to graduate early, so she and her roommate, Kari, had decided to spend their spring quarter traveling in Europe. With everything we had been through as a family, I couldn't help but be anxious and nervous for them, but I also had to remind myself I'd done the same thing at her age with one of my girlfriends. With a lot of prayers, I sent her off, confident she would be smart and safe.

The girls had a great time, and not long after returning from their trip, Kari introduced Amy to her cousin, Chris. Jerry and I first met Chris at a celebrity sports banquet for the Jacob Wetterling Foundation. This fundraiser took place each year around Jacob's birthday on February 17, which also happened to be the birthday of Minnesota Vikings head coach Dennis Green. For several years, he graciously served as honorary chairman for the gathering.

The JWF Celebrity Sports Banquet had become a popular event that attracted extensive media coverage, and we were so grateful to Jerry's high school friend Brett Lichty and the steering committee for generating this positive publicity for the foundation. However, this led to some incredibly unfortunate timing for our daughter Amy when she introduced us to her future husband for the first time.

"Mom, Dad, this is Chris . . . " The TV cameras suddenly turned in our direction, blinding us with their bright lights. Of all our kids, Amy especially hated being in the spotlight, so I knew how upsetting and awkward this was for her. Thankfully, Chris handled himself with such grace and professionalism. Both Jerry and I were impressed with him.

I could only imagine what it must be like for someone like Chris to marry into the chaos that had become our world. Jerry and I agreed that we needed this happy distraction and wanted it to be a big celebration. We encouraged Amy and Chris to invite all their friends, and with large families on both sides, we knew it was going to be a big wedding.

For the reception, they chose the El Paso Sports Bar and Grill in St. Joseph. It had a large banquet room big enough to hold all the guests, with the added bonus of being located right in the heart of St. Joe. Not only was this going to be a big wedding, it was going to be fun.

Amy and Chris were married on December 21, 2001, at First Presbyterian Church in downtown St. Cloud. My heart burst with pride as Jerry and I walked our beautiful Amy down the aisle together, surrounded by festive Christmas greenery and bright red poinsettias.

In spite of all the trauma and chaos, our kids had grown up to be amazing adults. Amy and Chris had remembered Jacob with a kind note in their wedding program, and we all carried him in our hearts throughout this glorious day. It was a perfectly joyful celebration—so fun, and so needed. Truly, I don't think I'd smiled that much, laughed that hard, or been that happy in the previous twelve years.

As 2001 drew to a close, I looked forward to starting the new year with a calmer, more manageable schedule. We had recently hired a new staff member at the foundation, Alison Feigh, who joined us as a child safety specialist. She was special to me for so many reasons.

Alison was a classmate of Jacob's, but she had been in Australia vacationing with her family at the time of his kidnapping. By the time she returned to St. Joseph a few weeks later, life as she knew it had changed completely. It affected her deeply—so deeply that by the time she graduated with the rest of Jacob's class in 1996, she decided to do something about it.

Alison chose to attend St. Olaf College in Northfield, Minnesota, and entered the Paracollege so she could design her own major in Child Abduction Prevention. Four years later, she graduated from St. Olaf and moved to Virginia to work at NCMEC. On September 11, 2001, Alison was riding a city bus on her way to work when the third plane crashed into the Pentagon, just a few miles away. She'd been forced to listen to the horror unfold on the bus driver's radio as he worked to reroute them away from the smoke and chaos. The trauma of that experience made Alison realize how much she wanted to return to Minnesota to fulfill her career goals closer to family and friends. She moved home, and later that year we hired her as a part-time employee at JWF.

Things were falling into place, and some of the burden was being lifted from my shoulders. I was still traveling a lot for JWF presentations, NCMEC board meetings, and Fox Valley trainings, but with key people now in essential roles, it all was starting to feel a bit calmer and more manageable.

In early March of 2002, I was scheduled to do a Fox Valley training in Birmingham, Alabama. I had an early afternoon flight, and as usual, I called my mom to let her know I was coming, so we could spend some time together in the morning before heading to the airport.

Mom had moved a few times after Bud's death in 1977, and she was now living in a nice two-bedroom apartment in a Minneapolis suburb near the airport. With all my travel, it meant so much to me that my mom was always willing to let me stay overnight and give me rides to and from the airport.

That particular March morning, I hadn't stayed overnight because I had a later flight. When I arrived at Mom's house, she was still in bed—which was completely out of the norm. She told me she wasn't feeling well and probably should see a doctor. I called my brother Russ and explained her symptoms.

"I need to catch a flight," I said. "Do you think you could get away from work to take Mom to the doctor?"

Russ worked for Delta Airlines at the airport, so he was close by and told me he'd be right over. I helped my mom get dressed and gave her a big hug and kiss.

"Russ is on his way and should be here shortly," I told her. I jumped in my car and drove myself to the airport to catch my flight.

It seemed like forever before my plane finally touched down. When I arrived at my hotel, I immediately called Jerry to check in.

"How's Mom?" I asked.

"She's in the hospital and she's comfortable. She had an intestinal blockage, which they fixed, but ... " He paused.

"But what?"

"They think it's pancreatic cancer. We have to wait for the tests to come back, but it's not good."

My knees crumpled. Mom was never sick. How could this be? I felt so guilty leaving her that morning and just wanted to turn around and go home. Jerry assured me she was comfortable and I should stay.

"How long?" I asked him.

"There's no treatment available for her," he said. "The doctor said we can hope for six months."

I hung up and fell apart. *Six months.* How would I ever survive this?

{ Chapter 27 }

The kids called her Gram, and through all life's ups and downs, she had always been there for us. Mom was the glue for our large family, and with her unfailing love, strong faith, and quiet wisdom, she had carried me through some of my darkest days. I couldn't imagine what life would be like without her steady presence.

Memories flooded through my mind on my long flight home from Birmingham. A few years earlier, I'd been asked to give a brief safety announcement during a pregame ceremony at a Minnesota Twins game. I was scheduled to be out of town so, on a whim, I asked Mom if she'd be interested in doing it instead. I knew this was *way* outside her comfort zone, but my mom loved the Minnesota Twins, and I had many fond memories of her listening to the games on the radio while she was gardening, fixing meals, or just relaxing on a lazy summer day in St. Paul.

It took a little encouragement, but eventually she accepted the offer. On June 24, 1998, my mom—a woman who seldom took center stage—stepped up to home plate at the Hubert H. Humphrey Metrodome in downtown Minneapolis, introduced herself as Jacob Wetterling's grandmother, and urged 15,000 Twins fans to talk to their kids about safety over the summer.

My whole family was there, and everyone told me what a great job she did. I was so incredibly proud of her for stepping up. As always, she was happy to help and willing to do whatever she could to help find Jacob.

When my plane finally landed in Minneapolis, it was so strange not to call Mom to have her come pick me up. My eyes teared up again as I wheeled my bag out to the curb and realized how much I missed her warm hug and welcoming smile. I picked up my car and drove straight to her apartment.

When I arrived, she was up and dressed and seemingly at peace with everything that was facing her. Trying to be strong, I gave her a big hug and asked how she was feeling.

"I'm okay. Comfortable."

I just nodded, not sure what to say.

"It's okay, Patty. I've lived a good life. I'm ready," she told me.

I could feel the tears coming and couldn't hold them back any longer. "No, Mom. Please. *We're* not ready! It's not time yet. You have to hang in there." I was already feeling the pain of losing her, even though she was standing right there in front of me. She nodded and tried to assure me.

"I'll hang around for as long as I can, but don't worry. You'll be okay."

I didn't know how any of this would ever be okay, but there was one thing I did know. I was committed to making the next six months as amazing as we possibly could for her.

I became more intentional about spending time with my mom, not just when I had to go to the airport. As spring arrived, we visited the Como Park Conservatory and took time to breathe in the fragrant spring flowers. We drove down to Hidden Falls Regional Park near her old apartment, and she shared with me how she and her neighbor, Audrey, would occasionally go there for a "weenie roast." We had coffee at her favorite pie shop in Highland Park, and we took short walks along the Mississippi River or Minnehaha Falls.

Whenever we could, we also got together for family dinners at Nancy's, Russ's, or Peg's. If Mom was feeling up to it, sometimes she would have us all over to her apartment for her famous beef brisket sandwiches. Nothing pleased her more than just having us all together.

By summer, we were three months into Mom's six-month prognosis and I felt like there was just never enough time in a day. Though I had scaled back on my speaking engagements and tried to spend as much time as I could with my mom, my work commitments still kept me extraordinarily busy.

On June 13, 2002, I joined state officials in unveiling the new AMBER alert system in Minnesota. The system originated in 1996 and was named after nine-year-old Amber Hagerman, who was kidnapped and murdered near her home in Arlington, Texas. Later, "AMBER" became an acronym that stood for "America's Missing: Broadcast Emergency Response" and by the summer of 2002, it was active in about a dozen states.

I'd heard about the AMBER plan and met Amber Hagerman's mom during a training in Texas, so I worked hard to push for the AMBER alert system in our state. The Minnesota Chiefs of Police Association and Minnesota Sheriffs' Association were both on board. The key was to get the information out to the public quickly. I'd learned that the first forty-eight hours after an abduction were the most critical for successfully retrieving a child. In our case, it had been eight hours from the time Jacob was abducted to the time news finally hit the airwaves. The AMBER alert would now be the first line of defense in getting the word out quickly and efficiently so the public could aid in the search. It would be three more years before all fifty states had operational AMBER alert systems, but I was proud of the way Minnesotans had backed the plan and pushed the legislation through well ahead of the curve. I was also especially proud that the system would get tested twice a year—on October 22, the day of Jacob's abduction, and on May 25, National Missing Children's Day.

Also, in 2002, the *Boston Globe*'s widely acclaimed investigation into clergy sexual abuse in the Catholic Church began to hit close to home. Several priests who had been on restriction at St. John's Abbey in Collegeville because of allegations of sexual abuse (including pedophilia) were now being investigated by the SCSO for any possible connection to Jacob's kidnapping and other crimes in the area.

None of this was news to us, but the national attention from the clergy abuse scandal drew added interest to Jacob's case. Suddenly, the media was clamoring for interviews and comments from me, and though I tried to accommodate them as best I could, the reality was there had been almost 30,000 leads in the past twelve and a half years, and this was just one more. It seemed incredibly far-fetched to me that a monk or priest would resort to kidnapping a random child at gunpoint from a dead-end road. Why would they need to go to the extreme of kidnapping a child when they had access to children all day long, at school, church, camps, and other programs at St. John's?

The investigation at St. John's Abbey got very real for our family when we learned that Father Tom Gillespie was on the abbey's list of eighteen monks who had been credibly accused of sexually inappropriate behavior with children. Later, I would also learn that Matthew Feeney had been convicted of criminal sexual conduct against young boys while serving as a camp youth counselor in the early 1990s. After continuing to abuse boys, he would eventually be civilly committed as a sexual psychopathic personality and a sexually dangerous person to the Minnesota Sex Offender Program.

These two men had visited our home together and offered their support the day after Jacob had been abducted. Father Tom had hosted the first community prayer services for Jacob, and he even had our family over for dinner at the rectory. I also remembered how Matti Feeney had given me his card after Jacob's kidnapping and invited our other kids to his house for movie night. Unbelievable. I found their predatory sexual behavior and abuse of power especially insidious.

Toward the end of August, Mom ended up in the hospital again and we knew she was nearing her end. There was little else they could do to help her, so after a week, Mom's medical team recommended we put her in hospice care.

Logically, we knew this made sense, but the term "hospice care" sounded so final. My siblings and I struggled with the decision, but after receiving some recommendations from the social worker at the hospital, we settled on a charming, home-like residence that was centrally located for all of us.

As Mom continued to grow weaker, I gathered Peg, Nancy, and Russ and said, "Barbi needs to come home." Everyone agreed, but we weren't sure how best to approach it. All of us were emotionally spent and nobody wanted to take on dealing with Barbi.

For years, Barbi had struggled with alcoholism. She had lived such a glamorous life—traveling the world, working as a flight attendant for Pan Am, meeting amazing people, and enjoying life to the fullest. But with Barbi, everything was larger than life, and that included her drinking. It had become such a part of her that we were all a little surprised when she agreed to go to treatment after very little resistance.

Barbi had learned a lot during her month at the Hazelden Treatment Center in Minnesota. She did a lot of writing and reflecting, facing her demons in her daily journal, then burning them nightly in the campfire. When we visited, she told us how much she enjoyed the meditations and reflection exercises, and she vowed to do her best to beat this disease.

Still, she had never been able to stop drinking completely, and all of us worried how she would cope with the stress of our mom's final days.

"I'll be in charge of Barbi," I said. "We can stay at Mom's apartment and keep each other company. She needs to be here."

Despite her struggles, Barbi meant everything to me. I still remembered how she had dropped everything to come to Minnesota when Jacob was kidnapped, and how much she had continued to help me on this very long journey. I wanted—no, I *needed* her to be home with all of us.

Barbi found a flight and joined us a few days later. I was so happy we were all together and I knew Mom would be too. For two weeks, my siblings and I visited Mom at hospice, and after long days of sitting by her bedside, Barbi and I returned to Mom's apartment, where she amazed me with her excellent cooking. She was in a good place and accepting of what was going on.

Mom slept a lot as hospice staff tried to keep her as comfortable as they could. Even though she never complained, we knew she was in pain. But, as always, she was strong right to the end.

On her last day, I found some time to be alone with her to say my final goodbyes. Her breathing was quiet but steady, and even though the cancer was taking her away, her big and generous heart just kept beating as strongly as ever.

I reached for her hand and cried as I begged Mom for one last request.

"Please Mom . . . let me know if Jacob is in heaven. I hate to lose you, but it comforts me to know that, if he's there, you'll be together. If you see him, please give him the biggest hug ever. And please, please, please . . . if you can . . . let me know."

Before leaving the room, I promised Mom I would carry her in my heart forever and asked if I could still come to her with questions or for support. Already, I knew I would forever miss her calm, loving, kind, and gentle spirit.

In the early morning hours of September 14, 2002, our Mom, our Gram, our Eunie, took her final breath and died peacefully in her sleep.

{ Chapter 28 }

On October 22, 2002—the thirteenth anniversary of Jacob's abduction—the *St. Cloud Times* ran the following snippet on page 1C of their "Central Minnesota Life" section:

History notes

On this day in 1989, St. Joseph resident Jacob Wetterling was approached by a masked man with a gun and kidnapped. His whereabouts are still unknown.

That was it. It ran under "The Hot Dish" column at the very bottom of the page and was the only mention of Jacob's abduction in the paper that year. The tiny article didn't even include a phone number for people to call if they had a tip.

It was a hard day anyway, and this just added to my sadness. After all my efforts to find Jacob, protect kids, educate parents, change laws, and support other searching families, Jacob had become a "history note" at the bottom of "The Hot Dish" column. How depressing.

I suppose I should have been grateful for any mention at all, but the truth was, I was still reeling from my mom's death and not handling any of it well. Just weeks earlier, I stopped by a liquor store near Lyndale and I-494 in Richfield to pick up a bottle of wine. As I walked through the parking lot, I happened to notice a cute little boy in a soccer uniform who was sound asleep in a running Suburban with all the windows rolled down. He was all by himself, and as I got closer, I noticed a bunch of soccer balls in the back. I realized this boy's mom or dad was probably the soccer coach and had just run into the liquor store to make a quick purchase before heading home.

Honestly. *When would people learn?* Were any of my efforts even making a difference? This person would never leave a fifty-dollar bill sitting on the seat of their running Suburban with all the windows open, so what in the world were they thinking when they left their *child* here all alone?

Years earlier, I'd met Tara Burke at a law enforcement conference. She was just three years old when her parents left her and her nine-year-old brother in the car while they ran into a hardware store on a quick errand. A man knocked on the window and told the kids their parents wanted them to come inside. As Tara's brother was helping her out of the car, the man grabbed Tara and sped away. She was held captive for ten months, and it wasn't until another young boy who was being molested by the same kidnappers was able to escape and get to police that they were finally caught.

This whole horrible scenario was running through my head as I stood guard, waiting to make sure this little boy was safe until his parent came out. After at least ten minutes, I finally saw the dad exit the store carrying a case of beer. He had risked his child's life for a case of beer. For a moment, I seriously thought about confronting this man and telling him how careless he had been, but I didn't trust myself not to fly off the handle. So, instead, I just let him wonder who had placed all the Jacob Wetterling "missing" flyers on the empty seats of his car.

I started 2003 with renewed hope for a better year. Amy was now working in Minneapolis as a job coach for people with disabilities. Trevor would be graduating from Colorado State University with a major in early child development, and Carmen—now a senior at UW Madison—would graduate with a major in human development and family studies, specializing in early child development. The previous summer she had met a wonderful young man from England named Kristian. The two of them worked together at Camp Friendship—a Minnesota camp for children and adults with disabilities—and both planned to pursue a career in social work following graduation. Jerry and I both really liked Kristian, and we could tell Carmen was crazy about him.

I now worked twenty to thirty hours a week from home, on top of my regular trainings and travel. We had recently hired a new executive director for AMECO after the first one had to be let go, mainly due to inexperience. As board chair, I was now spending a lot of time training in the new ED, while at the same time continuing to work as program director for Team HOPE—which by now had grown to over sixty parent volunteers.

To protect the safety and privacy of our volunteers, we had recently switched to a prepaid calling card system that allowed us to share a single 800 number versus individual pagers. Each month, we had to replenish the funds in the phone account so the volunteers and team captains could continue using their calling cards to make and return calls to families needing support. It was my job to review the monthly bills and submit them to the newly hired executive director of AMECO for payment. It was a lot of busy work, but I always made it a priority.

Because of the recent restructuring that had moved Team HOPE under AMECO, the new executive director was now technically my boss. We spoke on the phone regularly whenever she had questions about her new position. However, as time went by, it was clear the new director had her own ideas for growing AMECO. I was happy to give her some space while I stayed busy as program director of Team HOPE.

I was now managing a budget that was four times as large as the AMECO budget. My responsibilities also included preparing quarterly reports for OJJDP, overseeing expenditures, projecting costs, assessing future needs, searching for outside financial support, and monitoring the activities of the staff and volunteers. The work was rewarding, and I absolutely loved working with Abby, our office administrator. In addition to her many skills, she was also the parent of a kidnapped child. In 1997, her ten-year-old son, Sam, had been abducted by her ex-husband, and for over eight months, she didn't know where he was, or whether he was even alive. Thankfully, Sam was recovered after being recognized from a "Have you seen me?" postcard.

Because of our shared experiences, Abby and I were especially mindful of minimizing any vicarious trauma for our parent volunteers. We stressed the importance of self-care and worked hard to keep everyone emotionally healthy while doing this difficult work.

In February, Jerry and I were incredibly saddened to hear of Charlie Grafft's death. He had been the sheriff of Stearns County when Jacob was abducted and had been such an important part of our journey. From the very beginning, he had been right there with us, pulling in favors from every friend, officer, and agency to help in the search.

Jerry and I attended his funeral, which was packed with hundreds of law enforcement officers he had known throughout his fifty-year tenure. He was a legend who would be sorely missed.

We were now on our third sheriff in Jacob's investigation. One year earlier, in 2002, our second sheriff, Jim Kostreba, had retired so he could run for a seat in the Minnesota House of Representatives. Later that same year, on November 5, John Sanner, a captain with eighteen years of experience at the SCSO, had been elected sheriff in a tight race against the police chief of Waite Park. A few weeks after the election, Jerry and I had both met with the new sheriff, who shook our hands, looked us in the eyes, and promised to keep the search for Jacob a priority.

"We'll never give up," Sheriff Sanner assured us.

Elizabeth Smart was fourteen years old in the summer of 2002, when she was kidnapped from her home in Salt Lake City. In September of that year, Colleen Nick and I flew to our quarterly NCMEC board meeting a day early so we could meet her parents. Ed and Lois Smart were in DC to connect with legislators and also to meet with their case manager at NCMEC. He had suggested they also check in with Colleen and me—fellow parents of missing children—for guidance, hope, and support.

The Smart family had been doing an amazing job of managing the media and keeping Elizabeth's story alive. We talked with Ed and Lois about the investigation and also asked about their other five children, especially nine-year-old Mary Katherine, who had shared a bedroom with Elizabeth and pretended to be asleep on that horrible night when her sister was taken away at knifepoint. Before parting, we exchanged phone numbers and hugs. We also promised we would do our part to keep Elizabeth's story alive in Minnesota and Arkansas.

Six months later, on March 12, 2003—while Colleen and I happened to be together again for our quarterly NCMEC board meeting—we received the most joyous news: Elizabeth Smart had been found! The excitement was palpable throughout the building, and we shared hugs and tears with all the NCMEC staff. For us, Elizabeth exemplified the hope that we all carried in our hearts.

After so many years of searching and hoping, I absolutely thrived on learning how these kids were found, and I paid particular attention to what steps or actions had been successful in freeing them. Typically, there were three key factors: (1) keeping the missing child's story and photo in the media, (2) having someone come forward who had witnessed a situation between an adult and a child that just didn't feel right, and (3) making sure the police responded quickly to the tip. That's how Elizabeth was found, and it renewed my hope that it *was* possible for missing kids to come home.

About a year after our new AMECO director was hired, several Team HOPE volunteers began calling me to say their calling card wasn't working because there weren't any minutes left on the card. I had been regularly submitting the bills to the new director for payment, but they just weren't getting paid. Even after I spoke to her about it, the problem persisted, which shut down our ability to respond to requests for assistance.

Things got ugly. The AMECO director began hiring personal friends to take care of office business, and I became increasingly worried that she was making poor executive decisions on top of not paying the bills. After receiving more phone calls from frustrated volunteers, I finally called a few of the organization's board members to voice my concerns. These were people I knew and trusted, so I was confident in sharing my concerns with them.

They confronted our executive director about my concerns, but rather than admitting fault, she told them *I* was the problem. She said I was the one who hadn't been submitting bills and that my work for Team HOPE was "sloppy." Neither was true, and I was devastated that she said these negative things about me to my own colleagues, some of whom I had known for over fourteen years. I needed a chance to respond, so I asked to meet with the full AMECO board. They set up a conference call so everyone could listen and hear my side of the story.

I try so hard to forget this day.

Because I worked from home, I was fortunate to be able to dress casually much of the time, but not on this day. Even though I knew nobody would be able to see me, I put on a suit, heels, and makeup, just so I would feel confident and professional for this important phone call. When the conference call began, I spoke calmly, and once again expressed my concerns. I was well prepared and explained the situation in a concise and respectful manner. I was able to back up my claims with emails and other written documents, which I read aloud to the group. Afterward, I waited for their questions.

"That's not what she says," one of the board members told me. "She says you're not doing your job. You're the problem, not her."

I was flabbergasted.

"That's absolutely not true," I said. "You guys *know* me. You know how hard I've worked for these two organizations, and you know I'd never do anything to betray the trust I've built with our members and parents. If I say I'm going to do something, I do it. You *know* that. I've been here since day one. I helped *found* these two organizations. You know I value good work, and you need to trust me when I tell you, this director is not doing good work."

Before ending the conference call, the board told me they would meet and get back to me. Later that day, I received the call.

They had met as a group and discussed the situation.

They had already fired their first director and didn't want to fire a second one so soon after firing the first. They were concerned how this might look to the Office of Juvenile Justice and Delinquency Prevention, the organization that provided our federal funding.

So rather than fire the executive director, they fired me.

I couldn't believe it. I'd never been fired from anything before. How could this have happened? Not only had I been fired from the very organization I helped found, the people who fired me were close colleagues whom I considered friends. How could they not believe me? How could they have taken this other woman's word over mine?

When Ron Laney heard the news, he hit the ceiling.

"You can't fire Patty!" he told the board. "Find some way to work this out!"

It was too late. One of the board members did eventually call and offer me a different position with Team HOPE, but I declined. There was no way I could work with people who didn't believe in me.

What followed were some very dark days. Once again, I found myself home, isolated, and powerless. I had lost a job that I absolutely loved, from an organization I'd helped birth—all just before the holidays. I was such a mess: sad, embarrassed, ashamed. I had zero self-esteem, and I rarely left the house.

In time, I would learn this woman had been sabotaging me all along. Less than a year later, she was finally fired.

Maybe I should have been happy, but I wasn't. Life had taken another hard turn, and I was very far from happy.

{ Chapter 29 }

I spent my days alone, sitting in a rocking chair, just thinking and rehashing. I knew I hadn't deserved to be fired, but still, I was out of a job. I had worked so hard to build awareness, fight for positive change, and make the world safer for our kids, but now what? If I was no longer the director of Team HOPE, who was I? Where could I turn for support? Who could I even talk to? Not only had I lost my job, I had also lost a tremendous support system.

In the midst of all this, Jerry and I were also trying to wrap our heads around a new lead that had recently developed in Jacob's case.

A few months earlier, on October 21, 2003, a thirty-five-year-old local man named Kevin had come forward and admitted that, on the night Jacob was kidnapped, he had been listening to a police scanner and decided to go check out the scene for himself. He arrived at the abduction site before police got there and then drove into the driveway, possibly leaving his tire tracks at the crime scene.

From the beginning, it was assumed Jacob had been taken away in a vehicle, because his Nike shoe print had been found about seventy-five yards down the driveway next to a set of tire tracks. The toe of the print appeared to be dug in, as if Jacob had shown some resistance, and the footprints ended at that spot. Investigators assumed he had been forced into a vehicle and driven away. A witness at the farmhouse had further corroborated this theory after he reported seeing a small car driving rapidly down his driveway and then turning around at the time of the abduction.

Investigators were rethinking this theory, telling us that the car the witness had seen was now accounted for, and the tire tracks that had been left on the driveway belonged to Kevin, not the kidnapper. This could mean the kidnapper was someone local who had escaped with Jacob on foot, rather than in a vehicle.

It was a lot to process.

A year earlier, NCMEC had pulled together a team of investigators and done a cold case review of Jacob's abduction. The team had included two investigators from the SCSO, one investigator from the Minnesota Bureau of Criminal Apprehension, a detective with the Lexington Police Department in North Carolina, a member of the Naval Criminal Investigative Service, a retired officer from the US Secret Service, and a retired officer from the FBI. There were also six NCMEC employees who participated in the cold case review (including our case manager, Ron Jones), and two retired law enforcement volunteers from NCMEC's Project ALERT team.

Because of my work with the National Center, I was familiar with these types of cold case reviews, but even so, the investigators at Stearns County shared very little with us about the outcome of Jacob's case review. All we knew was that they would be circling back and taking a closer look at some of the early suspects.

Based on the questions the investigators were now asking us, we soon realized there were two suspects they planned to revisit. One was a former family friend who had close ties to Jacob and may have known about the boys' plan to go to the Tom Thumb store that night. The other was our neighbor, Dan Rassier—the witness who had seen the car turning around in his driveway that night.

Dan was a single guy who lived with his parents on the farm where Jacob had been abducted. We didn't know him, but we knew his name had been turned in by tipsters early in the investigation. Dan had never been married, and because he taught middle school band to kids the same age as Jacob, investigators saw him as a logical suspect. His parents, Bob and Rita, were active in the St. Joseph Catholic Church, and though I wouldn't have recognized them if I'd bumped into them walking down the street, I'd always heard they were nice people. They happened to be on vacation in Europe at the time of Jacob's abduction, so that left Dan home alone all night with no alibi.

All this new information was so confusing. If there was no car, and if Dan Rassier really was the abductor, what were we supposed to do with the fact that Jacob's footsteps stopped halfway down the driveway? Did that mean he just threw Jacob over his shoulder and carried him somewhere? Wouldn't the search dogs still have been able to track Jacob's scent?

It was just so hard to believe the abductor could have been living right down the street from us all these years.

The days continued to slip by, and suddenly, it was Jacob's birthday again. He turned twenty-six on February 17, 2004, and as always, I hurt as much on this day as I had on the day he'd been taken from us. Twenty-six years old. I wondered if he might be married by now, or a dad.

I spent the day at home, cleaning, sorting, reminiscing, crying. I talked to my friends Nancy and Donna and to all three of my sisters. When I called Barbi, she sounded so tired. Her alcoholism had finally caught up to her, and she was in very poor health. She'd actually been on hospice the previous summer, but through sheer willpower, she managed to graduate off hospice and come back to Minnesota with her husband, John, for a visit. We were all so happy to see her, yet it was hard to see our vibrant, larger-than-life sister looking so frail and weak.

Now, Barbi was back on hospice again. When I talked to her on the phone earlier that day, I thought it was unusual she hadn't mentioned Jacob's birthday. Every year, without fail, she sent a dozen roses on his birthday—eleven of them in some bright color, but always one white one . . . for hope. But by late afternoon, the flowers still hadn't arrived, and I wondered if Barbi really had forgotten Jacob's birthday.

Jerry had a meeting that evening, so I made Jacob's favorite peanut butter swirl bars and grilled a steak. As I ate dinner by myself, it suddenly felt like Jacob was right there, sitting at the table with me.

"Hey Jake. I miss you," I said with tears spilling down my face. "It's been so long."

I closed my eyes for a moment and took a few deep breaths.

"I can't even believe you're twenty-six now. That's crazy."

I paused and let that sink in a minute. Twenty-six.

"I just want you to know I'm trying so hard. Not a single day goes by that I don't think about you or wonder what more I could be doing. I promised I'd never give up, and I never will. I swear. Not until the day you're finally in my arms again. I love you with all my heart, Jake. Happy birthday."

The next morning, I decided I needed a boost, so I called to make an appointment for a haircut and highlights. I spent the afternoon unwinding and relaxing, then returned home a few hours later. When I walked in the door, our home phone was ringing, so I ran to answer it. It was my sister Nancy. She was crying.

"What's wrong?" I asked her.

"Barbi died today . . . "

No, no, no.

"She slipped into a coma during the night and her lungs filled with fluid in the morning. She died around 1:15 this afternoon."

I looked at the time on my cell phone and noticed I had five missed calls. My sister had died while I was getting highlights in my hair.

I hadn't been there for my sisters.

When Jacob had been taken, Barbi had somehow managed to fly out of San Francisco just days after the earthquake. She stayed for six weeks and *literally* took care of me.

Wear this.

Comb your hair.

Talk to this person.

Eat.

Barbi saved my life. She put me on my feet again and gave me a sense of direction. She helped us form the Jacob Wetterling Foundation. She contacted all those missing children organizations and filled out their very long and grueling applications, just to make sure Jacob's name and face was recognized all across the nation. She believed in me and my work. She talked to me about testifying before Congress to change laws, seeing something in me that I wasn't yet able to see for myself. I did it because of Barbi's constant and gentle nudging.

We were so close. Of all my sisters, Barbi and I were the nearest in age, and I absolutely worshipped her. When we were little, she had an imaginary friend named Sculthy Bin-a-Boo. Sometimes I wasn't sure if Sculthy was an imaginary friend or an alter personality, but it didn't matter much. I loved Barbi and Sculthy Bin-a-Boo all the same.

In high school, Barbi had the coolest friends, and I had the dubious distinction of being asked out by really cute guys who, it turns out, were more interested in Barbi. It was okay, though. I got it. She was gorgeous, funny, fun, and kind.

The one thing Barbi *couldn't* do well was tell jokes. Over and over, she'd make me sit and listen while she practiced a joke, repeatedly getting the punchline wrong. In the end, we always ended up laughing hysterically.

Barbi was always an infinite dreamer with such a deep and compassionate soul. She taught me to look beyond myself, to see possibilities, and to live with abandon. She was as fearless as she was vulnerable, and I loved her with every ounce of my being.

How could she be gone? She was only fifty-six years old.

February 17, 2004
Jacob's 26th birthday

Dear Jacob,

You're twenty-six today. Unbelievable. I tried to write you a letter this year to catch you up on all that you've missed and to reflect on how much we miss you, but words seem so shallow. I hurt as much on your birthdays as on the day you were taken from us. Other moms understand how indelible a birth stays in your mind and heart. You were one special little (well not little) baby and I treasure those memories!

I made your favorite peanut butter and chocolate chip bars, and I grilled a steak. Your dad had a meeting, so I ate alone but it was okay for the space that I was in. It was like I had you here with me for dinner. Just you and me.

My favorite moment of the day was when your kindergarten teacher, Lavonne Gitter-Skow, called. She told me she thinks of you often but especially today because she knew it was your birthday. She said "I'm sitting here with twenty-eight first graders who have something they want to say to you." Then, she held the phone up and they all shouted, "Thank you for keeping us safe!"

I nearly burst into tears. She said they'd just had their safety talk and she'd told them about you. She said she was just doing her little part and thanked me for doing my bigger part. I think she had it backwards. Working with little children and letting them know how

very special they are IS the biggest part. I know you loved her and
you loved school because of her.

I miss you so much during times like this, Jacob. Hang in there. I
wish I could give you a hug.

Love,
Mom

{ Chapter 30 }

In April 2004—just five months after I was fired from my job and two months after Barbi's death—our friend Jim Graeve called me and said, "Patty, we need you to run for Congress."

I laughed.

Jim was a local St. Joseph resident and an active member of the Democratic-Farmer-Labor (DFL) party. "I'm serious," he said. "We don't have a candidate, and you'd be awesome!"

The Democratic candidate for Minnesota's Sixth Congressional District, Janet Robert (an attorney from Stillwater), had just dropped out of the race—one day before the district convention. This left the local delegates scrambling to find a candidate who was willing to run against the Republican incumbent, Mark Kennedy.

Jim was convinced I was the right person for the job, even though I'd never had any desire to run for office. The more I listened, however, the more intrigued I became. Jim made some good points. People in Minnesota knew me. I had spent time in Washington and done work on a federal level. I had run two federal programs, applied for federal grants, and helped change federal law.

As I hung on Jim's words, I thought to myself, *well, what the heck?* What did I have to lose? I had been searching desperately for a reason to get up in the morning, and now here was an incredible opportunity that would allow me to start over and truly make a difference. Maybe I could be a child advocate in Washington. I agreed to consider it.

Within a matter of days, Jim pulled together a very convincing team of local DFL activists to come to St. Joseph and meet with Jerry and me at our house. They explained what a US congressional race entailed, who I was running against, what the DFL would provide, how it got started, and when we could make an official announcement. Everyone was so convincing, they actually made me believe I could win. As a US congresswoman, I could continue fighting for what I believed in. Kids needed a voice, and I knew I could be that voice.

"What do you think?" I asked Jerry.

"I think you should do it," he said. "It sounds like a great opportunity."

In a perfect world, our family would have had more time to discuss the impact of this important decision, but—as so often happened—someone leaked the news to the media, and it caught us all off guard. I confirmed my candidacy without realizing what was in store for me.

Suddenly, everything was moving at lightning speed. My immediate job was to study the issues and contact local delegates to gain the DFL endorsement. I had no idea what I was doing, but with my impressive team to guide me, I just kept moving forward. I announced my candidacy on May 11, 2004, and just eleven days later, I won the DFL endorsement at the Minnesota State DFL Convention.

I barely had time to wrap my head around the fact I was actually doing this before I started hearing from people who didn't support my decision to run for office. Many felt I was just "too nice," and they didn't want to see me getting caught up in the ugliness of politics. I could understand their concern; I didn't want that either. However, I wanted to be a child advocate in Washington and felt I was up to the challenge. With everything I'd been through in my lifetime, I was sure I could handle whatever came my way. Couldn't I?

I was so naive.

Each morning when I arrived at our campaign office in downtown St. Cloud, I found a bottle of holy water strategically placed in front of the door. I was never really sure what it meant—whether it had been left by a friend or a foe—but, given the choice, I decided to take it as a blessing. Each day, I said a silent "thank you" to the person who had left it for me, then went about my work. I always had several bottles of holy water lined up on my desk.

All day long—week after week—I studied the issues. I knew I wasn't an expert on everything, but throughout my adult life, I sought out people who *were* experts and asked for their counsel and advice. Unfortunately, it didn't work that way in politics. As congressional candidates, we were expected to know everything about everything.

Fundraising was also important, so every day my campaign manager sat me down in my office with a staffer from the finance team. They handed me a list of donors, each with a phone number and an "ask" (the target amount that person could afford and might be willing to give). The lists were generated from a public database of campaign donations, so if someone had ever donated to a political candidate in the past, their name was on the list.

It took some time to get used to it, but after a while I didn't mind making the calls. It allowed me to introduce myself to people, talk about why I wanted to run, and ask for their support. Everyone was friendly, and I got the sense people enjoyed hearing from someone they felt they knew. I had 91 percent name recognition in my district, which I attributed directly to Jacob. People truly cared and were still paying attention to my message, even after all these years.

The race in Minnesota's Sixth Congressional District was being closely watched, and I had the honor of being chosen as one of four congressional candidates to speak at the Democratic National Convention in Boston on July 27, 2004. In the three minutes I was given, I tried to connect with my party delegates on the issues that mattered most to me. I wanted to help pull the United States forward and represent the good, hardworking, everyday Americans who had carried and supported me. This was an opportunity for me to give back.

For the next several months, I didn't spend a moment by myself. The contrast between my days sitting home alone in my rocking chair and this new pandemonium was stark. It was hard to believe this was the same lifetime, let alone the same year. I brought in my best friend, Nancy, to become my scheduler and office manager, and my friend Kevin to help with the financial paperwork. Staffers picked me up in the morning to do "meet and greets" at the local cafés, then I spent afternoons back at the campaign office on the phone. Evenings were most often filled with house parties or community rallies, and even though Jerry couldn't "campaign" for me because of his Baha'i beliefs, he loved hearing about my busy days on the campaign trail.

I was endorsed by many of the national organizations that commonly supported Democrats, but I quickly learned these endorsements sometimes came with a price: the automatic assumption by some voters that I shared every belief those organizations supported. This was a huge challenge for me. Although I was happy to receive endorsements from organizations like the Minnesota Police and Peace Officers Association and the Minnesota

Teachers Association, there were other more controversial organizations that attached themselves to my campaign and caused headaches for me when I didn't wholeheartedly share their beliefs.

I didn't consider myself a hardline, left-wing liberal, and I didn't want to be seen as one, either. I was a centrist, and I was proud of the fact that many of the legislators who helped with the passing of the Jacob Wetterling Act were actually Republicans. Minnesota senator Dave Durenburger and congressman Jim Ramstad had both been strong supporters of my efforts and had worked hard at both the state and federal level to pass this important legislation.

Still, the Republicans continued to hammer me on two key issues: guns and abortion rights. I got criticized for not having a gun permit, and because I was a Democrat, it was automatically assumed I would vote to take away everyone's guns. Nothing I could say would change that. The hard right-wingers also tried to beat me up for not having a fishing license. They even went so far as to call the resort where our family vacationed every summer and ask the owner, a proud Republican, whether I ever fished or had a fishing license. He told them that, yes, Jerry and I always had a license, and not only did I fish, I often caught the *biggest* fish. I smiled when I heard this, but I secretly wondered—exactly how would this make me a better congresswoman?

I was also repeatedly attacked for my stance on abortion. After serving as an advocate for almost fifteen years, I had met and listened to many victims of sexual crimes, and I didn't believe the federal government should be deciding what these victims and their families should do during such a time of terrible duress. I'd seen both sides of this issue and recognized there was no blanket decision that could possibly cover every one of these very personal situations. I was advised to avoid the topic altogether.

Meanwhile, life didn't pause for my political campaign.

On Sunday, August 29, 2004, our youngest daughter, Carmen, was getting married, and just one month after that, our oldest daughter, Amy, was expecting her first child. This would be our first grandchild, and Jerry and I were so excited! I was busy 24/7 with the campaign, but I tried very hard to stay present for my family and was looking forward to these two important milestones.

Early on, I informed my staff I would need to take off the week of my daughter's wedding to attend activities and help with preparations. Unfortunately, they forgot to block it off on the calendar, which resulted in me having to cancel a debate that had been scheduled for six weeks. We offered five alternative dates, but Mark Kennedy's campaign staff refused to reschedule, using the opportunity instead to criticize me for canceling the debate. The local media caught wind of the conflict and repeatedly asked me to comment, but I refused to get caught up in the drama. I simply shook off any criticism and tried to remain positive. I needed and wanted to be there for Carmen.

Carmen and Kristian had a lovely wedding with close local friends, immediate family, and a small number of visiting British friends. It was held at the beautiful Great Hall in downtown St. Paul, a perfect venue that gave an elegant and historic feel to this very special occasion.

Once again, I struggled to hold back tears as Jerry and I walked Carmen—our baby—down the aisle. She looked so beautiful and confident, she absolutely glowed. Shortly after the wedding she and Kristian planned to move to England, and I had to remind myself I wasn't losing my daughter but gaining a son-in-law. Kristian was such a perfect match for Carmen—someone who made her laugh and feel safe. It made my heart swell to see them so happy as they began their married life together.

Few people would ever know the incredible challenges we had faced together as a family—the fear and the sadness, the hope and the heartbreak, the unwanted publicity, the horrifying leads, the embarrassment of having people you knew investigated as suspects.

Moments like this were more than just milestones for us. They were success stories. Against all odds, we were making it. Our kids were happy, successful, and in a good place. For me, that's what mattered most of all.

{ Chapter 31 }

On September 29, 2004, exactly one month after Carmen and Kristian's wedding, Amy called with the announcement we'd been longing to hear.

"The baby's on its way!"

I immediately called the campaign office and claimed the day as my own. Jerry and I drove straight to the Cities, both of us beyond excited to finally meet our first grandbaby. Carmen had stayed back after Kristian left for England to support her sister through the birth. She was already in the room with Amy and Chris when we arrived, so Jerry and I sat and waited anxiously with Chris's mom, Toni, and his sister Beth for ongoing updates.

Finally, early in the afternoon, our granddaughter Lili made her way into the world. She was so perfect. As I held Lili in my arms, she reminded me so much of Amy—those beautiful eyes and ears, little fingers and toes, and even tiny fingernails. All of it took me back to my own days of having babies and raising a family. I loved those days so much and was unbelievably proud and happy for Amy, Chris, and their beautiful new daughter.

Around 5:00 PM, after hugs and holds and endless pictures, everyone decided to go out for a bite to eat so we could give Amy and Chris some time alone with their new little family. I didn't join them because—although I'd claimed the day as my own—my campaign manager had encouraged me to stop by a house party later that evening, even if it was just for a short visit. House parties generated both dollars and support, so I decided to fit this in, assuring my family I would be back to meet up with them at the hospital by 7:00 or 7:30.

The party was in Minneapolis, not far from the hospital. As I drove along, my mind was very far away from my campaign. All I could think about was my beautiful little granddaughter and how anxious I was to get this commitment out of the way, so I could get back to the hospital and hold her again.

I stopped at a red light and heard the revving of a motorcycle behind me.

When the light turned green, I continued on my way until I reached the next red light. The man on the motorcycle revved his engine again, then pulled up to the left of my car—in the lane for oncoming traffic—and glared at me through the driver-side window. I could see only part of his face through his helmet, so I turned back and looked straight ahead, unable to figure out what he wanted. At the next light, he did the same thing, only this time, he kept revving his engine and pressed his face right up to the window, yelling, "Baby killer!"

I was terrified. I didn't move when the light changed, and because he was in the way of the oncoming traffic, this forced him to pull ahead of me. I followed him for about a block, then, very quickly, veered off onto a side road. I went a block or two, then turned again to make it difficult for him to backtrack and find me. I was lost and scared, so when I spotted a church, I sped into the parking lot, parked, and quickly ran inside. I found the office assistant and asked if I could speak to the minister.

"May I ask what it's regarding?" she asked me politely.

"I'm . . . just . . . really scared, and I need to talk to someone."

She returned shortly with the minister, who could see I was visibly shaking.

"Why don't we meet in my office?" he suggested gently.

I followed him back to a small, neat office, and he shut the door gently behind us as I settled into a chair opposite his desk.

"Are you okay?" he asked.

I didn't even know how to start, so I just jumped right in.

"This crazy motorcycle guy just pulled up next to me at a stoplight and started screaming 'Baby killer!' at me. When the light changed, he started following me and . . . I didn't know what he was going to do," I blurted out, trying to hold back tears. "Maybe he was trying to intimidate me because I'm running for US Congress. I don't know. But—my daughter just had a baby this morning . . . our first grandchild . . . and this guy . . . "

I got so worked up I couldn't stop talking. I went on to tell him about Lili, then about my sister's recent death, then my mom's death, then Jacob's kidnapping. Finally, I told him my family was expecting me back at the hospital in an hour, but I needed to get to this campaign party first, and I was too scared to get back in my car.

"Wow," he said. "Any one of those things is monumental on its own, but the combination is overwhelming. I'm so sorry. I know about Jacob, and

I'm familiar with what your family has gone through. If you'd like, you can sit in the sanctuary for a while. It's beautiful, it's quiet, and it's a good place for prayer."

The minister said a prayer with me, then guided me to the sanctuary.

"I have a meeting, but please feel free to stay as long as you want," he said. "The junior high youth will be arriving for youth group in about twenty minutes, so that will probably end your peaceful silence. But feel free to go back to my office if you need more time."

I thanked him and found a quiet pew where I could sit and breathe. He was right, the sanctuary was beautiful and quiet. I took several deep breaths and continued to wipe away tears as I said a prayer and reflected on my whole crazy day.

I finally felt safe again, and I was so grateful to be sitting in this place of worship—surrounded by God. When the junior high students entered, I was comforted by the sound and normalcy of their laughter. I found my way back to my car, and soon after, I arrived at the house party. Everyone knew I was anxious to get back to the hospital, so we made the most of my short visit. Afterward, my campaign manager walked me to my car and told me it was the best house party speech I'd ever given. Perhaps that was because, in that moment, I absolutely knew why I was running.

For Lili.

{ Chapter 32 }

On November 2, 2004—my fifty-fifth birthday—I went to the polls to cast my vote for myself for the US Sixth Congressional District seat.

As I stood in line outside our township hall that morning, I was suddenly aware of every piece of my journey that had led me to this point. I was that scared little kindergartener who had felt so lost after my dad died. I was that excited second grader who was so happy when my mom married Bud and he became our second dad. I was that proud big sister when my new baby brother was born. I was one of five happy kids growing up in St. Paul. I was the soda jerk, cheerleader, college student, war protester, teacher, wife, mom . . . and the victim of a terrible crime. Now, here I was: an advocate, an American citizen, and a candidate for US Congress.

Wow.

I quietly made my way to an open voting booth and finally got my first look at the official ballot. There, under incumbent Mark Kennedy, I was listed as the second candidate for US Congress in the Sixth District. I smiled a moment, then darkened the circle next to my name.

In just over five months, our team had set up an office with seventeen staff members and hundreds of volunteers. We had raised nearly $2 million and run a high-profile race that brought the president of the United States to St. Cloud for the first time in history. I had done my very best to further the discussion of building a safer world for children, and I felt good that I'd honored all three promises I'd made to myself before agreeing to run. I hadn't promised more than I could deliver, I hadn't lied, and I hadn't sacrificed my integrity to win this election. I worked hard to study the issues and acquired a massive amount of knowledge on things like taxes, small business, labor unions, farming, jobs, education, the economy, government spending, partisan politics, conservatives, liberals, political conventions, and delegates— not to mention all the inner workings of a political campaign. I felt like I'd been cramming for finals for five months straight, and by the end of this day, it would finally be over.

I finished marking the ballot, then made my way out to the scanning machine that would read and tabulate my votes. I smiled as an election judge handed me an "I VOTED" sticker. Never in all my years of casting votes had that little red sticker meant so much to me. I stuck it on my coat and headed out the door with a sigh of relief.

Barbi's husband, John, had flown in from California, and Trevor was also home from Colorado to join us for election night. Carmen had left already to join her new husband in England, but Amy, Chris, and Lili all came up from the Cities that evening. We joined friends, family, campaign staff, and loyal supporters at the Del-Win Ballroom to wait for the election results. Throughout the evening, we anxiously watched as the returns trickled in. It remained a close race, but when the votes for Anoka County finally came in and it was clear I couldn't win, I grabbed the second of the two speeches I'd prepared—the one I hoped I wouldn't have to read—then called Mark Kennedy to congratulate him on his victory.

When all was said and done, I had received 46 percent of the vote to Mark Kennedy's 54 percent. Aside from the millions of dollars we raised locally, our campaigns had also received a lot of national support from the Democratic and Republican Campaign Committees, making this the most expensive congressional race in Minnesota history. I campaigned hard for six months and was often asked, "How can you possibly do this in such a short amount of time?" I usually laughed and replied, "Who would ever do this for a *longer* amount of time?"

The truth was, even in defeat, I was already being asked if I would run again in 2006. I couldn't even imagine starting all over again and keeping up this pace for another two years, but I wasn't ready to completely rule it out.

Shortly after winning the election, Mark Kennedy announced he would be leaving his House seat at the end of the term and running for the US Senate in 2006. I was so put off by this, I actually began to consider another political run. Kennedy had just started his second term as a congressman representing the Sixth District, and now he would be spending the next two years campaigning for US Senate? I felt he had betrayed the very people who had voted for him, and I—more than anyone—knew how much time and how many resources these campaigns required.

I also knew from our own polling during my campaign that I would have beaten Mark Kennedy in a statewide race. As a whole, Minnesotans tend to be more liberal than those in the Sixth District, and many people in the highly populated metro districts didn't respond favorably to Mark Kennedy's nasty attack ads on me. If I could go head-to-head with Kennedy in a statewide race for Mark Dayton's open Senate seat, I was sure I could win.

I would be competing for the DFL ticket against two other candidates— Hennepin County attorney Amy Klobuchar and Ford Bell, the president of the Minneapolis Heart Institute Foundation. I knew it was a bold move to run for United States Senate, but I was certain I could do a better job than Mark Kennedy, so I felt compelled to try.

Once again, I began studying the issues, fundraising, and meeting with people from all over the state. I also got to know the other candidates and found them both interesting. I knew Amy Klobuchar from her work as the Hennepin County attorney, and many times we saw each other at Democratic fundraising events. In the summer of 2005, we both attended a gathering at the home of Ruth Usem, a loyal Democrat who helped fundraise for many DFL candidates. Recently, Ruth had been to Chicago and met a newly elected, up-and-coming US senator who had impressed her so much, she—like many others—believed he would run for president one day. She invited Senator Barack Obama to attend a fundraiser at her lovely home on Lake Harriet in Minneapolis, so others could hear him speak and get to know him.

When I arrived, there were more than 150 people mingling outside on the lawn, enjoying fancy appetizers and beverages. Just before 7:00 PM, Amy Klobuchar and I were ushered into the kitchen so we could be introduced to the crowd, ahead of Senator Obama. As we waited for the guests to file into the house, Amy and I got a chance to speak briefly to the Chicago senator and share a little bit about who we were. Senator Obama was so impressive—intelligent, confident, warm, and engaging. I could definitely picture him running for president one day.

Amy Klobuchar and I continued to meet on the campaign path, and soon it became clear that she had been working for many years to build a strong political backing. Still a newbie to the political scene, I didn't have that same deep support. Though I had strong polling numbers, Amy was leading in both fundraising and endorsements, and to be honest, I really liked her. She had been good to me and had also supported my congressional run. She was intelligent, funny, and caring, and when I heard her stump speech, I often found myself standing in the back of the room laughing at her jokes. I admired her confidence and respected the experience she brought to her campaign.

I announced on January 20, 2006, that I was withdrawing from the US Senate race and would, instead, be supporting Amy Klobuchar in her candidacy.

Following my announcement, I was highly encouraged to try again for the now-vacant US House seat in the Sixth Congressional District. If I agreed, I would have two opponents—Republican state senator Michele Bachmann from Stillwater and Independence Party candidate John Binkowski, a twenty-seven-year-old college student from St. Mary's Point, near Afton.

I decided to go for it, so I made my announcement at the Anoka County Government Center on February 4, 2006. I won the DFL endorsement a few months later, on May 13.

John Binkowski was Jacob's age and was smart, funny, and blunt. I admired his desire to jump into the race and make a difference in the world, but I'd been told that Independents tended to pull votes away from the Democratic candidate. That worried both me and my team. Regardless, I still really liked John, and as the campaign went on, we often joined forces to call out our opponent on her misstatements of fact.

About a month out from the election, news came from Washington that rocked my world. US representative Mark Foley—a well-known advocate for child safety who had led the House caucus on missing and exploited children—resigned abruptly after allegations arose that he'd been sending sexually explicit emails and instant messages to underage congressional pages. I had worked with this man several times on sex offender legislation, and now he was being accused of the same type of predatory behavior we had worked so hard to prevent. Not only that, but I learned there were other congressional leaders who had known about Foley's behavior for over a year and had covered it up. I was livid.

I held a press conference on October 2, 2006, calling for a criminal investigation of Mark Foley, as well as the immediate expulsion of any members of Congress who had known about his conduct but refused to take action. I kept imagining myself as the parent of one of those pages. What if I'd encouraged one of my own high-school-age kids to be a page in Washington? These kids were young, vulnerable, and so far from home. Mark Foley exploited their trust, and I found the entire situation reprehensible and unacceptable. I demanded change.

Suddenly, I was thrown into the national spotlight. I was invited to give the Democratic response to President George W. Bush's weekly radio address and was contacted by several TV networks and national newspapers about the scandal. I felt strongly this was an important issue that needed to be addressed immediately, but after speaking out, I was accused by my Republican opponent of rushing to judgment and exploiting the situation for political gain. Unbelievable. This was my life work, and I certainly wasn't going to stay quiet just because I was a political candidate.

I continued to run a hard race—speaking of my desire to be an advocate for children in Washington, while at the same time trying to rise above Michele Bachmann's often erratic statements.

On Election Day, November 7, 2006, I retraced my route to the St. Joseph Township Hall and once again voted for myself for Minnesota's Sixth Congressional seat. This time, we rented space upstairs at the Red Carpet Event Center in downtown St. Cloud to watch the results come in. The media was all there, and I was sitting on a couch with my kids when, once again, I knew I was done. I had received 42 percent of the vote, John Binkowski 8 percent, and Michele Bachmann 50 percent.

The people of the Sixth Congressional District had spoken. Although I wasn't the extreme liberal my opponents painted me to be, the voters made it known they wanted someone more conservative to represent them in Congress.

Twice now, my family had witnessed the amount of time and effort it took for me to run a political campaign. They'd seen all the negative ads and heard all the horrible criticism, so if I had ever wanted to run again, I'm sure they would have had me committed.

No more politics. I needed a job.

{ Chapter 33 }

One day, out of the clear blue, I received a call from a friend who told me the director of sexual violence prevention at the Minnesota Department of Health (MDH) was leaving her position. I'd previously worked with the director on an MDH grant the foundation had received, so I decided to call her and get more information about the position.

As director of the program, I would be responsible for overseeing an $800,000 federal prevention grant and managing projects funded by the National Centers for Disease Control and Prevention (CDC) to prevent violence against women. It sounded perfect, so I filled out the application and sent it in. After several interviews, I was offered the position in July 2007.

My new office was located in the Golden Rule Building in downtown St. Paul. Not only was I back in my hometown, it made me smile every single day to go to work doing sexual violence prevention in the *Golden Rule* Building. Jacob had always been all about fairness, so this was perfect. Each morning when I entered the building, I was reminded to treat others as you would like them to treat you.

It wasn't long before I realized the magnitude of work I had cut out for me. In 2005, Minnesota spent nearly $8 billion responding to sexual violence. That included everything from medical and mental health care to time lost at work. Even more staggering, the number of Minnesota children and adults who had been sexually assaulted in 2005 would nearly fill the Metrodome. That would be over 60,000 people in just one year.

Thankfully, I had a great team. After traveling around the state to meet many of the key partners that had already been identified in the new Sexual Violence Prevention Network, I also worked with other team members to pull together many local nonprofits, public health officials, and public health nurses.

We hosted a retreat in August 2007 to start defining the problem of sexual violence and finding ways to prevent it from happening. We established different committees who met regularly over the next two years, and in June 2009, we released our report: "The Promise of Primary Prevention of Sexual Violence: A Five-Year Plan to Prevent Sexual Violence and Exploitation in Minnesota."

I loved my job and the people I worked with. Our entire team believed in our mission and truly felt we could prevent sexual violence by changing social norms. We needed to raise our teenage and young adult children to have healthy relationships, and to encourage the public to recognize and speak out against the sexualization of younger and younger girls in marketing and media.

I worked long hours, and the daily 180-mile round-trip commute was exhausting. So when the housing market crashed in 2008, I started looking for options. I was able to buy a small house on the east side of St. Paul in the spring of 2009 at an unbelievably low price. The interest rate was low, the payment was affordable, and now that I was working full time, Jerry and I both viewed this as a sound financial move. I began spending Mondays through Thursdays there. I made it cozy with leftover furniture and other necessities from home, then filled in the gaps with items donated by my siblings or purchases I made at an amazing thrift shop in the neighborhood. It was fun, and Jerry enjoyed staying with me in the little house whenever we had weekend plans in the Cities.

On July 11, 2008, Trevor and his girlfriend, Trish, were married at a beautiful outdoor wedding in Littleton, Colorado.

They met as students at Colorado State, and Jerry and I both felt incredibly lucky to be adding this perfect daughter-in-law to our family. Trish was stunning and funny. She understood Trevor in a way no one ever had before, and she brought out a fun, playful side of him that made us love her all the more.

The wedding took place at Arrowhead Golf Club in Littleton, with Jerry presiding. He had been so honored when Trevor and Trish asked him to officiate, and now with the golden glow of the sun setting against red sandstone rock formations behind them, the ceremony couldn't have been more perfect.

When it was my turn to be seated, Trevor walked me down the aisle—and off in the distance, we saw a fox pause to watch us. We glanced at each other and shared a knowing smile. As we neared the front, I looked up at Jerry, who appeared nervous. Our eyes met, and I nodded reassuringly. He had presided over only one other wedding in the past, for a friend, but this was different. This time it was for his own son, and I knew he wanted everything to be perfect for Trevor. I gave him one more "you got this" smile as I took my seat and Trevor took his place next to his dad.

As the music changed, we all stood and looked back to see Trish coming down the aisle. Just then, three deer appeared, seemingly out of nowhere, and started walking ahead of her. We watched in hushed silence, mesmerized, as Trish paused for a moment, then slowly followed the deer until they reached the last row of guests and then ran off to the side, letting Trish take center stage. It was absolutely magical, and not one person broke the special moment with a sound or even a photo.

Jerry did a beautiful job presiding over the wedding, and when it was over—more magic. An eagle circled over all of us before soaring off into the sky.

I finally broke into tears, knowing without a doubt that Jacob was there with us, sharing the joy.

In the fall of 2009, our family was once again forced to recognize another huge and difficult milestone. October 22, 2009, would mark twenty years since Jacob had been taken from us.

Twenty years. It was unfathomable.

Jerry and I found ourselves looking back to the very beginning and remembering what had given us strength all those years ago. Clearly, it had all started with two key people—Vern Iverson (who had coordinated the early media response) and Red Grammer, whose song "Listen" had become a symbolic anthem for our search. Together, they helped us build a powerful circle of hope by rallying the community and providing a constant source of information to keep media engaged.

We asked Vern if he could reach out to Red and see if he might be available to perform a concert at St. Ben's. Our plan was to hold it at the thousand-seat Benedicta Arts Center at the College of St. Benedict, and we hoped to sell enough tickets at five dollars each to raise proceeds for the Boys and Girls Club of Central Minnesota and the Jacob Wetterling Resource Center (which had undergone a name change just one year prior).

With a lot of work from friends and family, it all came together. "Twenty Years of Jacob's Hope: A Celebration of Children Concert with Red Grammer" was scheduled for October 17, 2009, and—once again—we were so grateful for the support of our community. It would be a near-sellout performance.

There was only one glitch.

About an hour before the concert, just as we were leaving the house, everything went dark. We scurried out, assuming it was only a neighborhood thing, but as we reached the St. Joe city limits, we could see the entire city was dark, including the college campus. We were experiencing a regional power outage, and no one could tell us how long it would be before it was fixed.

As we arrived at the auditorium, we could see many people milling about, waiting for the doors to open. Staff at St. Ben's couldn't let anyone into the building while the power was out, so all we could do was wait and hope. Finally, about twenty minutes before the concert was supposed to begin, the power miraculously came back on and security officers quickly opened the doors for the hundreds of people who were waiting. There would be no sound or light checks, but amazingly, the event went on as planned.

During the concert, I read from a book I'd recently written for our grandchildren—now three of them. Amy and Chris had added another daughter, Izzi, to their family in 2007, and in January 2009, Trevor and Trish welcomed their first son, Jake, who was named after his uncle, Jacob.

It was important to me that our grandkids knew about their Uncle Jacob, and I wanted to share his story in a way that wasn't frightening. I included many fun family photos, which were projected onto the screen behind us as Jerry and I narrated.

Grandma Patty and Grandpa Jerry had four wonderful children—Amy, Jacob, Trevor, and Carmen. We love them very much, and we had lots of fun when they were little.

You know a lot about Amy and Trevor and Carmen. Now I want to tell you about Jacob.

Jacob liked to play hockey and soccer and football, and he loved to go fishing.

Jacob liked to tell jokes and do fun things with his friends.

Jacob liked school and learning to play the trombone.

He loved dogs.

Jacob believed that things should be fair and that we should all
be kind.

The book described what happened to Jacob in a gentle way that wouldn't
scare our grandkids, but provided enough information so they would feel
comfortable asking questions.

Next, I focused on all the good things that had happened to our family
over the past twenty years, including the birth of baby Jake.

Baby Jake will grow up and be unique and special, just like you are.
He will also help us remember our missing Jacob.
Whenever we see him, our hearts will smile.
We will hug him and hold him, and tell him that we love him.
We will play with him and teach him to be kind and fair.
And to dream big dreams and hope big hopes.

Finally, I ended with a special message of hope for all of our grandchildren, both now and in the future, so they would always know how much we
loved them.

You never met your Uncle Jacob, but he is always with all of us.
When you see a rainbow, when you blow out a candle and make
a wish, or tell a funny joke . . .
When you hug your best friend, or your little sister, and when
you go to sleep at night . . .
You can know that Jacob is smiling inside your heart.
We call that special place in your heart "Jacob's Hope."

After the reading, everyone enjoyed Red Grammer's music, as well as
performances by Douglas Wood (who sang his song "Jacob's Hope"); Minnesota singer and songwriter George Maurer; and Beats on the Block, a local drum group from the Southside Boys and Girls Club. The concert was
like a twenty-year reunion with old friends, and it warmed our hearts to see
so many of Jacob's classmates and closest friends in attendance.

In addition to the concert, media coverage of the twentieth anniversary
also helped generate hope. I always called this time of year "the annual shaking of the tree." Though we didn't call on the media nearly as often as we

had in the beginning, we always reached out on October 22 and reminded people to leave their porch lights on for Jacob and all missing kids.

This year, Aaron helped out as well. He had recently returned home after serving in Iraq with the Army Reserves, and for the first time, he shared how it felt to live with his survivor's guilt. The Minneapolis *Star Tribune* featured Aaron in a cover story by Richard Meryhew titled, "Gone 20 Years, But With Him Every Day." It was hard for us to read about all the pain Aaron was still working through, but he did a great job with the interview and was a strong voice for all Jacob's friends who were also struggling with so many unanswered questions.

Even now, 20 years later, Aaron Larson plays it back daily, wondering what he might have done, said, or seen to make things turn out differently.

What if he and the Wetterling boys—Jacob and Trevor—had just stayed at the Wetterling house that night instead of biking to the store for candy and a movie? What if the moon had been full and there'd been enough light for the boys to spot the man lurking in the weeds? Or, what if the man with the gravelly voice who stepped from the dark had somehow lost his nerve—or taken Aaron instead of Jacob?

"It's difficult to think about all the things that might have been," Larson said softly. "It's something I think about every single day."

The *St. Cloud Times* also had extensive coverage of the twentieth anniversary. They interviewed key investigators on the case, including Sheriff Sanner and Captain Pam Jensen with the SCSO and Special Agent Ken McDonald with the Minnesota BCA. The sheriff shared how they were now focusing on local suspects and the possibility that the kidnapper may have escaped on foot. They explained how they had developed this theory after the driver of a car had come forward in 2003 and admitted to driving through the Rassier property shortly after Jacob was abducted, unintentionally leaving his tire tracks in the driveway.

Jerry and I still struggled with this whole "escaped on foot" theory. Six years after they had learned about Kevin, the sheriff's office seemed to be no further along in its investigation.

Did Dan Rassier do it, or didn't he? Why couldn't they just rule him in or rule him out?

{ Chapter 34 }

For years, I had wanted to walk down the Rassiers' driveway, just to see for myself where Jacob's footsteps had stopped. His Nike shoe print was the last known trace of him, and I wanted to get a sense of this place that had haunted me for so long.

The long gravel driveway went down a slight hill, then took a ninety-degree turn past the tree line, making it impossible to see the farmhouse from the road. I had started walking up the driveway a few times in the past, but then always talked myself out of it. I didn't really know the family, so I never felt comfortable enough to just walk up to the house, knock on the door, and introduce myself. However, one day, on pure impulse, I decided to do it.

I started walking down the gravel driveway toward the house, but with each step, I became more panicked. Barbi once told me that in the early days of the investigation, she dreamed that Jacob's body was buried on the Rassier property. What if it was true? What if Dan Rassier *had* taken Jacob? What if he was dangerous? I hadn't even bothered to tell anyone where I was going, so if anything were to happen to me, who would know? I quickly backtracked and made my way back to 91st Avenue.

Logically, I found it hard to believe Dan Rassier could have had anything to do with Jacob's kidnapping, but Sheriff Sanner seemed convinced he was their number-one suspect. I asked if there was any way I could just talk to him.

"I just want to sit across from him, look him straight in the eye, and have him tell me he didn't do it," I told the sheriff.

It took some convincing, but finally, he agreed. I would wear a wire, and investigators would be listening.

I met with special agents from the FBI, who went over all the details. They explained where they would be and how they would make sure I was safe. They chose an office plaza in St. Cloud as the meeting place for my conversation with Dan. It was the site of the MDH's district office, and I had an office there which I used frequently during the winter months. It also had a gym on the main floor where Dan was a member.

On Tuesday, October 20, 2009, just three days after our Celebration of Children concert and two days before the twentieth anniversary of Jacob's abduction, Jerry and I met with agents from the FBI and the BCA at the Stearns County Sheriff's Office to go over the operation. They put a small microphone on me, tested it, then explained that Jerry would be with them in a car close by. If anything happened, or if at any time I felt uncomfortable, I was told to just get up and leave.

Oddly, I wasn't even nervous. I'd been wanting to talk to Dan Rassier for so long, I was actually looking forward to it. I sat in my office upstairs and anxiously waited for the call to let me know when Dan was leaving the gym. When it finally came, around 8:30 PM, I left my office, hurried down the stairs, and almost ran right into him.

"Are you Dan?" I asked him.

"Yes. Hi Patty," he replied.

"I need to talk to you. I need ten minutes."

"Sure. Do you want to sit down somewhere?"

We made our way over to the benches in the building's common area and sat down.

"You work upstairs?" he asked me.

I explained that I worked at MDH in St. Paul most days, but also worked here at the district office on occasion.

I took a deep breath. Dan had a young, boyish face and showed no sense of skepticism about our meeting. He was tall with a slim build, and there was nothing about him that made me feel afraid or physically threatened.

"I just . . . I need you to talk to me. I need you to tell me what happened that night. You were home, you were the last person close to Jacob."

"I'm just going to say as clear as I know how," he said. "The police, the FBI, are idiots. I'm sorry to say that, but that's how I feel. The news people came out and made me look like a jerk. They changed my voice on TV, they filmed me at school, and they made me look like I didn't give a crap about it."

I knew what he was talking about. About five years earlier, a reporter from the local FOX network had confronted Dan in the parking lot of the school where he taught.

"But they said you went back to bed that night . . . " I interjected.

"Yeah," he said, defensively. "I went back to bed after I went through all the buildings. I walked around with a flashlight, I looked around, and eventually I did go to bed. But they made it sound like I didn't care and just went back to sleep."

"Yeah, they did," I agreed.

"And this guy that came forward fourteen years later and said he was the driver of the car—I have a picture of the kind of car that turned around. I know it was involved with the whole thing."

"I thought it was dark? I thought because it was really dark . . . "

"No," he interrupted me. "See, you don't even—they didn't even tell you. There was a car in the afternoon. This car comes zooming down the hill, dirt flying, does a fast U-turn, and takes off again. No one has ever done that, and I've lived there basically all my life."

"But why would they do that?" I asked him.

"I remember running to the side of the house to watch it go up the hill, and I go . . . man! So, the day goes by, I leave, and I come back at night. And then, around quarter after nine, a different car comes and does the exact same thing."

"How do you know it was a different car?" I asked. "It was really dark."

"We have a yard light. It was a dark, smaller car. It wasn't the same car, but it was the same driver. The coincidence of someone coming in like that two times, in one day . . . "

"I never heard about the first one," I told him. "Did you tell them?"

"Yeah, I told them that thirty times. And five years ago, when they had me in there for a couple hours, they just basically said to me, 'Why don't you just admit that you did it?' "

I could tell he was angry, but I kept going.

"Well, it's troubling because you were closer to them than anybody, and you were home alone, and you teach kids Jacob's age. I would think if they came pounding on your door . . . did they come to your house that night?"

Dan sighed.

"So, okay, I saw that happen—the car—and it's just weird. Then, I go to bed. It was 10:00, 10:30, I don't know exactly. But I remember sleeping and the dog barking. My parents are gone to Europe . . . first time they've ever been gone . . . that's another whole thing. I get up and look out and found out why she's barking. It's because all these flashlights are in our woods and by the woodpile. Immediately, my heart's going. I thought somebody was stealing wood, so I called 911."

"You did?" I asked. "That night?"

"That night," he told me. "I called 911."

"Wow," I replied. "What time do you think that was? I mean, I know they responded quickly, but . . . "

"They have a record of what time I called. But the lady said, 'There's been a boy taken out there.' So, I walked out the door, I go up the hill, and I met one officer. He said there's a boy that we think has been taken. I don't know if he asked where I live, but I go back to the yard and looked around in the buildings."

I wasn't sure if I believed him.

"Weren't you concerned that they were just combing your parents' property with . . . "

He interrupted me again. "Well, of course I was concerned. But what . . . "

Now I interrupted him. "I would just find that really horrifically traumatizing."

"That they were up there looking?" he asked me.

"Well, I meant, yeah, I guess I would have been out there with them, trying to figure it out."

"Well, I went through the buildings," he told me. "They never came down, they never came in the yard, they never knocked on the door."

"The whole night they didn't?" I was shocked.

"No."

I pressed on.

"Do you think Jacob could have been on your property? Do you think somebody else could have dragged him? I don't know what happened. I am . . . you know . . . this time of year is hell. And it's kind of been hell for you too. I mean, as a suspect . . . "

"Yeah," he said. "It's been harder on my parents."

"Did you know Jacob?" I asked him.

"I never knew Jacob. I only knew Jerry from a few games of basketball."

"My sister had this dream that Jacob was buried on your property," I said. "She said, 'You have to go down there, Patty!' And I can't tell you how many times I started walking down your driveway, just to talk to you, and your parents, and whatever. And then I'd feel rather foolish because I'd never done that before, and I didn't know what I wanted to say. But I just wanted you to look me in the eye and say you had nothing to do with Jacob's . . . "

He stopped me. "I had nothing to do with that."

"You would never have harmed Jacob?"

"I only feel that if I would have been more alert, I could have stopped it. I could have saved him if I would have known it was that car. I mean, when it turned around, I really feel that I saw Jacob looking out the window of that car. I have that memory of somebody looking out the window, and that's why I would like to talk to that guy who says he was the one that drove that car."

"So what do you think happened?" I asked him.

"I think the person that did it either did a test run in the afternoon, or the mission failed in the afternoon. And he came back at night and got his chance."

"But who?"

"I mean, it's possible it's connected to that boy in Cold Spring that was mentioned in the article . . . "

"Jared? I remember Jared from a long time ago."

Jared Scheierl was the twelve-year-old boy from Cold Spring who had been abducted, assaulted, and released just nine months prior to Jacob's abduction. I had met him five years earlier, when he came forward and shared his story. He and I were interviewed on a local TV network just before the fifteenth anniversary.

"You know," Dan continued, "Maybe this time the guy panicked, with all the publicity, and, you know, he couldn't risk . . . "

"So where would he be?" I asked.

"Well, if that's really the scenario, I actually feel—because the police make me feel so guilty—that if other people would know that, they could go on our property and bury Jacob. You know what I'm saying?"

I didn't know what he was saying.

"They could do it so easy," he continued. "You know, Patty, I mean . . . "

"How could they?" I didn't understand what he was trying to tell me.

"They could come . . . there could be a deer hunter . . . we have people that go down there and hunt . . . "

"And you wouldn't notice?" I asked.

"We wouldn't. We might not even see him drive down in the meadow. Or, they could park their car and just walk through the woods. Bury him, I mean. I found a . . . well, I won't say."

"You found what? I need to know."

"Well, I go down in the gravel pit and do a lot of recycling metal. Maybe you were the one that called it in."

"I didn't call in anything. I've never been on your property."

"Well, anyway, I was down there digging one time a couple years ago and the police came out to investigate what I was digging.

"It wasn't me. I've never . . . "

"Hey, you know, even if it was you, I wouldn't blame you. I mean, you don't know me. But anyway, someone could come on the property very easily and bury a body."

Up until this point, I'd been perfectly calm. Now he was starting to freak me out.

"That's pretty scary," I said. "I can't imagine that. Honestly, I'm just having a hard time grasping that you're saying that. Why would they choose your property?"

Now he seemed to backtrack a bit.

"I mean . . . no . . . I . . . I actually . . . I'm just being negative here. Negative paranoia. The police were always asking me that first year, 'Is there somebody that's really upset with you?' It's one of their questions they kept pursuing."

I was confused. "But why? That makes no sense either. Why would somebody take my son and then bury him on your property so that you'd get . . . "

He stopped me. "I don't think that's what happened, but I'm saying that if somebody knew they were looking for somebody local . . . "

"I do law enforcement presentations," I told him. "I've sat through a lot of investigative stuff, and you always start right where it happened. And that's why it's hard for me. I hear it over and over—you start where it happened and then you can broaden your circle. But the circle starts . . . I mean . . . it's dead-center on your property. That's disconcerting, and that's one of the reasons I just wanted to talk to you. Plus, it's October 22 this week, and I just . . . "

"Yeah," Dan replied.

"I need to know. Our family needs to know answers. And *you* need to know, and your family needs to know."

We talked for several more minutes before I decided to wrap it up. "Well, I'm heartbroken. I don't know what to do . . . twenty years . . . "

"Twenty years, I know," Dan said. "And they can't solve it because . . . "

I cut him off. "I don't even care about that. I don't care about them. I care about me, I care about our family, I care about Jacob. I need to know. I need to know what happened. Was he tortured? Was he drugged? Was he killed? Is he alive? Did somebody adopt him and just want a friend to be with him? You know? Did somebody take him as a prank and then it went terribly wrong and they didn't . . . "

Now he cut me off. "No, I don't think that. I don't think that was the situation. But . . . "

"Did they plan it? Have they done it before? Have they done it since? If it's somebody within ten miles, why haven't they done it again? You know? There haven't been any others . . . "

"It's possible that he's still alive," he told me. "The hope is that he is."

"But where would he be and how could we reach him?" I asked. "I just don't know where to go. And then, just today, I thought maybe our calling in the media right away worked against us, because somebody might have kept him alive, but then they got freaked. Because the response was so quick."

I knew I was rambling, but I didn't care. It was as if all the questions I'd ever wanted to ask were just spilling out and I couldn't stop them.

"It's just so hard," I said. "It's hard to go back. That's why time gets to be your enemy."

"Yeah," he agreed. "It gets worse and worse."

I had been pretty calm throughout our whole conversation, but just as we were wrapping things up, Dan's brother came out of his office on the second floor where he worked and alerted Dan that there was a guy leaning over the railing above us, listening to our entire conversation. I assumed this guy was probably an FBI agent, and now I worried that Dan's brother may have become suspicious of the situation. I started shaking, suddenly very nervous. I got up to go and told him I needed to use the restroom.

"Thank you, Dan," I told him. "Nice to meet you."

"Nice talking," he replied.

After washing my hands and gathering my wits, I headed out to the car that was waiting for me.

"I really don't think he did it," I told the FBI agent. "He didn't seem mean enough or devious enough . . . so, he's either a psychopath or he's innocent."

It didn't matter what I thought. The sheriff's investigation into Dan Rassier was just starting to ramp up.

The Earley sisters—Patty, Barbi, Nancy, and Peggy—at Christmas 1951.

The sisters with their adoptive dad, Russell Farrar King, on the day he married their mom, 1955.

Patty and Jerry pose with Patty's family at their wedding, 1973. Eunice King, Patty's mother, is in front. The others, from left: Nancy, Peggy's husband Glenn, Peggy, Russ, and Barbi.

The Wetterlings at the sign for Jerry's office outside their Victorian home in St. Joseph, Minnesota, 1982.

Wetterling family photo, 1988. Jerry, Patty, and Amy in back; Carmen, Trevor, and Jacob in front.

Jacob in his goalie gear, 1988.

Jacob blows out the candles on his eleventh birthday while his friend Nick Larson and cousin Kevin watch.

The Wetterling kitchen, October 1989. Patty is hidden in a friend's embrace; Eunice is at the sink; and Jerry reads a document. *Mike Knaak, © St. Cloud Times—USA Today Network*

Investigators at work in the command center in St. Cloud. *Mike Knaak, © St. Cloud Times— USA Today Network*

Jerry and Patty with Carmen at a silent auction fundraiser at the Del-Win Ballroom on November 1, 1989.

Patty, Trevor, and Jerry at a balloon release. *Mike Knaak, © St. Cloud Times—USA Today Network*

On the first anniversary of Jacob's abduction, Patty ties a white ribbon onto a tree planted in Jacob's honor at Centennial Park in St. Joseph. *Stearns History Museum*

Outside the White House after the signing of the 1994 Jacob Wetterling Act.
From left: Eunice, Patty, US Representative Jim Ramstad, and Jerry.

Patty receives NCMEC's Tenth Anniversary Award, 1994. From left: Ernie Allen, Dr. Dan Broughton, Patty, John Walsh.

Patty meeting President Bill Clinton in the Oval Office, June 1996.

Patty holding the Olympic torch as her mother shares the moment, 1996.

Patty testifying before a Minnesota legislative committee with the mothers of murdered teens Katie Poirier and Cally Jo Larson, December 21, 1999.

Stearns County Sheriff John Sanner with Patty, 2004.

Patty speaking at the Democratic National Convention in Boston, during her first run for Congress, July 27, 2004. *Chris Maddaloni/CQ-Roll Call, Inc. via Getty Images*

Patty speaking at a news conference outside the US Capitol to announce the Sex Offender Registration and Notification Act, May 17, 2005.

The Wetterling family on the twenty-fifth anniversary of Jacob's kidnapping, 2014.

Patty reviewing letters collected over twenty-seven years, 2017. *Shelley Paulson Photography*

Joy and Patty at the first Running HOME for Jacob 5K run, sponsored by the Jacob Wetterling Resource Center, October 22, 2016.

Joy, Jerry, Patty, Jared, April 2017.

{ Chapter 35 }

In mid-June 2010, Carmen was scheduled to attend a work training in St. Cloud and was looking forward to spending some quality time with her dad at home in St. Joe while I was working in St. Paul. She was about four months pregnant at the time and had just learned she was having twins. Jerry and I were so excited for her and Kristian, and we couldn't wait to welcome two more grandbabies to our family later that fall.

On Wednesday, June 30, Carmen left our house to head to her training and was shocked to see sheriff's cars, a BCA mobile crime lab, a K-9 unit, and several media vans parked at the abduction site. Panicked, she immediately grabbed her phone and called Jerry.

"Dad, what's going on at the abduction site? I just went by and there's a whole bunch of police and media there!"

We'd been told that investigators were planning to search the Rassier property once again, but we had no idea how extensive the search would be. The property had already been searched twice before, so frankly, we didn't expect much. We also didn't realize the media would catch wind of it, and by the time we learned about the search, several reporters were already there.

Jerry managed to calm Carmen down, but the trauma of seeing all those squad cars and media vans surrounding the very spot where her brother had been taken really unnerved her. Jerry called me as soon as he hung up with Carmen, but there was no way I could get home. I had broken my right ankle in a bicycle accident a few weeks earlier and couldn't drive.

By the next day, the news had hit in full force. The story had been picked up by all the local TV stations, and front-page articles about the search had appeared in the *Star Tribune*, the *St. Paul Pioneer Press*, and the *St. Cloud Times*. This was turning into a very big deal, and I needed to be there. I took the day off work and asked my sister Nancy if she would drive with me up to St. Joseph.

On the way, I tearfully shared with Nancy a dream I had recently had. I was pushing Jacob in a wheelchair, trying to outrun a guy who was chasing us. At one point, Jacob turned to me and asked, "Mom, when did you get so old?"

Now, I wondered if it had been a sign. It had been such a long time. Could this really be it?

I still found it incredibly hard to believe that Dan Rassier had anything to do with Jacob's kidnapping, but, by the looks of this search, it was obvious the sheriff did. What did he know that we didn't?

When Nancy and I arrived at the site, the reporters all scrambled to talk to me. Although I tried, I really couldn't answer most of their questions.

"I don't know what to think," I told them. "And I don't know what I want. Do I hope they'll find something? I'm not sure. Do I hope they don't? That's not good either. It's a really confusing place to be."

I expressed our gratitude that the search was continuing and tried to remain hopeful.

The search of the Rassier farm had turned into a very public display, and the whole town was in shock. The Rassiers were well known and respected in St. Joe, and I couldn't help but feel sorry for them. On the other hand, we had waited so long for answers, and Dan had remained a top suspect since Sheriff Sanner had been elected to office in 2003. Maybe this search would finally yield some answers—one way or another.

Following the search, six large truckloads of dirt and ash were hauled out of the Rassiers' dump pit and taken to the Stearns County Public Works Building for further analysis. For the next month, investigators sifted through the dirt looking for anything that might provide clues to Jacob's disappearance. In late July, they reported that some "items of interest" had been sent to the crime lab for further testing but declined to tell us any further details or how long it would take. Again, we waited.

In the meantime, it was hard to witness the fallout from the very public search. The *St. Cloud Times* reported that parents at one of the schools where Dan taught music were now uncomfortable with his position. He had been teaching for the Rocori School District since 1978—over thirty-two years—and had never once received any complaints or disciplinary action. Yet now the school would require a paraprofessional to be present in his classroom to appease concerned parents. If Dan was innocent, I couldn't help but feel awful for what he and his family were going through. On the other hand, if he did have some kind of involvement in Jacob's disappearance, didn't we have the right to know? It was impossible to sort out my feelings, so I just tried to keep my mind occupied with happier things—like knitting double sets of baby booties for Carmen's twins.

By the end of September, we finally received word from the sheriff's office. The forensic tests had come back and failed to reveal any new evidence from the dirt and ash they had collected from the Rassier farm.

I hung up, uncertain how I felt. Should I feel happy? Relieved? Disappointed? At least now we could be confident that Jacob wasn't buried in our neighbor's dump pit, but where did that leave us? Another dead end.

A few months later, Jerry and I became proud grandparents for the fourth and fifth time when our twin granddaughters, Maizie and Belle, were born. They were so tiny—less than half the size Jacob had been when he was born—but so much work! Carmen and Kristian rose to the challenge, and I often watched in awe as they pulled double duty: double the feedings, double the diapers, double the needy cries—but with half the sleep. I loved to help during the evenings since my place in St. Paul was close by, and Carmen was always grateful for a chance to get out of the house.

The twins added new joy and energy to our lives, but as usual, it wasn't long before our peaceful world was rocked with madness once again.

{ Chapter 36 }

Friday, April 12, 2013, had already been such a busy day. As I sat on my flight from DC to Minneapolis, I realized I still had a long way to go before it was over.

I was returning from three days in Alexandria, Virginia, attending the board meeting of the International Center for Missing and Exploited Children (ICMEC). I was now an ex-officio member of the ICMEC board after taking over as board chair for the National Center for Missing and Exploited Children one year earlier. I was NCMEC's first female board chair and was extremely honored to be named to this position, but it wasn't long before I began to recognize the magnitude of what I'd taken on. On top of my full-time position at the MDH, I was now helping lead a national organization of 350 employees with offices in DC, California, Florida, New York, and Texas.

As my plane touched down at MSP International, I grabbed my cell phone and checked the time. In a few hours, I was scheduled to speak at a charity fundraising gala in Willmar, Minnesota. I had explained to their executive director that I would be returning from DC earlier that same day, but assured her I'd be back in plenty of time to attend the gala later that evening.

"Plenty of time" may have been a bit optimistic. As soon as the flight attendant gave us the okay to disembark, I grabbed my carry-on and made my way out of the terminal. I found my car, tossed my suitcase into the back seat, and did my best to make the mental shift from *DC mode* to *gala mode* as I began the two-hour drive to Willmar.

When I arrived, I checked in and met briefly with the tech people. Everything appeared to be in order, so I made my way to the ladies restroom to change into my gala outfit. Finally, I had a chance to exhale for a moment. What a day.

The truth was, I sometimes found it extremely difficult to be a keynote speaker at events like this. People were there to socialize and have fun. They came early, had a cocktail or two, made bids on a variety of silent auction items, enjoyed a nice dinner that was usually accompanied by music or other entertainment, and then . . . it was my turn. How could I talk about difficult topics like child abduction and sexual exploitation without taking all the oxygen out of the room? It wasn't always easy for people to understand the true *depth* of my hope—how I clung to it and was fueled by it. I was happy if I could just leave them feeling empowered and committed to building a better, safer world for our children.

I ended my keynote with one of my favorite stories.

I once got a letter from a second grader named Dalton. He wrote:
"Jacob will be fine. If he isn't all right you'll see him in heaven. My dog died. If Jacob is gone he can play with my dog. Everyone in the world wants him back."
Dalton's words gave me an image I could live with. I was so grateful.
Not all wishes come true, and not all hopes are realized, but we owe it to our children to try.

As the event wrapped up and I prepared to leave, I was greeted by a tall, blond woman who appeared to be in her mid-forties.
"Hi Patty. I'm Joy Baker. You were amazing."
I thanked her and we shook hands.
"I was just wondering if I could give you my card," she said, somewhat nervously. "I'm not sure if you've heard of me, but I have a blog called *Joy the Curious*, and I've been writing about Jacob's case for the past few months."
She handed me her business card, and I reached into my purse to give her one of my own.
"I know it's late, and you have a long drive home," she continued. "We can talk about it another time. I just wanted to introduce myself."
Over the years, I'd been handed many cards by people who had written books, articles, short stories, or poems, but blogging was new to me. I'd never read a blog. Who was this Joy Baker, and what the heck was she writing?
When I got home, I mentioned it to Jerry, but was so exhausted I could

barely think. I went straight to bed and figured I would deal with Joy Baker in the morning.

On Saturday morning, I slept late and woke to find Jerry in the family room, reading Joy's blog.

I walked over to him and stared at the computer screen as he read the first entry out loud.

> Where are you, Jacob? Twenty-one years, and still no trace.
>
> It was 21 years ago yesterday, October 22, 1989, that eleven-year-old Jacob Wetterling was abducted by a stranger while riding his bike home from a convenience store in St. Joseph, Minnesota.
>
> Twenty-one years.
>
> I think everyone in Minnesota knows and remembers Jacob. I was 22 years old and had just graduated from the University of Minnesota when this story broke. I remember the constant media coverage, the white ribbons, the "Missing" posters . . . and I remember seeing Jacob's parents on the news, begging for their son's safe return. My heart broke for them.
>
> We all wanted to help. There were composite sketches of a bald-headed man with piercing eyes. And then we learned of a white work van with no windows. For weeks, I scoured every white van on the road, hoping to find a scary bald man at the wheel. To this day, when I see a white work van with no windows, I think of Jacob. . . .
>
> Weeks passed, then months, then years. As a state, a nation, and a generation, we were shook. Jacob's abduction changed the way we raised our children. We taught them to be wary of strangers, to be home before dark, and to scream and fight back if someone ever tried to pull them into a car. Our parents didn't need to have this conversation with us; but this is how we live in the post-Jacob years.
>
> I've been doing a lot of thinking about Jacob lately. This case has stuck with me all these years, and like many I'm sure, Jacob and his family are never far from our thoughts. Then, out of nowhere, last summer we learned that a farm property was being searched, near the spot where Jacob was abducted . . .

"So, wait a minute," I interrupted. "She wrote this in 2010? After the dig at Rassiers' place?"

Jerry scrolled back and checked the date of the blog post.

"Yep, October 23, 2010," he confirmed. "Two and a half years ago."

"So, why haven't we ever heard about this before?" I asked.

"I don't know. Do you want me to keep going?"

"Whatever." I walked into the kitchen and poured myself a cup of coffee.

Jerry continued, sounding calm and even enthralled by Joy's writing. I was simply blown away.

It turned out Joy had actually come to St. Joseph, found the abduction site, and driven down toward our house. Though she admitted feeling "stalkerish" at that point and never did actually turn into our circle, the whole thing felt creepy.

Yet it was clear she had done her homework, and her details were surprisingly accurate. She had scoured newspapers, gone to the Stearns County library, and searched old microfilm. She had even looked up the weather report for October 22, 1989, and found out the moon hadn't risen until midnight on that date, so at 9:00 PM, she confirmed it would have been totally dark.

Joy wrote about Jacob's case for three weeks in 2010 before moving on to other topics that piqued her curiosity. Then, just two months ago, in February 2013, she'd started up again after being contacted by—of all people— Dan Rassier.

Joy met with Dan, and he told her about Kevin, the thirty-five-year-old man who had come forward in 2003 and admitted to leaving his tire tracks in the driveway on the night of Jacob's abduction.

Joy got Dan and Kevin together, so they could chat and compare stories. She told Dan's story in full detail on her blog, then she told Kevin's story . . . both in multipart posts. There were many details that had never been shared with the public before, and some were even new to us.

By the time Jerry finished reading all eleven blog posts, I was completely floored. This "blogger" had been interviewing key suspects, challenging details, and—in my mind—meddling. I found myself asking, over and over, who the hell was this woman?

Jerry helped me get some perspective. We agreed that Joy was an incredible researcher. She wasn't going off in a million different directions, but was instead concentrating her efforts on the site of the abduction. She was asking questions about what did and didn't happen, and she was talking to people who had firsthand knowledge of the case. She was open to talking to anyone, and possibly because she *wasn't* law enforcement, they seemed willing to talk to her. I had to respect that she'd nailed most of her facts. Obviously, she was a good writer, but I couldn't understand how anyone other than us could write our own story.

Jerry and I set up a call with Joy on Sunday afternoon. I didn't trust myself to be nice, tolerant, or receptive to what she had to say, so I let Jerry take the lead in asking questions. I felt like she had to prove herself to me. She said she wanted to help find Jacob, but in my mind, so did everyone. What made her any different?

Joy was open about her own confusion as to why she kept "thinking Jacob," and explained she simply felt compelled to push on. At one point, she even said, "If you want me to stop, I'll stop," but the truth was, I didn't know what I wanted.

We talked for nearly two hours, and by the end of that first phone call, I wanted to believe I could trust her. She had an openness and honesty that seemed genuine, but after twenty-three years of searching, I'd met so many dishonest, unscrupulous, and dangerous people, I didn't just hand out my trust easily. She would have to earn it.

Like it or not, we now had a blogger in our lives.

{ Chapter 37 }

We didn't hear from Joy for a few weeks. Then, on May 5, 2013, we received an email from her telling us that Esme Murphy, a reporter from WCCO-TV in the Twin Cities, wanted to do a story with her and Dan Rassier. Joy wanted to know our opinion before agreeing to do the interview.

I had done several interviews with Esme in the past, and, though she could be aggressive in her pursuit of a story, I had always found her to be kind and respectful. She was one of several Twin Cities reporters I now considered friends.

Still, I wasn't quite sure how to respond to Joy. Even though she'd made it clear in her blog that she didn't believe Dan Rassier was guilty, she wanted to make sure we knew her primary goal was to find Jacob, not to help Dan clear his name.

Joy also went on to give us an update on her blogging. She was hoping to line up interviews with two former investigators on Jacob's case who were "friends of friends," and she'd also been talking to a woman who had lived near the Tom Thumb convenience store at the time Jacob was kidnapped. The speed at which she was working was alarming to me.

I replied: "Wow! Lots to catch up on! You have really good instincts. I'd be happy to meet in person. I go to DC this week, but I think I'm in town next week. I have some questions too. We need to talk soon."

Ultimately, Joy declined the interview with WCCO, but Esme moved forward with her story on Dan Rassier, anyway. While much of the interview focused on Dan's frustration with law enforcement and their refusal to investigate the tip he'd given them about the two cars he'd witnessed in his driveway, Esme did give a shout-out to Joy and her blog: "In the past year, Rassier has begun working with a local blogger, Joy Baker, to put out information about what he really did and saw that night."

And so, there it was. Joy Baker and her blog had made the 10:00 PM news.

I had to admit, I was worried how this was all going to play out. We'd been burned and exploited by a few wannabe investigators in the past, and even though Joy seemed on the level, the truth was, I had no idea who this woman was or what her real intentions were.

On top of all the dust Joy Baker was stirring up with her blog, I was still busy working full time in St. Paul, while also putting in many extra hours as board chair for the National Center. Then, when I didn't think I could possibly handle one more thing, our world was rocked once again. In late June we received two large manila envelopes in the mail—one addressed to me, and one addressed to Jacob. They had been sent from the Victim Assistance Program of the United States Attorney's Office in northern California.

Now what?

I sat down and opened Jacob's envelope first. After twenty-four years of turmoil and chaos, not much surprised me anymore—but this did.

The letter was in reference to a court case against someone named Behzad Mofrad.

Dear Jacob Wetterling,

The enclosed information is provided by the United State Department of Justice Victim Notification System (VNS). As a victim witness professional with the United States Attorney's Office, my role is to assist you with information and services during the prosecution of this case. I am contacting you because you were identified by law enforcement as a victim during the investigation of the above criminal case.

Charges have been filed against defendant(s) Behzad Mofrad. The main charge is categorized as Identity Theft.

Are you kidding me? *Someone stole Jacob's identity?*

My heart was pounding and my hands shook as I ripped open the other envelope. It held a copy of the letter that had been mailed to Jacob. I tried to compose myself, but the rage, sadness, confusion, and anger were too much to contain. I was stunned and furious. How could this have happened?

I dialed the number listed at the end of the letter and was caught off guard when a woman answered on the second ring. I gave my name and started to explain that my son, Jacob, wasn't able to respond since he *had been kidnapped* twenty-four years earlier.

I broke down. Several minutes went by before I could talk or even listen to what this woman had to say. She apologized profusely and told me she knew all about Jacob. She explained that she had wrestled with even sending the letter, but had been required to by law.

She explained that Behzad Mofrad had stolen Jacob's identity and had acquired driver's licenses in his name in California, Florida, and New Jersey. He had rented a post office box in Lafayette, California (also in Jacob's name), and somehow managed to convince car dealerships to let him take expensive cars out for test drives without leaving deposits. He then drove the cars to Mexico to sell. He had done this several times, all while using Jacob's identity. I was horrified.

To make this whole nightmare worse, he had already done the same thing once before. Years earlier, he had stolen Kevin Collins's identity in California and served thirty-three months in a California prison. Kevin's dad was David Collins, the man who had generously flown to Minnesota right after Jacob's kidnapping and helped with our first mass mailing of "Missing" flyers. David had also lent his expertise in helping us set up the Jacob Wetterling Foundation.

As I listened to the woman on the other end of the line, it took some time for everything to sink in. This had happened *twice*?

Behzad Mofrad was finally caught when he tried to apply for a passport using Jacob's name. This had required a birth certificate, so he called the Todd County Recorder's Office claiming to be Jerry, but he couldn't give them what they needed to prove he was Jacob's dad. Next, he called back pretending to be Jacob, but fortunately, the clerk knew Jacob's story and notified authorities.

On June 6, 2013, Behzad Mofrad pled guilty to identity theft, and I was given the opportunity to write a victim impact statement to be read at sentencing. I found his actions so despicable, I couldn't even begin to explain the horror of what he had put us through. It was so hard to find the words, but I tried my best, between tears and sobs.

When I received the letter from the US Department of Justice regarding the identity theft of my son Jacob, my heart broke. Truly, you stole him from us all over again.

Ours is an unimaginable pain, often dubbed "a parent's worst nightmare." I have been forced to look at a darker side of life—the life of criminals, child molesters, and exploitation—yet, I have known few who have stooped lower than to take the opportunity to hurt those who are already hurting and use it for personal gain. This cruelty is among the lowest that I have seen.

You have hurt us. You stole our child from us. You have damaged the reputation of Jacob, who was an eleven-year-old child, heinously kidnapped. You are not worth even the smallest tie to this wonderful person.

I hold out little hope that anything I say can impact how you feel, but my hope is that the judge will hear, a jury will hear, other inmates will hear, and that you will spend a lot of time "missing" from everything you hold dear in life.

On October 22, 2013, it will be twenty-four years since we have seen our son. We hurt every day. Maybe that is an appropriate amount of time for you to think about the harm you have caused and the heartache to all who know and love Jacob.

As a family, we did our very best to move on—once again—and put this horrible experience behind us.

{ Chapter 38 }

Joy Baker and I had been trying to arrange a meeting for three months, but it hadn't worked out. When I had to cancel yet another time, I emailed Joy and told her I'd been reading everything she sent me, and I had some insight to share. I also added, "I've just been on my own painful journey dealing with someone who stole Jacob's identity."

Within moments, Joy replied, "So sorry. I read about that a while ago. Take your time. I'm not in any rush."

Wait a minute. What? I was so confused. How could Joy Baker have known about Jacob's identity theft? I had just received the letter earlier that week. What was going on?

She told me she'd found out about Jacob's identity theft in an online article from the *San Francisco Chronicle* dated December 8, 2012. That meant the media knew about it six full months before we—his *parents*—had learned about it. How could that be?

I had always taken pride in being actively involved in Jacob's investigation, realizing I knew more than most parents in our position because of my work with the National Center for Missing and Exploited Children and Fox Valley Technical College, as well as my participation at law enforcement trainings. As I became aware of new techniques and tactics, I always passed them along to Captain Pam Jensen at the SCSO (our family contact and the lead investigator on Jacob's case). She would often respond jokingly, "So, you've been to another seminar . . . "

I usually took her joking in stride, but now I was really frustrated. Why wasn't she sharing more with us? Why had Joy known about Jacob's identity theft before I did? Over the years, Jerry and I had worked hard to earn the trust of Stearns County investigators. We had never acted irresponsibly or burned them in any way because we *needed* them.

Now, I was exhausted, sad, and overwhelmed. I no longer knew where to turn. For the first time, I was starting to get the sense that Joy Baker was working harder to find Jacob than anybody else on the planet.

In the months since I'd first met Joy, she had been talking to all kinds of people related to Jacob's investigation—witnesses, suspects, neighbors, former neighbors, former investigators—you name it. I hadn't heard from her since our last exchange about the identity theft case, then I received an email from her one evening in late July:

> Hi Patty,
>   I met Jared tonight. On a whim, I decided to contact him on Facebook last week and told him my story. He agreed to meet with me, so I invited him to my house for pizza and a beer (it turns out we have a mutual friend, so I figured he was a pizza-and-beer kind of guy).
>   Jared mentioned that when he met you during the KARE-11 interview in 2004, you had suggested that he get together with Trevor and Aaron to talk about their mutual experiences. He still, very much, wants to do this. More than anything, he wants to help find out what happened to Jacob, and he thinks that by comparing notes with Trevor and Aaron, it may spark some memory that could be helpful. I think he strongly believes that his abductor and Jacob's abductor were the same person . . . the deep voice, authoritative manner, threat of a gun, and similar commands.
>   Anyway, I wondered if you might want to get a hold of Trevor and Aaron and give them the heads-up . . . to let them know that Jared is legit.
>   Let me know if I can help in some way. Thanks.
>
> —Joy

No way. That was it. I was drawing the line. First of all, it felt weird to have these two people meeting behind our backs and talking about us. Second, I was deeply protective of our kids, and I was certain that meeting Jared would be too hard on Trevor and Aaron. I just didn't see the benefit. Finally, I was worried that by sharing his story on Joy's blog, Jared would end up feeling re-traumatized and re-victimized. I supported him and understood his passion for answers, but I also felt the need to protect him.

I didn't reply to Joy right away. Instead, I decided to sleep on it and let things digest a bit before getting back to her. Finally, around 2:00 PM the next day, I responded.

> Hi Joy,
> I have to tell you that I'm struggling with you contacting everybody all around us. I know you have an "interest" in solving Jacob's disappearance, but it sometimes feels like stalking or something . . . like you are continually going all around us and then telling us who you've met and how it went, and sometimes even giving suggestions of what we should/could do next.
> You have no idea what it's like to have people float in and out of our lives with strong interests . . . sometimes strong suspects . . . and we absolutely can't drop our efforts to live our lives because someone new comes along. When I don't drop everything and follow up with you or with someone else, I get the feeling that others may think we've given up or aren't doing whatever we can to find Jacob . . . and yet NOBODY can live their lives in high gear for twenty-three years and survive.
> I am very protective of Aaron, Trevor, and our other kids. I'm just going to suggest for a moment that you think about what it would be like if I were to do this to you . . . to talk to your neighbors, friends, any law enforcement people you know, etc. It just isn't feeling very good right now.
> I feel you are shaking things up and maybe you can be helpful in some way we haven't tried, but I don't know where to go with this. I just had to share with you my struggles . . .
>
> Thanks,
> Patty

It was several hours before I heard back from Joy.

Patty,

I have a dilemma. Jared just messaged me and asked for your phone number. I have no idea what to tell him.

I wish I could undo this, but I can't. And now I'm left in a huge quandary.

All I can tell you is this. You have no reason to trust me . . . you have no idea who I am or why I care so much. I don't even understand it myself. All I can tell you is, I'm a caring person. And honest, and kind, and smart, and prayerful. I have a loving family, many wonderful friends, and a respected career. You can ask anyone who knows me, and they'll tell you I'm truly just a nice, normal person. To have someone think otherwise of me is really unsettling.

So, I can lie to Jared and tell him I don't have your number, but I think he would know I'm lying. I can be honest and tell him you're a little freaked out by the idea of getting the three boys together, but I'm afraid that would be really hurtful.

So, you can see my dilemma. I honestly don't know what to do here.

—Joy

Instead of replying with another email, I decided to just pick up the phone and call Joy. I gave her my permission to give Jared my cell number, and I tried to explain some of my concerns. We hung up after a short, tense conversation.

Not long after, Jared called.

It had been almost nine years since we first met during that TV interview in 2004. I remembered him as being personable and funny, and I was impressed with all the interesting things he'd done with his life, in spite of the horrible trauma he experienced as a twelve-year-old child.

Now, all these years later, conversation with Jared was still easy. We talked about his three kids and his work as a commercial plumber for a large plumbing and HVAC company. I told him how much I appreciated his willingness to put himself out in the public eye and share his story. I knew it was a big decision for him, and it wouldn't be easy.

After we chatted and caught up a bit, he reiterated his desire to meet Trevor and Aaron.

"I just don't think that's a good idea," I told him.

"Will you at least ask them?" he pleaded.

"I'll think about it," I said, but admitted I still wasn't convinced how it would help.

I decided to change the subject.

"So, what do you think about Joy Baker?" I asked.

I was curious to hear his impression of her, and I wondered how he felt about sharing his very personal story on her blog.

Jared explained that he and Joy shared a mutual friend, which is partly why he agreed to meet with her in the first place. We talked about his meeting at Joy's house the previous night, and he felt confident she was truly just trying to help. He was amazed at how much research she had done and how much she already knew about his case. He also agreed with her that his case and Jacob's had to be connected. Although he was anxious, he was also excited about using her blog to get the details of his kidnapping out to the public in a new way that might help generate tips in both our cases.

"Well, good," I told him. "Go for it. Somebody knows something."

It was clear to me that Jared needed to tell his story, and after my initial misgivings, I was glad Joy was the one to help him do it. I was incredibly proud of him for opening up like this, and after talking to him, I could tell Joy was protective of him too. Like them, I also felt Jacob's and Jared's cases had to be connected, and the more attention Jared's case got, the greater chance we had of getting our own answers.

{ Chapter 39 }

Joy and Jared went back and forth several times before she finally published his story on her blog on August 11, 2013. For the first time, Jared shared several details about his kidnapping that hadn't been made public.

He explained how it had been a Friday night—Friday the thirteenth—when he and about ten friends had gone ice skating at an outdoor rink near his house. Afterward, they walked to a local café for some hot chocolate and a bite to eat.

Around 9:30 PM, they started heading for home. Some got rides, while others walked. The café was only about a quarter mile from Jared's house, so he decided to walk. On his way home, a man in a car approached him, rolled down his window, and asked Jared if he knew where the Kraemers lived. Jared knew the family well, since they lived only a few houses away from him. He approached the car, giving directions as the man slowly got out. When Jared turned to point, the man suddenly grabbed him from behind by the shoulders and in a deep voice said, "Get the f— in the car. I have a gun and I'm not afraid to use it." He pushed Jared into the back seat of the car and told him to pull his stocking cap over his eyes so he couldn't see where they were going.

Jared gave other specifics the public hadn't heard before, including a very detailed description of his kidnapper, an updated description of the car, comments the man made to him, and the location where Jared had been let go. Most chilling of all, Jared explained how the man had told him, "Run and don't look back, or I'll shoot." The last part was the same phrase, word for word, that Jacob's kidnapper had used with Trevor and Aaron.

Joy's blog story about Jared's kidnapping and assault generated several new comments but no solid leads. However, Joy had also begun researching an early suspect in both Jared's and Jacob's case—Duane Hart. He had been arrested on January 24, 1990, after several young men from the Paynesville area had come forward and told police how they had been sexually molested by Duane Hart as young boys. They all agreed to testify against Hart because they felt he may have been responsible for Jacob's kidnapping. To avoid a public trial, Hart pleaded guilty to six counts of criminal sexual conduct and was sent to prison.

Joy had been scouring through newspaper archives trying to find a photo of Hart to show Jared, but so far had been unsuccessful. What she *did* find was an article from a 1987 issue of the *Paynesville Press* about five attacks on young teenage boys in Paynesville. The descriptions of these attacks were eerily similar to both Jacob's and Jared's cases, so she immediately sent a copy of the article to Jared, asking if he had ever heard of these cases before.

He had not.

Paynesville Press
May 26, 1987

Local police seek help in accosting incidents

The Paynesville Police Department is seeking public support in apprehending a man that has been accosting young men in the Paynesville community. So far there have been five different incidents reported.

Sergeant Bill Drager, Paynesville Police Department, said, "We need help, all the help we can get."

According to Sgt. Drager, the incidents began last summer, there were two more incidents during the winter, one incident occurred this spring and another last week.

The police are taking these incidents very seriously.

Sgt. Drager stated, "After this guy grabs the boys, he tells them, 'Don't turn around or I'll blow your head off' and in at least one instance he used a knife." The man then makes sexual advances to the boys.

The young men that have been assaulted range in age from 12–16 years of age. "The kids are scared," Sgt. Drager said.

There doesn't appear to be any pattern to the area that the attacks take place. One incident happened by the river, another in the hockey rink area, downtown Ben Franklin area, middle school playground, and the alley between the middle school and the hospital.

The last incident happened when two young men were riding their bikes home. One young man was grabbed off of his bike and the other young man went for help.

In every instance, the young men had been downtown before they were accosted. "I think he's picking them out downtown and then following them home or lying in wait for them to go home," Sgt. Drager said.

Every instance occurred on a weekend night after dark— between 9:30pm and 2:00am.

The suspect wore a mask on several occasions. Sgt. Drager said one young man described the mask as looking like it was made out of indoor-outdoor candy-striped carpeting.

The man is supposedly 5'11" tall, not fat, but chunky. In the last incident, he had blackened everything—so that you couldn't make out anything on his face. He can run fast, according to witnesses.

The police are encouraging people to call in if they see anything strange or suspicious. "If someone is lurking around or walking on your property—call us," Sgt. Drager said.

Jared was astounded and asked Joy to send a copy of the article to the SCSO. The next day, Captain Jensen replied to Joy and said she would be very interested in talking to Jared and looking into the Paynesville cases.

"I was unaware of those," she wrote.

Jared called us right away. After telling us about the article, he talked a lot about Duane Hart—a name all three of us were very familiar with. He also told us he was planning to set up a meeting with Captain Jensen to go over details about his case. We were surprised to hear he had never met with her before, even though she was the lead investigator on both his and Jacob's cases.

Ten days later, Jared met with Pam Jensen for the first time. In preparation, he had called to get my input on what questions he should ask.

"Just say whatever is in your heart," I told him.

When he asked Joy the same question, however, she gave him an entire list.

- Between August 1986 and May 1987, there were five separate instances of Paynesville boys between the ages of twelve and sixteen

who were accosted and sexually molested/assaulted. Was anyone ever convicted in these cases?
- Was DNA collected after my assault, and if so, was it tested to see if it matched Duane Hart's DNA?
- Was Duane Hart ever put in a lineup before me?
- Has Hart definitely been ruled out as a suspect in my case or Jacob's case?
- Is my case still active?
- Is there a statute of limitations on my case?
- Is it true there were fibers similar to the ones from my snow-mobile suit found in the back seat of a suspect's car? [Joy had learned of this possibility after reading a 2010 memoir written by former FBI Special Agent Al Garber.] If so, whose car was it?
- What kind of car was it?
- Besides Hart, what other suspects have been interviewed in my case?

Pam had also done some research, so when they met, she gave him some new and astounding details about his case.

First, during one of the Paynesville attacks, a baseball cap had been left behind at the scene when the victim fought back and knocked it off the per-petrator's head. The cap was taken into evidence, but had somehow been misfiled. After a detailed search, they had now found the cap and would be submitting it to the crime lab for DNA testing.

Second, as DNA technology improved over the years, clothing that Jared had been wearing at the time of his assault—a snowmobile suit, sweatshirt, and T-shirt—was being periodically sent to the BCA for analysis.

Third, when Jared asked about Duane Hart, he was told that Hart had been released from prison in 1995 and was currently living with his mother in an apartment in St. Paul.

This last tidbit made Jared and Joy especially nervous, so rather than share any information about Hart on Joy's blog, they quietly began their own investigation into the 1986–87 Paynesville attacks.

Not long after Jared was assaulted in Cold Spring in 1989, his family had moved back to Paynesville—his parents' hometown, about eighteen miles from Cold Spring and twenty-eight miles from St. Joseph. By now, he knew almost everyone in town, so he and Joy started asking questions. One by one, they found people who were willing to come forward and talk to them. Their process was simple but effective. Jared reached out to these victims and bravely shared his own story, then Joy followed up so she could document the details and provide additional research.

The more people they talked to, the more cases they uncovered, but— even though all the victims said they had made formal reports to police— none of those reports could be found, since the document retention period had long since run out.

Of course, all of this raised the bigger question. What in the world had been happening in Paynesville in the years just prior to Jacob's kidnapping?

{ Chapter 40 }

Throughout the summer and early fall of 2013, Joy and Jared continued searching for and talking to additional victims of the Paynesville attacks from the late 1980s. Joy had prepared a new blog post about their findings, and for the first time since publishing Jared's story almost three months earlier, they were ready to go public with what they had learned.

Although we had still not managed to meet in person, I really liked Joy. She was honest. She was real. She was a great writer, incredibly smart, and committed to helping us find Jacob. She was also someone I could confide in. I knew I could ask her questions without being judged, or feeling like I was being brushed off, as I often did when I talked to people at Stearns County.

I also knew there had been several opportunities for Joy to reveal leads or other sensitive information on her blog that might possibly compromise the investigation or make Stearns County look bad. Yet she had chosen not to. When Jared had shared with Joy that Duane Hart had been released from prison and was living with his mother in an apartment in St. Paul, she had questioned the accuracy of that information and found several sources of information that proved Duane Hart was still being held at the Minnesota Sex Offender Program in Moose Lake. When Jared shared this information with Captain Jensen, they investigated further, and, in an ironic twist of fate, discovered Duane Hart's identity had been stolen.

Joy's blog article about the Paynesville attacks was published on October 22, 2013—the twenty-fourth anniversary of Jacob's abduction. Over the past few months, Jared had been calling to give Jerry and me updates on what he and Joy were doing, but there were so many names and details, it was often confusing and hard to follow. Now as I read the 1987 *Paynesville Press* article for myself, plus all the added details Joy had provided, I realized the full scope and magnitude of what they had uncovered. I was left feeling shocked and exasperated. Didn't these law enforcement people ever talk to each other? Paynesville, Cold Spring, and St. Joseph were all in Stearns County. What was going on?

As word began to spread, more victims of similar attacks in Paynesville came forward to share their stories with Jared and Joy. It was a lot to keep track of, so in January of 2014, Joy put together a Google map that pin-pointed the location of each of the six attacks they had discovered so far, along with a detailed description of what had taken place at each site. Just seeing the number of blue pins on that map—along with their proximity to one another—was astounding. If Stearns County hadn't been paying atten-tion earlier, I got the sense they certainly were paying attention now.

Later that same month—just days before the twenty-fifth anniversary of his own abduction—Jared wrote a letter to the editor of the *Paynesville Press* asking for the public's help in finding more victims from these attacks. He called it "Embracing the Past," and with Joy's help he put together an im-passioned plea asking anyone who had details about these attacks to please come forward. He ended the letter by saying:

> I have lived with the stress of this event all my life, and, in ways, it defines who I am. I suspect other victims live with the same stress, and I would like to speak with them. People with information can call the Stearns County Sheriff's Office. If you are a victim, they will refer you to me.

Between Jared's letter and Joy's blog, people were starting to take notice and share information with the two of them. While some victims were reluctant to talk or reveal their identity, others were grateful that someone was finally listening. In the twenty-six to twenty-seven years since these young men had been victimized, nobody had been charged with these crimes, and to make matters worse, many victims felt they had never been taken seriously. As a vic-tim advocate, I knew how important it was for victims to be believed and for someone to be held accountable. None of that had happened in Paynesville.

I was finally realizing that Joy was reaching all kinds of people with her blog that I would never have reached using traditional media. Over the years, we'd used television, radio, newspapers, and magazines to get the word out about Jacob's kidnapping. I did interviews with the nightly net-work news programs, Pat Robertson of *The 700 Club*, John Walsh, Joan Riv-ers, Phil Donahue, Maury Povich, and Nancy Grace. I'd been in *Reader's*

Digest, People Magazine, Good Housekeeping, and *O* (Oprah's magazine). We even reached out to truckers' magazines and flea market publications to try to reach a broader audience. The one thing I'd never done was blog. It was a world unknown to me.

The Paynesville lead had breathed new life into both Jacob's and Jared's investigations, and Joy was receiving comments on her blog from people who had key information. She regularly passed along tips to Captain Jensen, but what followed was a complete lack of response from the sheriff's department. It was as though they were no longer looking into any new leads that were coming in, either from Jared and Joy or from us.

It was clear to us that Sheriff Sanner's favorite "person of interest" was still Dan Rassier, while Jared and Joy seemed to be zeroing in on Paynesville. What was happening? Who were we supposed to believe? We were getting pulled from both sides, and it was overwhelming.

Suddenly, it felt like the twenty-four years of trust we had so carefully built with law enforcement was now broken. This wasn't easy for me to swallow. Not only had I always supported the SCSO, I had also worked with law enforcement agencies all over the country—training first responders, police chiefs, and sheriffs, as well as keynoting at some of the nation's largest conferences on missing and exploited children. Now, by simply working with Joy and Jared, I felt like I was somehow betraying the very people I had trusted the most—or, even worse, I worried they thought I was betraying them.

Jared was in a similar position. After his story had become so public, he'd been approached by several people with different theories, and his mind was racing in a million different directions. There were those trying to convince him that his attacker had been one of the priests or monks connected to St. John's. Others in Paynesville were convinced it was Duane Hart, while a large community of online sleuths were contributing all kinds of bizarre theories. We'd already lived through a lot of this craziness, but Jared was newer to it, and I worried about his willingness to talk to anyone and everyone. I knew Joy was struggling to keep up with him too.

Still, Jared and Joy were a breath of fresh air. Between Joy's investigative skills and Jared's desperate quest for answers, they were asking questions that had never been asked and were truly making a difference. Now, we just needed to figure out how we could all work together.

{ Chapter 41 }

It was April 13, 2014—almost a year to the day since I'd first met Joy Baker at a fundraising gala in Willmar. We had talked on the phone and exchanged several emails, but never managed to get together. Now, Jared had finally taken it upon himself to set up a meeting with all four of us—Joy, Jared, Jerry, and me.

Jerry and I were both anxious to hear how Jared and Joy's recent interview with Esme Murphy had gone. She contacted them after learning about the Paynesville cases the previous October, while working on a story about the twenty-fourth anniversary. After patiently sitting on this new lead for almost six months, WCCO-TV planned to air a two-part story about Jared and Joy's work starting May 14.

We agreed to meet at Joy's house on a Sunday afternoon. Jerry and I stopped by Jared's house to pick him up on the way, and before we headed to Joy's, he gave us a quick tour of Paynesville, showing us where some of the attacks had happened.

We drove past the former Ben Franklin building downtown, where one boy had been assaulted on the stairway that led to an apartment above the store.

Next, Jared pointed out a house near the river, where two brothers had been chased off their own porch by a man who was hiding and waiting for them as they walked home after dark.

We continued toward the middle school playground, where a boy had been playing hide-and-seek with friends when he was attacked from behind.

From there, we drove down an alley near the hospital, where another brutal assault had taken place.

Finally, Jared pointed out a large field near the Catholic church where two boys had been attacked while biking home after dark. A man dressed all in black had been hiding in some spruce trees, then jumped out and chased after the boys, pulling one of them off his bike while the other boy went for help.

My heart raced as I listened to Jared share these stories. For the first time, I began to realize the absolute terror these kids must have faced while living here in Paynesville during the late 1980s. We'd seen Joy's Google map, but visiting these sites in person suddenly made the terror seem very real and incredibly relevant.

When we finally arrived at Joy's house, fourteen miles away in New London, she came out to meet us in the driveway.

"Hi, I'm Joy," she said as she and Jerry shook hands.

"It's so nice to finally meet you," Jerry said.

"Thank you both for coming," Joy said, as she reached for my hand next. I decided to bypass the formality.

"I'm a hugger," I said with my arms outstretched.

Joy walked us to the front door and welcomed us into a lovely split-level home that reminded me so much of our own house with its entryway full of shoes. I loved the familiarity of it. We met Joy's husband, Ross, and their black lab, Zoey, then settled into the living room so we could visit.

I hadn't realized that up to that point, I'd been holding my breath with anxiety. I was grateful to sit and exhale, sensing the normalcy of their home. I asked about their two boys, whose photos were proudly hung in the hallway, and enjoyed listening to Joy talk about their older son, Jordan, who was in his first year of college, and their younger son, Cole, who was a junior in high school.

As we wrapped up our small talk, Jared explained why he'd called this meeting.

"Joy and I have been talking to a lot of people and gathering a lot of new information. So I wanted us all to meet together and get on the same page so we can figure out what to do next."

In their many conversations with current and former Paynesville residents, Jared and Joy had been learning more about Duane Hart, as well as other people Hart used to hang around with. They told us stories about drug running, arson, and bar fights. They also told us about a makeshift camp Hart had built at the base of a steep bank on a lake in Paynesville. He often lured boys there to swim, fish, and party. Then he molested them.

Next, Joy shared details about Hart's January 1990 arrest for criminal sexual conduct against six boys—four in Kandiyohi County and two in Stearns

County. She also shared details about his civil commitment trial that began in 1993, just months before his scheduled release from prison. She had recently obtained documents from the Kandiyohi County Courthouse and told us about the six young men, childhood victims of Hart's, who had testified against him at his trial. Because of their courage in speaking out, Hart had been committed indefinitely to the Minnesota Sex Offender Program at Moose Lake, where he remained.

"Duane Hart's name isn't new to us," I said to Jared and Joy.

I explained how we'd been told way back in 1989 or early 1990 that investigators didn't believe it was Hart because he had a totally different MO than the person who had taken Jacob. Hart was a groomer who targeted vulnerable children, bribed them with drugs and alcohol, and then sexually molested them.

"We were also told Hart didn't drive because he didn't have a car," Jerry added.

"Oh, he definitely had a car," Joy countered. "At least, according to the testimony these guys gave at his civil commitment trial . . . and other people we've been talking to."

I went on to explain how, in the very beginning, investigators always talked about Duane Hart and Danny Heinrich, another suspect from Paynesville.

"It seems like they were almost always mentioned in the same sentence— 'Hart and Heinrich.'"

Jared and Joy mentioned they were already familiar with Danny Heinrich and had considered reaching out to him, but hadn't gotten around to it yet.

"We're trying to figure out if there were any more attacks after Hart was arrested," Joy added.

Eventually, we moved on from Hart and Heinrich, but Jared couldn't stop chattering. He told us he'd been talking to a few web sleuths who had filled his head with all kinds of plausible but outrageous theories. It was a fast and furious conversation that was confusing, frightening, intriguing, and upsetting. When Ross finally called out that the hamburgers were ready, I was the first to jump up.

"Sounds great. I'm starving!"

We tried to talk about normal stuff over dinner. By this time, I had spoken quite a bit to Jared, but really didn't know Joy or Ross very well. Joy shared a little bit about her work as the head of marketing at the local hospital, and Ross told us about his work as a turkey farmer.

After dinner, we sat around the kitchen table, continuing to talk. No matter which direction the conversation went, we always returned to Paynesville. Everything seemed to be connected, and we were all convinced it had to be the same guy. So now what?

Jared told us he wanted to bring together a group of "informed people," which worried me a bit. We'd been through so much, and I just didn't trust people as easily as I once did. I cautioned Jared about sharing everything with everybody, and Joy was quick to agree. I admired her instincts and was grateful for her natural caution; Jared sometimes seemed so vulnerable in the way he just put himself out there. I worried he might get swept away by some of the crazies. If we were all going to be on the same page, we had to come to some type of understanding about what that meant and who we were working with.

Eventually, we ended the meeting. We thanked Joy and Ross and got back in the car for our fifty-minute ride home. After dropping Jared off at his house, Jerry and I sat quietly for a while as we each tried to process what had just taken place. It had been such a powerful meeting, and my head was still spinning.

On that one Sunday afternoon, I had now become acutely aware of how many other stories and other victims were potentially tied to our search for Jacob. What did it mean? What would happen next? It was all a bit scary to think about, but by the time we left the Baker home that evening, I felt like we were truly a powerful team.

My heart was full, my spirit was hopeful, and after getting beaten down for so long, both Jerry and I felt energized for the first time in years. We had been joined on our journey by the most unexpected of companions—a plumber and a blogger. Now, we were speeding down a road not yet traveled, fueled by a common belief: Together, we could find Jacob.

{ Chapter 42 }

For so long, Jerry and I had been pushing a boulder up a mountain. We always had help, but for the past few years, it often felt like we'd been pushing on our own, with very little assistance from the sheriff's department. Never had this felt more pronounced than that spring.

On April 22, 2014, just nine days after our meeting with Joy and Jared, NCMEC hosted its first-ever Long-Term Missing Children's Summit, "Time to Bring Them Home." It was held at NCMEC's headquarters in Alexandria, Virginia, and nearly two hundred participants attended the four-day conference, including representatives from local, state, tribal, and federal law enforcement agencies; specialists in forensic science; medical and mental health professionals; survivors; victim advocates; and others with experience or specialized knowledge of missing child issues.

The goal was to provide ideas and strategies for keeping investigations and searches active, even after so many years had passed. I was chair of the NCMEC board of directors at this time, so I made sure that our sheriff was invited.

Despite receiving the mailed invitation, an email invitation, and personal follow-up calls from NCMEC staff, Sheriff Sanner never responded. I was exasperated. Jacob had been missing for nearly twenty-five years, and here was an unprecedented opportunity for law enforcement and other professionals to share and learn from each other about how these long-term missing cases get solved. Why wasn't our sheriff willing to go?

I shared my frustration with Captain Pam Jensen.

"The sheriff doesn't do those types of meetings," she told me. "But I'll go."

"Great!" I said. "I'll forward them your contact information and make sure they send you an invitation."

A few days later, I called back to confirm that Pam had received the invite.

"I guess I won't be going after all," she said.

Not only would our own sheriff not be attending, he wouldn't allow the lead investigator on our case to go, either. It felt like a huge slap in the face.

Still, I was determined not to let my disappointment overshadow my excitement. On the first day of the summit, I was surprised to run into our local FBI agent, Shane Ball. He'd been one of the agents who was with Jerry and me when I'd worn a wire to speak with Dan Rassier.

"Hi Shane, I'm so glad you're here!" I said, giving him a hug.

"Of course," he said. "It's good to see you."

I felt so much better knowing there was at least one person investigating Jacob's case who was making an effort to learn new strategies for finding missing kids.

The summit opened with words from Bob Lowery, vice president of NCMEC's Missing Children Division.

> This summit was inspired by the recoveries of long-term missing children whom doubters didn't believe were even alive. But as the months and years went by, these brave young people were fighting for their lives against captivity and torture. Today Elizabeth Smart, Shawn Hornbeck, Jaycee Dugard, Amanda Berry, Gina DeJesus and Michelle Knight are free. . . . They are living proof even in the worst of situations, when all leads are dry and it feels like all hope is lost, we must never, never give up looking for our missing children.

I had met many survivors over the years, yet it was always monumental to be in the same room with these amazing people and their families. Just a year earlier, on May 6, 2013, I had been on a work trip in Washington, DC, with Colleen Nick (my good friend and fellow searching parent) when once again, we shared astonishing news: Amanda Berry, Gina DeJesus, and Michelle Knight were recovered in Cleveland after being held captive for nearly a decade. Colleen and I heard the news, looked at each other, and completely flipped out. We started hugging, smiling, laughing, and crying all at the same time. Being at NCMEC for this type of historic moment—again—was absolutely electric. The hope and joy were palpable, and we could see it on the faces of every single person who worked there.

Now, it felt electric once again to meet these survivors and learn from law enforcement about what went right and what went wrong in their searches for missing children. All these success stories confirmed what I had been screaming for years. There *are* missing children still out there, and it is up to *us* to find them. These children couldn't be expected to rescue themselves. They were traumatized, terrified, and constantly told that they or their loved ones would be killed if they ever tried to escape. They survived on the hope that we were still searching for them. We couldn't give up.

As I returned home later that week, feeling proud of all we had accomplished, it was once again hard to fathom this strange dichotomy that had become my life. Sometimes it seemed like I was living in parallel universes. Whenever I was in DC or at the National Center, I always felt like I was relevant, impactful—that the work I was doing was truly making a difference. Yet, in my own hometown, I felt powerless, insignificant, and brushed aside whenever I tried to ask questions or get updates about the sheriff's investigation of Jacob's case. How did we get here? What more could I do?

On Wednesday, May 14, five weeks after Jared and Joy had recorded their interview with Esme Murphy, the first part of the series was finally scheduled to air during the 10:00 PM newscast. It didn't really surprise me that WCCO had waited to broadcast the story during May sweeps—a Nielsen ratings period. Jerry and I were very familiar with the fact that Jacob's story was often highlighted during sweeps. But for Joy and Jared, the long wait had been stressful. It seemed like every day they were finding more victims, and the story was constantly evolving.

About a week before the story was scheduled to run, Esme asked me if I would also be willing to take part in the story. I didn't want to take away anything from Jared and Joy's powerful message, so before agreeing to the interview, I reached out to them to get their thoughts. Both encouraged me to do it, so Esme and I made arrangements to meet at my house in St. Paul one day after work. While I knew my participation in the story might further complicate my relationship with the Stearns County Sheriff's Office, I wanted to recognize all of Jared and Joy's hard work and to validate their efforts. It seemed like the least I could do.

Two days before the WCCO story was scheduled to air, we received a text from Joy saying a reporter from FOX-9 News had just contacted her at work about a story they were doing on the Paynesville attacks. Although she declined an interview, she seemed stunned that another network had caught wind of the story and was now running something ahead of WCCO.

That night, we all watched anxiously as FOX-9 ran a story titled "The Paynesville 5." The reporter explained that, because of Joy's work, investigators were now taking a new look at a series of child molestations in Paynesville that had occurred in the years leading up to the Wetterling abduction.

"In fact, they've already reinterviewed some of the victims and are working with the blogger who brought the information to light," he added.

I had to laugh. Stearns County was definitely *not* working with Joy, and Pam Jensen had only reinterviewed some of the victims earlier that same day. I also knew Joy had been very protective of these victims and would never have referred to them as "The Paynesville 5." The whole story felt sensationalized.

By the next day, KARE-11, the NBC affiliate, had also picked up the story, so by the time part one of Esme's story aired on Wednesday, we were all on edge. Just before 10:00 PM, Jerry and I tuned in to WCCO as the intro began.

There is a new development in one of Minnesota's most infamous unsolved crimes: the abduction of Jacob Wetterling.

A masked stranger grabbed the eleven-year-old as he biked home from a store in St. Joseph nearly twenty-five years ago. Now, WCCO-TV has learned that a cluster of at least six unsolved sexual assaults on boys were never looked at as a possible lead in Wetterling's case.

For four years, Joy Baker, a blogger from New London, has written a detailed blog about the Wetterling case. Last summer, her research uncovered articles in the *Paynesville Press* in 1986 and 1987. They detailed six unsolved sexual assaults on boys just two years before Wetterling's abduction.

The story cut to video footage of Esme and me sitting at the kitchen table of my house in St. Paul. "We did not know about these cases until Joy Baker put it on her blog," I told her.

Next, they cut to footage of Esme and me reviewing two police reports she had recovered from the Paynesville Police Department. "Some of these were taken from a group of boys. That is really rare," I commented. "The threat of a gun, the age of the victims . . . they were close to Jacob's age. I do think there is a strong possibility they are connected to Jacob's case."

I went on to say it was frustrating to learn so many years later about the Paynesville cases, but I was also understanding. "It was a different world back then. We didn't have the internet. We worked hard so that each law enforcement agency had a fax machine."

Sheriff John Sanner agreed and explained that the lack of the internet and the fact that small-town law enforcement agencies often acted independently may have kept the Paynesville cases from becoming a significant part of Jacob's investigation. "We can't look back. We are actively investigating these cases now. We want anyone with any information to come forward, no matter how small. You could hold the key."

I couldn't help but roll my eyes. So *now* he was paying attention? We were still stinging from the lack of communication, and I could only hope the sheriff was serious about following up on these leads and finally letting his investigators reinterview the Paynesville victims.

Part two of Esme's story aired the following evening and focused on Jared's story. He did an amazing job, and I was so proud of him. Even though WCCO didn't share his last name, everyone from Paynesville knew Jared. He'd lived there for most of his life, but most people didn't know his full backstory. Now, everyone would know, including his own kids. I was amazed at his courage, as well as his kindness. I knew he was doing this to help find Jacob.

"I apologize to the victims . . . about bringing up twenty-seven-year-old repressed memories," he said. "But their involvement in this case could matter."

The story cut to another shot of me speaking to Esme from my house in St. Paul. "I am so grateful to Jared and Joy digging. I do think there is a strong possibility they could be connected. Every one of these victims needs answers. Are they tied to Jacob? Let's find out."

{ Chapter 43 }

Following the media blitz about the Paynesville attacks, all hell seemed to break loose. The number of visits on Joy's blog went from about a hundred per day to over 30,000. She was also receiving all kinds of tips and comments, including several from Paynesville residents that had a recurring theme: "Look into Delbert and Tim Huber."

Back in 2011, there had been a lot of media coverage when eighty-one-year-old Delbert Huber shot and killed a well-liked teacher over a trespassing dispute. He and his forty-five-year-old son, Tim, conspired to cover up the murder. They were eventually convicted and sent to prison, but because of all the new publicity surrounding the Paynesville attacks, many people from the area were coming forward again and saying the Hubers may have been involved in Jacob's kidnapping.

Very early in the investigation, Delbert Huber's name was turned in as a potential suspect in Jacob's case because of his strong resemblance to one of the sketches. He looked like the "bald man with a piercing stare" who had been spotted at the Tom Thumb store the same day Jacob was abducted.

This led to a whole slew of follow-up stories by WCCO and several other media outlets. It was all moving so fast, and all the new attention to Jacob's case was incredibly stressful for our whole family. Could the Hubers really be the ones who had taken Jacob? Why? What would have brought them to St. Joseph?

Jared had told us the entire Huber farmstead had been razed just six months earlier. If Delbert and Tim had been in prison since 2011 . . . then where was Jacob? Clearly, there was no good ending here.

We'd already been through so many tough leads over the years. The boy's body found in the Mississippi River. Bones found in the woods in northern Minnesota. A Milwaukee barber who had kept sexually haunting journals and one of Jacob's "Missing" posters in his home. A pair of brothers from

St. Joseph whose family members turned them in. A report that Jacob was in a mental hospital in London; another report that he had been seen in Amsterdam.

Jerry knew I had a vivid imagination, and he always recognized how these leads tore at my spirit. "Let's go camping," he said. "Nothing is going to get done over the weekend anyway, so let's just get out of here and try to keep our minds off of it."

He was right. A weekend up north sounded better than biting my nails at home.

We drove to the resort in northern Minnesota where our family had been going every year since 1988. Camping at this peaceful place had always been therapeutic for us, but it was also bittersweet. Jacob had loved this resort, and I could picture him running back from the boat with fish stories, playing Marco Polo in the pool, or making new friends with other kids in the cabins.

After we got the tent set up, Jerry and I sat next to the campfire and let ourselves be mesmerized by the flames. Without all the distractions of our everyday lives, it was easier to face some of the hard questions. Could it be the Hubers? What if all the rumors and suspicions about them were really true? We tried to talk about other scenarios with less horrible endings. How about this guy? Or that guy? What about *those* guys?

Over the years, we had become accustomed to the whirlwinds that brought new waves of horrible possibilities. This time, though, I was thinking about Joy. We hadn't heard from her in several days. With all this attention to her blog and the fact that her name was now associated with Jacob's investigation, I worried about how she was dealing with the stress.

We didn't know it, but Joy had been devastated by many of the same thoughts we were having. A few days after we returned, we finally heard from her.

Patty & Jerry,

Well, I have to be honest . . . these past two weeks have been really hard on me . . . which makes me worry how incredibly hard they must have been on you. I've been so upset over all those stories about the Hubers, mostly because I think about what must be going through your minds . . . and that's been almost unbearable for me.

The other thing I was completely unprepared for was the sheer number of tips that came in. It was a huge responsibility trying to keep up, filter, and disseminate all this information and get it to the appropriate people without messing up.

All in all, I've been kind of an emotional wreck. After fumbling around for most of the weekend trying to get a hold of myself, I finally did something that made me feel better. Well, two things, actually. First, I made a huge batch of chocolate chip cookies, and I admit, that did help a little.

Second, I went through all the tips I've received over the past two weeks and organized them into one big spreadsheet. Next, I prioritized them from most important to least important, then sorted them all according to suspect. All told, my blog has generated 69 different tips so far. I have no idea how many Stearns County and NCMEC have received, but all together, that seems like a lot. (Is it?)

So, now I'm wondering what to do with this massive spreadsheet. I hesitated to even tell you about it because I don't know how much you want to know.

Pam did reply to one of my emails last week to say that they are taking all these leads very seriously, but I'm not sure what to believe anymore. Jared and I would be willing to follow up with some of these people, but I don't want to upset the apple cart either.

So . . . anyway. I just thought I'd check in and let you know what I've been up to. Mostly, I'm just really worried about you and I hope you're okay.

—Joy

I smiled when I read the line about baking chocolate chip cookies, but I could sense that Joy was really struggling. I responded.

Thanks Joy,

Ironically, I shared with Jerry over the weekend that I was worried about you being in this position. We are somewhat numbed, thick-skinned, and skeptical about everything as we have been on this path for so long. But you haven't, and how overwhelming to have the sheer volume of responses to deal with. Wow. Thank goodness you are so organized!

Don't worry about us, we'll be okay, but do take care of yourself.

We went camping/fishing on Friday and just walked away from everything. It was awesome.

I would LOVE to see the spreadsheet. Yes, that is a lot! I get so frustrated by Pam thinking she is "protecting" us from things. What if we knew some of these people but she never asked! You can always send us stuff. If I am overwhelmed, I might not read it right away, but at least you have shared. Jerry reads most of it right away.

Personally, I probably don't know enough about the Hubers. I still struggle with the fact that these were two hermit-like, ornery people living out in the country, often bickering with neighbors. They shot someone over $50. There is a giant leap from that personality type to the type who kidnapped Jacob. I just don't know. And if it was them . . . why did it stop? No other boy victims before or after Jacob? Or if they were tied to the Paynesville abductions/ assaults, again, why did it stop?

Their faces are eerily like the composites, however. If you know of any ties to us, to St. Joe, or possibly to Jacob, fill me in and I might be more open to them as suspects.

Baking chocolate chip cookies has been my one consistent solace. Some days are double batch days . . .

Let's try and reconnect this week and see what's next.

Thanks so much. You have brought more energy and life into this investigation than I ever dreamed possible at this late date. With that, I remain, hopeful.

Patty

Later that evening, Joy sent us a copy of the spreadsheet. She had stopped sharing the tips with Jared or Esme and was paralyzed by the thought of revealing something that might somehow compromise the case. Many of the leads were graphic and disturbing, and some just made my skin crawl. Although I claimed to be toughened up to this kind of activity, I acknowledged it was impossible for me—Jacob's mom—to ever have the capacity to hear these implied horrors about my child and not have it chisel away a piece of my heart.

I had begged for answers, but honestly, could I ever prepare myself to hear what happened to Jacob that night?

{ Chapter 44 }

On June 11, 2014, Delbert Huber died in prison, just weeks after responding to reporters and being questioned by Stearns County investigators. An autopsy report revealed he died of natural causes, but this did little to console me. Time was slipping away, and people were dying. If Delbert Huber had any answers about Jacob's disappearance, he took them to his grave. Another door slammed shut.

But what bothered me most was this ongoing silent treatment from the SCSO. Finally, I'd had enough. After voicing my frustrations with Pam Jensen for the millionth time, I called to schedule a sit-down with the sheriff.

In early July, Jerry and I met with Sheriff Sanner in his office at the Law Enforcement Center in St. Cloud. I came prepared with several pages of notes, just to make sure I wouldn't forget anything we wanted to cover. As we sat down at his large conference table, I tried to briefly explain what a trying year it had been.

"We get all our information from the outside world, and we get nothing from you. We have Paynesville victims calling and telling us they're not being heard. We have people calling to turn in tips because you weren't willing to follow up on a lead. And we have Joy and Jared stirring up more information and energy in Jacob's case than we've seen in the past ten years."

The sheriff sat quietly and stared blankly as I continued.

"We know that everyone cares and wants to help," I said. "But we don't know who's doing what—if anything—or who's coordinating efforts, or what's the best way to move forward. It feels like you just keep waiting for the perfect lead to drop down out of the heavens instead of digging for it. We get that you can't share everything with us, but being completely cut off from all communication with you for the past year and a half has been agonizing. We need to know what's happening."

Sheriff Sanner tried to assure us investigators were not intentionally trying to keep information from us. "There are data privacy issues," he said. "Because Jacob's case is still an ongoing investigation, we can't share information . . . even with the two of you."

"But the previous sheriffs would always talk to us," I replied. "What's changed? Right now, there's a lot of energy around finding Jacob. We need to capitalize on the momentum and keep people coming forward."

When he didn't answer, I continued.

"We realize everyone's busy, but we need to know more about what you're doing. From day one, I've always been law enforcement's biggest cheerleader. I've never burned you, but it gets hard when Jerry and I only hear from the outside world about what *hasn't* been done, and who *hasn't* been talked to. If everything is being done to find Jacob and we just haven't gotten the right information yet, I can sleep nights. But without hearing from you, I don't know that."

"I assure you, everything is being done to try to find Jacob," the sheriff said. "We've never quit, and we never will."

"Honestly, I don't know if I believe that," I said. "Tell me the downside of allowing the National Center for Missing and Exploited Children to come in and do an extensive case review. They have a lot more experience solving these types of cases, and I'm totally baffled by your refusal to talk to them."

I rattled off a bunch of statistics and key findings from the National Center, and tried to explain how hurtful it was that he'd refused to attend the Long-Term Missing Children's Summit earlier that spring.

"I need to know that you have a plan," I said. "Witnesses and suspects are dying. Information is being lost. You keep saying you're protecting the case, but maybe that's getting in the way of solving it."

I pulled out my notes and read a short list of things we wanted to see happen.

1. A meeting with the FBI and Minnesota BCA to strategize on how to move forward
2. The go-ahead to have NCMEC's long-term missing team come and do a case review
3. Improved communication

As we left the Stearns County Law Enforcement Center that day, I was grateful for the meeting, but I still felt depleted. Even though the sheriff had looked both of us in the eye and told us he would never quit trying to find Jacob, I could tell there was no passion behind his words. After nearly twenty-five years of searching, twelve of them under his leadership, I got the sense he was tired and—perhaps—just going through the motions. We also knew he was still locked into Dan Rassier as a person of interest.

I desperately clung to two shreds of hope from our meeting. First, Sheriff Sanner promised to call a follow-up meeting between us, the SCSO, the FBI, and the Minnesota BCA so we could make a plan for moving forward. Second, I was happy to hear the sheriff was at least willing to consider allowing NCMEC's long-term missing team to come to Minnesota and review Jacob's case. It was a start.

On August 15, 2014, Jerry and I made our way down to the Stearns County Law Enforcement Center for a meeting with "the team." These were the people who had been with us at the very start—the SCSO, the FBI, and the BCA. For so long, we'd been begging for this meeting, and now it was actually happening.

Representatives from the sheriff's office included Sheriff Sanner, Captain Jensen, Chief Deputy Bruce Bechtold, and two newer investigators that neither Jerry nor I had worked with in the past. The FBI sent Special Agents Rick Thornton and Chris Boeckers. Our local FBI agent from the St. Cloud office, Shane Ball, was also in attendance. Representatives from the BCA included Ken McDonald (our regional BCA agent) and BCA Superintendent Wade Sutter.

As we took our seats around the table in the Jacob Wetterling Conference Room, I looked forward to this rare opportunity to share, brainstorm, and strategize on Jacob's case. I also hoped to discuss plans for the twenty-fifth observance of his disappearance.

Sheriff Sanner opened the meeting.

"Thank you all for coming. We're here because Patty is frustrated and has some questions. Go ahead, Patty."

I stared at him, completely taken aback.

Really?

I took a deep breath, grateful I had come prepared. I was not going to squander this opportunity. As I unfolded my notes, I made direct eye contact with each person around the table.

"Yes, *thank you* to each and every one of you for coming today," I told them. "Our family is so grateful for all that's been done to help us find Jacob over the years, and yes, I am frustrated, and I don't know what to do with another October 22. But this isn't about me. It's about Jacob. Twenty-five years is too long. A lot has been happening this past year, and Jerry and I both feel like we may be closer to finding answers than ever before. That's why I wanted to have this meeting. We need answers."

I talked about the rough year we'd lived through and the lack of communication from the sheriff.

"There are data privacy issues," Sanner interrupted.

"Yes, we've heard that," I said. "But this has never been a problem before. So, why now?"

BCA Superintendent Wade Sutter jumped in to back Sanner up.

"Minnesota has some antiquated data privacy laws that need to be corrected," he told us. "But the sheriff is right. For now, we can't share anything with you."

I didn't press him, since that wasn't really what this meeting was about. Instead, I moved on. I shared some of the work I was doing with NCMEC and made a point of thanking FBI Special Agent Shane Ball for attending the Long-Term Missing Children's Summit. I tried to put into words what it was like to meet Elizabeth Smart after having worked with her parents for nine months, strategizing on ways to find her. Or what it was like to talk to Gina DeJesus and Amanda Berry about how they were reclaiming their lives after being kidnapped and held captive at a house in Cleveland for ten years. Or what it was like to sit with Jaycee Dugard's mother, Terry, and hear about the many challenges they were now facing since Jaycee's eighteen years in captivity.

"These families are real," I told them. "These children came home because nobody gave up on them. The National Center for Missing and Exploited Children has resolved some very old cases. They've found fifty-six children who were recovered after more than twenty years, and in most cases, the answers were right there within the first week of the investigation. We need to go back."

They were mostly quiet as I talked, but I could tell they were listening. After I finished addressing the group, Sheriff Sanner gave us a brief update. He said they were continuing to follow leads as they came in, and they were still following up with Dan Rassier. That was about it. There was nothing specific, and we still had no idea if the Paynesville leads were being seriously considered as a possible tie-in to Jacob's case.

Jerry, who seldom spoke up, challenged Sheriff Sanner. "It feels to me like we're being penalized for Patty being chair of the board for the National Center for Missing and Exploited Children. Is that why you won't talk to us anymore?"

The sheriff just stared at us blankly. He had no response.

Rick Thornton from the FBI stepped in and offered to engage a CARD team to reexamine Jacob's case. He paused to explain what a CARD team was for Jerry and me, but we were already well aware what it stood for: Child Abduction Rapid Deployment.

In my work with Fox Valley doing law enforcement training, I had the unique privilege of hearing some of the amazing work CARD teams were doing all over the country. FBI CARD teams consisted of highly trained experts who were specifically experienced in the subject of child abductions. The teams included FBI agents, intelligence analysts, and behavioral analysis profilers. CARD teams also utilized resources from the National Center for Missing and Exploited Children and provided investigative and technical assistance during non-family child abductions, ransom child abductions, and mysterious disappearances of children.

I was so excited. Because of my hands-on knowledge of CARD teams and the work they did, I also knew the only way to deploy them was via a direct invitation from local law enforcement in charge of a case. Now, in front of everyone, the offer had been made. The deal was on the table, and Sheriff Sanner really had no choice but to accept. This was absolutely the greatest outcome I could have hoped for from this meeting.

As the team continued to talk and strategize, I could feel their energy. People leaned forward over the table. They asked questions, offered suggestions, and seemed willing to drop their jurisdictional loyalty in an effort to come together and figure this out, once and for all.

As we wrapped things up, I emphasized how badly I wanted to find Jacob.

"My wish is that he's one of the success stories . . . one of those long-term missing kids who gets to come home. It *could* happen . . . and it *does* happen. But whatever the ending, we just need to know, where's Jacob, and who did this?"

Not long after this multiagency meeting, the vice president of NCMEC's Missing Children Division, Bob Lowery, called Captain Pam Jensen to ask a few questions about the Paynesville cases. As he pressed her for details, she gave him a reply that he read as an invitation. In short—if he felt his team could do a better job investigating the Paynesville incidents as they related to Jacob's case . . . go for it.

Bob leapt at the chance. He knew about the renewed energy in Jacob's case because of the Paynesville leads, so at the very least, he hoped they could light a fire under the sheriff to follow through and reinterview these victims. After confirming the invitation with Sheriff Sanner, Bob quickly put together a group of Team Adam volunteers and booked their flights.

The consultants who volunteer with Team Adam (named after Adam Walsh) are retired law enforcement professionals who have several years of experience at the federal, state, and local levels. They deploy to sites where cases of missing and abducted children are unfolding and provide on-the-ground technical assistance to local law enforcement, all free of charge. These investigators also have experience with long-term abductions and have successfully assisted in many cold case resolutions by working with local authorities.

In mid-August, NCMEC sent a team of seasoned investigators that included Bob Lowery (vice president of the Missing Children Division), Rich Leonard (senior forensic case manager on Jacob's case), Dave Wurtz (a Team Adam consultant from Michigan), and Dave Byington (a Team Adam volunteer from California).

After meeting with Sheriff Sanner and Captain Jensen, the team carefully reviewed the case file from the very beginning, then headed out to Paynesville. The whole team felt strongly these cases had to be connected to Jacob and Jared, and they became laser-focused in their investigation. They talked to several key people, including Jared, Joy, victims of the 1986–87 Paynesville assaults, members of the Paynesville Police Department, and former associates of Duane Hart.

Bob Lowery provided brief overviews at the end of each day. I was so grateful for these updates, which reminded me of our daily calls from Al Garber during the early weeks of Jacob's investigation. Finally, I felt like we were back in the loop.

Before the NCMEC team left and headed back to DC, they stopped by the house and shared some of their thoughts and frustrations. They were impressed with the Google map Joy had put together that showed where and when each of the Paynesville attacks had taken place. There were so many similarities between those cases, Jared's case, and our case, Bob reiterated that there was a high probability all the attacks were done by the same man.

"We just don't see pockets of boy victims like this very often without them being tied to the same perpetrator," Bob told me. "The victims were all about the same age and lived within such a small geographic area. These cases have to be connected," he repeated.

Before he left, Bob had one more idea to share with me that he felt would tie in nicely with the upcoming twenty-fifth anniversary. NCMEC had connections with some outdoor advertising partners, and he was hoping to put up five or six billboards in the area to generate more tips and keep the momentum going. We'd recently received a new age-progressed photo of Jacob at age thirty-five, so Bob suggested showing this new photo alongside Jacob's more familiar fifth-grade photo with a headline that said "STILL MISSING" across the top. Ideally, the billboards would be strategically placed in high-traffic areas of towns associated with the investigation—St. Joseph, St. Cloud, Cold Spring, and Paynesville.

I loved the idea and thanked the whole team for their inspiration and generous contribution of time. Their excitement further fueled my new sense of hope.

{ Chapter 45 }

The energy was building as the twenty-fifth anniversary approached, and though we hadn't planned one big event to commemorate this sad milestone, I was starting to feel better about the things we *had* done.

On August 31, 2014, John Walsh featured Jacob's story on his new CNN series, *The Hunt*. Earlier that summer, a team of producers had come to Minnesota to interview me, Jerry, Sheriff Sanner, Joy, Jared, and a few of the Paynesville victims. John was incredibly sensitive in telling Jacob's story, but it was still hard to see our family's pain "Hollywood-ized" on national television.

It was one of the few times we had ever seen a staged reenactment of Jacob's kidnapping, and everything about it felt weird. I had to sit and watch while a woman pretending to be me, in a house that wasn't mine, reacted and responded to the most traumatic moment of my life—all while being surrounded by a husband and kids who didn't look anything like my real husband and kids.

Of course, I was nitpicky about the details. Over the years, I had been absolutely adamant about getting the details right whenever a reporter interviewed me about Jacob's kidnapping. Now as I watched, I could tick off the inaccuracies one by one. The bikes "Jacob, Trevor, and Aaron" were riding looked like they were from the mid-'70s, not the late '80s. They showed a full moon, even though it had been completely dark. They showed a man in a full face mask, even though the kids had never been able to describe exactly what kind of mask the man had been wearing. And probably the most annoying: the home video they showed of Jacob playing the piano (both at the beginning of the show and at the end) *wasn't even Jacob*. It was Amy.

The reenactment of Jared's story was easier for me to watch, even though it showed him being kidnapped on a beautiful summer day, when it had actually taken place on a cold winter night in mid-January. I had to remind myself the average viewer wouldn't care about these little details. The point was to engage the audience and get them to feel, to care, and most importantly, to call if they had any information.

The show intensified when Joy and Jared were interviewed and began sharing their research on the Paynesville attacks. After displaying a map where each of the incidents had taken place, they showed Joy driving around Paynesville and pointing out the sites as she gave dates and details for each attack location. By the end of the driving tour, the map showed a cluster of eleven pins—over twice the number of incidents than the original five that had been reported. Their research was thorough, and the questions they raised were compelling.

The show ended with me asking the very question that had bothered me the most, ever since I'd first learned about the Paynesville attacks.

"What was going on in this region that was so deeply and intensely harmful to boys?" I asked. "I want answers. I want to know what happened."

In September, I reached out to Alison Feigh, Jacob's former classmate and program manager at the Jacob Wetterling Resource Center (JWRC). I wanted to brainstorm with her about what JWRC could do to observe the twenty-fifth anniversary of Jacob's abduction. Alison was smart, creative, and brilliant at grabbing an idea and running with it.

I shared with Alison how, in my darkest of times, I'd always refused to let go of the world we knew before Jacob's abduction. It was a world of hope and promise, and I felt we owed it to our kids to never lose sight of that world. So, when I suggested putting together a list of twenty-five things that would help families build and sustain this hope, she jumped right on it.

To honor Jacob on the twenty-fifth anniversary of his abduction, we asked all grown-ups to create a better, safer world for children by helping them build hope and confidence together.

25 Ways to Build Hope in Children
1. Help me build a fort.
2. Stop at my lemonade stand.
3. Read to me.
4. Listen without distractions.
5. Join me in finding animal shapes in the clouds.
6. Model kindness.
7. Create art.

8. Teach me empathy.
9. Put an encouraging note in my lunch.
10. Do something with me to make our block more beautiful.
11. Sing to me.
12. Remind me to share.
13. Be a voice for youth.
14. Celebrate differences.
15. Dance with me.
16. Teach me something new.
17. Help me create a family of snow angels.
18. Tell me campfire stories over s'mores.
19. Take technology breaks.
20. Ask me my opinion.
21. Create a scavenger hunt.
22. Volunteer somewhere together.
23. Put together a neighborhood event.
24. Take me on a bike ride.
25. Talk to me about online and body safety.

The billboards were going up, and I agreed to do interviews with all the Twin Cities TV stations. A reporter from the *St. Cloud Times* did an intensely emotional interview with Jerry and me at North Junior High, Jacob's school at the time of his abduction. He photographed us in front of the tree Jacob's classmates had planted that first spring after he was kidnapped. This tree, which had been the height of an average sixth grader at the time it was planted, now towered over the school at thirty feet tall and provided shade for the "Jacob's Hope" garden that was planted underneath. It was all such a stark reminder of how incredibly long Jacob had been gone from our lives.

On Wednesday, October 15, 2014, we held a joint press conference at the Law Enforcement Center in St. Cloud with the SCSO, BCA, FBI, and NCMEC. I was so happy to have NCMEC CEO John Ryan in attendance, as well as John Bischoff, executive director of the Missing Children Division. NCMEC was the one agency that truly *never* gave up on missing children. Their presence validated the impact Jacob's abduction had made on national child safety reform, and also recognized my work as board chair for the past two years.

As I took the podium to speak that day, I tried to set the scene from twenty-five years ago. "It was right here, in this very room, where investigators and dispatchers were answering calls and collecting tips. It's been renamed the Jacob Wetterling Conference Room, but twenty-five years ago, this was the command center." As I continued, I told the throng of reporters, "And that is our primary message today. We're still asking people to call."

When it was John Ryan's turn to speak, he shared what I had been saying and repeating for years. "Missing kids are still out there. From 2009 to 2013, more than 160 kids who were missing between eleven and twenty years were found," he said. "During that same time frame, forty-two children who had been missing more than twenty years were found."

Next, John introduced the billboard campaign and revealed a sample of what the billboards would look like. They showed Jacob's picture at the time he was abducted, the new age-enhanced picture of what he might look like at age thirty-five, and the phone number where people could report tips—800-THE-LOST. John also listed the location of all six billboards in St. Joseph, Cold Spring, Paynesville, and St. Cloud.

As the press conference came to a close, Sheriff Sanner wrapped things up by saying, "If we get tips today, we treat this case as if it happened yesterday. We'll treat it with the same energy and enthusiasm as if it was one day old, not twenty-five years old. We will continue to do that."

I made a sideways glance at Jerry, who casually turned and looked down at the floor.

Yes . . . one could only hope.

On a crisp fall morning, twenty-five years to the day since our entire world fell apart, I walked downstairs and turned on our front porch light in hopes that Jacob—and all our missing kids—might one day find their way home.

For the past year, I had been absolutely paralyzed by the thought of this anniversary. I simply didn't know what to do with it. Now it was here, and for all the buildup and worry, the day itself was rather quiet and uneventful. Our kids came home to visit—just as they had every other October 22. We were always so grateful to be together on this day, and after twenty-five years, we had learned it was much easier to face the sadness together. Of course, they also brought our beautiful grandchildren along with them, who always put smiles on our faces.

A few close friends dropped by throughout the day, many bringing flowers, gifts, and treats. We received a white rose with baby's breath from our former neighbors, Trish and Bruce, just as we had every year for twenty-five years.

More flower arrangements arrived throughout the day, adding color and vibrance to our home. Our Lakota friend, Frankie, came over to perform a healing ceremony for us and for Jacob. It involved smudging and prayer, and it provided deep, spiritual strengthening for all of us.

Later, Joy and Jared stopped by and had a chance to meet our kids and grandkids for the first time. They didn't stay long, but Jerry and I were grateful they were able to make it. We shared with each of them how meaningful they had become in our search for Jacob, and we were proud to introduce them as our dear friends.

That evening, after everyone had gone home, Jerry and I lit a candle and played the songs that reminded us most of Jacob—"Listen," "Jacob's Hope," and "Somewhere Out There" from the animated movie *An American Tail*. We prayed for our son's safe return, just as we had on this same night so many times before.

Yet, something felt different this year. I felt lighter, and I was filled with a sense of new possibilities. I knew this was because of Joy and Jared. They brought hope. They brought fresh energy and new ideas. Together, they had lit a fire under Jerry and me, and the constant flow of communication was both energizing and refreshing.

I thought back to the early days of Jacob's investigation, when every moment was filled with high energy and incredible effort. Sheriff Charlie Grafft had been so supportive. He would stop by for coffee from time to time and always shared funny stories about his early days of police work. One time, he stopped over and gave me a microcassette player. He told me to keep it with me and use it often.

"Talk into it when you have an idea, so you don't forget," he instructed. "You have good ideas."

I was thrilled. Back then, I really did feel like I was a valued part of the investigative team.

Then came John Sanner. Intentionally or unintentionally, he had relegated us to being victims. After so many years of searching, learning, and advocating, I felt like I no longer mattered. I wanted to scream, "I'm Jacob's mom! That should mean something! Why won't you talk to me?"

It felt like I'd been getting sicker and sicker for years, never realizing how worn out I really was. Now I felt like I'd received a blood transfusion and could feel myself getting stronger and stronger.

That's what Joy and Jared brought to the table. The four of us had become a force—energized, empowered, determined, undeterred, and undaunted. Jared and Joy seemed to know everything about the goings-on in Paynesville and were committed to finding as many victims as they could who were willing to talk to them. They asked a million questions, did follow-up interviews, and sought experts when they got stuck. Jared was so passionate in his quest for answers, everyone wanted to help him. And Joy was so friendly and forthcoming, people seemed willing to talk to her.

This joining of forces felt bigger than all of us, and somehow, we just knew we would find our answers. As I checked the porch light one last time that evening of October 22, 2014, my heart was warmed by a stronger sense of hope than I'd ever felt before. I couldn't really explain it, but this time, it just felt different.

This time . . . it was time.

{ Chapter 46 }

On November 3, 2014, the CARD team that Sheriff Sanner had requested at our July meeting with SCSO began its comprehensive review of Jacob's case, which included a close look at Jared's case, the Paynesville cases, and all the collected evidence.

Captain Pam Jensen and Detective Dennis Kern from SCSO and Special Agent Shane Ball from the FBI office in St. Cloud were joined by Special Agent Chris Boeckers from FBI-Minneapolis and Special Agent Mike Beaver from FBI-Oklahoma. Chris and Mike were both FBI child abduction team members who had worked together in November 2006 when Tristan White and Avery Stately went missing from the Red Lake Indian Reservation in northern Minnesota. Both had exceptional FBI careers, and we were so grateful for this deep dive into Jacob's case by a qualified team of experts.

By this time, we knew that the baseball cap that had been left behind during one of the Paynesville attacks had been sent in for DNA testing. We also knew that Pam Jensen and Ken McDonald from the BCA had reinterviewed Duane Hart at the MSOP facility in Moose Lake back in December 2013 and collected DNA swabs. When the DNA report came back, we were told Hart couldn't be excluded as a contributor to the profile on the cap, but the results were inconclusive. We never heard anything more, so we weren't sure if Duane Hart was still a viable suspect or not.

It had been seven years since I first accepted my position at the Minnesota Department of Health (MDH) back in 2007, and I was ready for a change. Still, that didn't make it any easier when I announced that I would retire on May 1, 2015.

I truly loved the people I worked with at MDH and had always felt at home in my position there. At my retirement party, I received many well wishes from coworkers, but I still wasn't quite ready to accept the term "re-tirement." Yes, I was retiring from state government, but I still planned to continue my work in sexual violence prevention, and I didn't consider my-self officially retired. Between my speaking engagements with JWRC, law enforcement trainings with Fox Valley, and my board chair position with NCMEC, I knew I would be plenty busy.

For reasons I couldn't quite explain, there was one other thing I wasn't ready to let go of . . . my cute little house in St. Paul.

The house fit me perfectly. It had three small bedrooms, one bathroom, a kitchen, and a living room. It was cozy, convenient, and only five blocks from Carmen's house. But there was something else. This little house on the east side of St. Paul had come to represent the "me" I had somehow lost along the way.

Before starting my position at MDH, my life had become all about leads, sightings, media, speaking events, and travel. I was always in response mode—prioritizing, triaging, and constantly waiting for the other shoe to drop. It was physically and emotionally exhausting. This little place gave me space to breathe, dream, and imagine. I could almost remember what it was like to live like a normal person again. I was able to pause, slow down, and ask myself, "Who am I?" I was confident and happy, and I absolutely loved this little place.

So, at sixty-five years old, I became a landlord once again. I had to laugh when I realized this seemed to be a recurring theme in my life. Back in Davenport, about two years before Amy was born, Jerry and I had purchased a triplex home and rented out the two lower-level apartments to cover our own monthly mortgage and utility payments. From that original triplex in Davenport to the old Victorian home in St. Joe (where we still rented out the living space above Jerry's office), to this cozy house in St. Paul . . . it seemed like I'd always been a landlord.

I looked forward to spending the summer working on my little house and preparing it for renters, so happy to hold on to this little piece of myself that had become so important to me.

In July, Captain Pam Jensen from the SCSO called to request a meeting with us. When she asked if she could stop by the house, both Jerry and I were a little thrown. This never happened.

When she arrived, I invited her in, and the three of us sat down at the kitchen table. I offered her a cup of coffee and tried to make small talk, wondering why in the world she was here. Eventually, Pam got to the point.

"We're working on a lead . . . a local guy . . . Danny Heinrich. He's been a suspect for a long time, but we have some new evidence, so we're getting a warrant to search his house. This will probably happen in the next week or two, so I just wanted to give you the heads-up."

"What new evidence?" I asked.

Pam told us that, during the CARD team's review of Jacob's case last November, Danny Heinrich had reemerged as a key suspect. In January, members of the team met with a forensic scientist at the BCA and requested that an unknown DNA sample from Jared's sweatshirt be compared to DNA from Danny Heinrich. They had just recently received the results—it was a match. They now knew without a doubt it was Heinrich who had assaulted Jared.

Jerry and I both gasped. It took a moment before either of us could speak.

"Does Jared know?" Jerry asked.

"No. Not yet."

Pam explained how they had talked it over as a team and made the difficult decision to hold off on telling Jared until after the search was complete. They just couldn't risk a leak.

"We weren't sure if we should tell you either, but I didn't want you to hear it from someone else. You know how it is. Whenever we go in, the neighbors talk, they call their friends, and somehow the media finds out . . . especially if they think it's related to Jacob. We're sealing the search warrant, but you never know what might leak out."

"So . . . what are you looking for?" I asked her.

"Anything related to Jacob or Jared," she replied. She didn't elaborate.

We tried asking a few more questions, but Pam wouldn't give us any more details.

"It's not Heinrich," I told her assuredly. "He let all of his victims go."

We knew Danny Heinrich and Duane Hart were both from the Paynesville area, so it made sense that one of them had been behind the Paynesville attacks . . . possibly Jared's too. But whoever had committed these crimes had always let the boys go. So, why not Jacob? And why St. Joseph? It didn't make any sense to me.

The truth was, I didn't want to hear what she was saying. If Danny

Heinrich did it, there would be no good ending. For self-preservation, I brushed off the possibility. Instead, I chose to focus on more positive scenarios—"alive scenarios," as Jerry and I called them. We had maintained hope for so many years, and until we found Jacob or learned what truly happened, I would continue to cling to it.

Later that day, Jerry and I took a walk and tried to make some sense of what Captain Jensen had just told us. We both hurt for Jared. He had lived with fear and unknowns for so long. How would he take this? How were *we* supposed to take this? After so many years of waiting and wondering, what if Jacob's case really *did* get solved? Would it make us feel any better to know what happened? No . . . not if this was the ending. On the other hand, did we want to continue living in limbo without ever knowing? No. That wasn't good either.

Amazingly, in over twenty-five years, we had never had this gut-wrenching talk about "what ifs." We were aware of the statistics, but we also knew that missing kids *do* come home, even after long periods of time. I knew their stories because I'd read every last one of them. I clipped them, saved them, and studied them endlessly. I had that whole three-ring binder filled with their stories, and I'd even met many of these survivors. It could happen.

On July 28, 2015, investigators executed a search warrant on Danny Heinrich's home. We heard nothing more.

{ Chapter 47 }

In late October, Jerry and I were looking forward to our upcoming trip to Colorado to visit Trevor and his family for Halloween. We couldn't wait to see our grandsons, Jake and Finn, and I'd come up with the perfect costumes for Jerry and me—Mary Poppins and Bert the chimney sweep. I was just starting to pull some things together when Pam Jensen called.

"Can you and Jerry come down to the sheriff's office on Wednesday morning?" she asked.

We were leaving for Colorado on Thursday, but anything related to Jacob's abduction was always a priority, so of course we agreed. Pam gave up few details.

On Wednesday morning, October 28, we arrived promptly at 9:00 AM, and the receptionist let Captain Jensen know we'd arrived. Pam greeted us in the lobby and told us to follow her.

"We're meeting downstairs," she said, "in the Wetterling Room."

Jerry and I gave each other questioning glances. This wasn't typical. If it was just a sit-down visit with Pam and/or Sheriff Sanner, we met at a table in one of their offices. When we walked into the Wetterling Room, we saw the whole team . . . SCSO, FBI, BCA. Seeing them all sitting there, quiet and stoic, I knew this was serious. They didn't gather like this just for ongoing updates.

I felt my adrenaline explode as they directed us to our seats. There was no levity or small talk. We sat down, and Sheriff Sanner began.

"We want to talk to you about what we've been working on in the search for Jacob."

FBI Special Agent Chris Boeckers turned on a projector and all eyes turned to the screen at the front of the room as he began to speak.

"In 2012, the BCA found an unknown DNA sample from the right sleeve of Jared's sweatshirt. They preserved that sample for future testing."

He showed a slide of Jared's hooded sweatshirt from 1989 with a patch from the right sleeve cut out. Agent Boeckers continued.

"Back in 1990, when Danny Heinrich was first being investigated, detectives collected several hair samples from him and kept them as evidence. On January 13, we brought those hair samples down to the BCA, along with Jared's clothing, the Paynesville cap, and Heinrich's shoes."

My heart was pounding. Over the years, we had been through several hundred leads, but not once had they zeroed in on one single suspect like this. Not ever.

"Ken, Dennis, and I met with forensic scientist Katie Roche. We went over what we wanted tested and why. It took a few months before we learned that none of the hairs in this initial batch had a root bulb suitable for DNA extraction. Detective Kern went back through the evidence and was able to find another hair sample from Heinrich that had been preserved under a glass slide. We brought that slide back to the lab in May, and it was determined to be suitable for testing. Heinrich's DNA was then compared to the unknown sample that had been collected from Jared's right sweatshirt sleeve. On July 10, we received the results. It was a match."

"We conducted a formal search of Danny Heinrich's house in Annandale on July 28 looking for any evidence related to Jacob or Jared. These are some photos from that search."

The next several slides were photos of Danny Heinrich's home. The house looked small, but neat. There was a photo of a sword collection mounted on the wall.

"When we conducted the search of Heinrich's home, we found it to be fairly orderly. We didn't find any articles of clothing or 'trophies' related to Jacob or Jared."

Next, he played one of Heinrich's home videos that showed a handgun inside a safe in his home. It was black . . . just like the gun Trevor and Aaron had described. It had not been inside the safe when they did the search. They were now working to track it down.

Finally, he showed a photo of nineteen binders of child pornography they had found in locations throughout the house.

"We haven't found any photos of Jacob or Jared in his collection, but we can't be entirely sure because many photos have been morphed or photoshopped. We're still working with NCMEC on photo analysis, but there are no photos of Jacob or Jared at this point."

Next, they showed us a photo of a footprint that had been taken at the crime scene. It was a clear print left in the sandy dirt of the Rassiers' driveway.

"In 1990, investigators obtained Heinrich's shoes. Here's a photo of the bottom of his shoe."

He clicked the forward button on the PowerPoint, and the next slide showed a transparent photo of Danny Heinrich's sneaker transposed on top of the crime scene footprint.

"Here's the mold of the footprint Detective Steve Mund took on the Rassier driveway."

They looked like an exact match. Goosebumps went up and down my spine. It was him. In that moment, I knew Danny Heinrich had been at the crime scene.

"Also in 1990, investigators seized the tires from Heinrich's car and analyzed them."

They overlaid a photo of Heinrich's tire treads onto the crime scene photo of the tire treads.

"To our eyes and yours, I'm sure you can see this looks to be his tire. Forensically, this isn't enough evidence to convict or even to make an arrest, but between the shoe and the tire, it looks to be him."

My head was splitting at this point. It was his shoe. It was his tire.

"In 1990, investigators vacuumed Heinrich's car and collected fibers and hair. These have been sent to the BCA, and the examiner is looking at over seventy hairs for potential DNA. It is a labor-intensive and time-consuming process. We don't have any results back from that yet."

Jerry and I both knew how long it took to get DNA results. In our experience, it had taken up to six months, and that was just for *one* sample of DNA. I couldn't imagine how long it would take to test *seventy* samples of hair, one by one.

They explained that, even though they now had definitive DNA proof that linked Danny Heinrich to Jared's abduction and assault, the statute of limitations that existed for those crimes back in 1989 had run out, so there was nothing they could do to bring justice for Jared. They were still working hard to find more to tie Heinrich to Jacob, but so far they didn't have anything. DNA tests on one of the hair strands vacuumed from Heinrich's car might come back to be Jacob's, but that would take time. In the meantime, they had a plan.

"We're going to arrest him on federal charges of child pornography, which carry longer sentences than state law. We hope the charges will cause enough stress for Heinrich that he's willing to talk and give us information to help find Jacob. We're all hoping for a quick resolution, but we can't know for sure how he'll respond."

Everything they were saying was surreal and terrifying. Jerry and I had been on this gut-wrenching journey for twenty-six long years, but still, we weren't ready for this.

"It's imperative that you don't tell a soul about any of this. We don't want to alert Heinrich in any way."

They told us we could tell our kids, but that was it. They planned to arrest Danny Heinrich the next day, and they needed to catch him off guard.

"We'll be talking to Jared right after we finish this meeting. We're planning to show him the same presentation we showed you, and we'll share the same facts."

It was overwhelming. I just wanted to put my head down and cry, but I couldn't do that here. Instead, I sucked it up and gathered as much stoicism as I could possibly muster. For once in my life, I was utterly speechless.

It was Jerry who finally spoke.

"Okay. So . . . I just want to know—person by person—do you really believe this is the guy who took Jacob?"

One by one, they went around the table.

SCSO Captain Pam Jensen: "Yes."

SCSO Chief Deputy Bruce Bechtold: "Yes."

SCSO Detective Dennis Kern: "Yes."

BCA Special Agent Ken McDonald: "Yes."

FBI Special Agent Chris Boeckers: "Yes."

FBI Special Agent Shane Ball: "Yes."

Finally, it came back around to Sheriff Sanner. He paused, swallowed, then, looking down, he said, "Yes."

I couldn't believe it. This was the same sheriff who had been locked into Dan Rassier as his "person of interest" for the past thirteen years. If Sanner was convinced, that was telling.

We drove home in stunned silence. I was so lost in my own fear and denial, I couldn't even speak. Jerry dropped me off at home, then headed back to his office.

As I sat there alone, my head and my heart were at war with one another. Heinrich's behaviors didn't fit the pattern of most predatory offenders. If it *was* him, his behavior had kept escalating: first stalking, then attacking and molesting, then abduction and sexual assault. And then what? He just quit and went back to child pornography? None of that made sense.

Danny Heinrich had let everyone else go, so why didn't he let Jacob go? Something must have gone terribly wrong. I had a million different scenarios racing through my head . . . all of them horrible. I shook my head and walked around the house screaming, "No! Not him, not this!" But no one was home to hear or respond.

An hour and a half later, I got a call from Jared.

"I need a hug. Can I come over?"

When he arrived at my front door, he looked like a scared twelve-year-old boy. I wrapped him up in my arms.

I loved this man. We had been on this same frightening journey for such a long time, and today, he had been all alone as he sat through that same horrifying presentation we had seen just hours earlier.

We couldn't talk to anyone else, so we talked to each other. Jared had a million questions, most of which I couldn't answer because I didn't know either.

He was upset that the investigators had known about his DNA match for months but had decided not to tell him. Because of my background with NCMEC and Fox Valley, I knew why investigators couldn't tell victims everything. At this critical point of the investigation, I also knew they had to protect the safety of everyone involved.

Jared fired more questions at me. When exactly did the investigators know? When did *we* know? Could they have charged Heinrich earlier on his own kidnapping case? Or were they just delaying it so they could catch him on Jacob's kidnapping?

Jared had known for a long time that the statute of limitations had run out on charges for his assault, but he'd always been told that he would still be able to prosecute on kidnapping charges, since that crime had no statute of limitations. But just today, he'd learned that wasn't true. Back in 1989, when his assault had taken place, Minnesota *did* have a statute of limitations for kidnapping—three years—and even though there was no statute of limitations today, the law from 1989 was what applied.

I could feel Jared's rage and confusion. This was a crushing blow. He had worked so hard to help us find answers, and even though we still didn't know where Jacob was or what had happened to him, Jared now faced a new and harsh reality. He *did* know what had happened to him and who had done it, but he would get no justice. Because of Minnesota's archaic laws back in 1989, Danny Heinrich could not be prosecuted for any of the life-changing harm he had caused Jared.

I could see Jared's mind racing in a million directions. After a brief PowerPoint presentation, he suddenly had to let go of all the other suspects he'd been carrying around for so long. It wasn't a priest, or a monk, or the railroad guy, or the junkyard guy, or the campground guy. Most surprisingly, it wasn't Duane Hart. Jared had spent a lot of energy going after Hart because he knew Hart had victimized so many other young boys during that same time period. Many of these victims also had him convinced that Hart had taken Jacob. Now what was he supposed to think or feel?

I felt so bad for him, and I was scared for both of us. What if Heinrich didn't confess? What if he got off? Then what?

Jared didn't stay long, but before he left, he gave me another big hug. I knew this deep and caring man would be part of our lives forever.

Jerry and I decided to wait until he got home from work to call our kids and tell them about Heinrich's impending arrest the next morning. However, that plan fell through when Pam Jensen called around 6:00 PM.

"Change of plans. We're on our way to arrest Heinrich right now."

We hurriedly arranged a conference call with Amy, Trevor, and Carmen and prayed they wouldn't hear anything about it before then.

When we were finally able to connect, I tried to speak calmly as I explained what was going on, even though, on the inside, I was torn apart. If it was Heinrich, we all knew the ending wouldn't be good. However, we also knew there would be a lot of media attention when his arrest was made public, and we needed to figure out what to do.

After talking it over, we decided it would be best for Jerry and me to stick with our original plan and leave for Colorado the following afternoon. I would work with Alison Feigh at the Jacob Wetterling Resource Center to prepare a family statement.

In the meantime, I would continue to focus on hope. Tomorrow, I would pack my carpet bag, umbrella, and lace-up boots, along with a scarf and tam for Jerry. The wind was about to change, and I told Trevor to prepare for our arrival.

{ Chapter 48 }

As expected, the arrest of Danny Heinrich sent shock waves through the state of Minnesota. On October 29, 2015, US Attorney Andrew Luger, along with Stearns County Sheriff John Sanner, FBI Special Agent in Charge Richard Thornton, and BCA Superintendent Drew Evans, held a joint press conference at the US District Courthouse in Minneapolis to inform the public about Heinrich's arrest on federal child pornography charges. He was also named a person of interest in Jacob's abduction, but Andrew Luger made it clear that Heinrich had denied any involvement and was not being charged with that crime. However, they also made it clear it was still an active investigation and encouraged anyone with knowledge of Danny Heinrich's activities during the late 1980s and early 1990s to contact them.

The criminal complaint against Danny Heinrich and the search warrant for the July 28 search of his Annandale home were also released to the media at the time of the press conference. Both were lengthy documents that went into detail about both Jacob's and Jared's cases, as well as the cluster of attacks on young teenage boys in Paynesville during the late 1980s. Between these two documents, the media now had an incredible amount of background information that would allow them to hit the ground running in pursuit of this developing story—which they did, in earnest.

We knew very little of this, because we were already on our flight to Colorado. When we arrived in Denver, Trevor picked us up at the airport and I finally felt like I could exhale. Jake and Finn were so happy to see us, and we had two full days to laugh and play with them before Halloween. In the evenings, while Trish got the boys ready for bed, we talked to Trevor and tried to sort through everything we were facing. We had so many questions. What now? What would happen at the preliminary hearing? If Heinrich really *did* take Jacob, how long would it take before we got answers? He was facing up to sixty years in federal prison for child pornography. Was that enough to make him talk?

After the kids went to bed, Trish joined us and we continued talking. We spoke to Carmen and Amy on a three-way call from Trevor's, and they shared some of what was happening in Minnesota. This was big news, and people were riveted. The principal at the school where Amy taught told her to take time off if she needed it, and Carmen's supervisor did the same. They told us about all the support they were receiving from friends, and it felt good to talk through things together.

Halloween came to Trish and Trevor's neighborhood, and it was absolutely magical. Many of the houses had elaborate decorations, and everything seemed so innocent and normal compared to the scary and bizarre life we were currently living back home. It reminded me of how Halloween used to be in St. Joe before Jacob was kidnapped. Parents often dropped their kids off on the main drag, then picked them up about a mile down the road when they were done trick-or-treating. Some parents even met up at the bar for a beer while they waited for their kids. But all that went away after 1989. Neighborhood trick-or-treating was replaced by Halloween parties at the schools or trick-or-treating at the mall. Kids no longer went alone.

Later that night, after everyone had fallen asleep, I had trouble settling down. I hated the sense of powerlessness I felt. It was like being back at the very beginning, when I wanted to *do* something—to help search for Jacob—but I wasn't allowed to.

I was grateful to Alison Feigh for speaking on our behalf at the press conference after we left town, but as the week wore on, I realized I *did* have some thoughts I wanted to share. I wondered if maybe we should hold our own press conference when we returned. At least that might help me overcome this sense of powerlessness.

The next morning, I talked it over with Jerry and the kids.

"I think you should do it," Trish spoke up.

Jerry and Trevor agreed.

When we spoke to Amy and Carmen, they were also supportive.

We asked Alison at JWRC to put out a news release stating we would hold a press conference at our home the morning after we returned from Colorado, on Tuesday, November 3.

The next day, on our flight home from Colorado, Jerry and I talked about what we should say. What exactly did we want to accomplish? What was our main message? After going round and round a bit, we finally ended up on the same page.

First, we wanted to keep the focus on Jacob, not this awful man who harmed kids. I hated when the media showed Heinrich's mug shot right next to Jacob's smiling fifth-grade photo. That man didn't deserve to be on the same screen as our innocent son. We still didn't even know if Danny Heinrich had anything to do with Jacob's kidnapping, yet there they were, side by side in almost every news story. A week earlier, no one had even heard the name Danny Heinrich; now it felt like every reporter in the state was scrambling to learn more about him. They were making him into a celebrity. We wanted to change the narrative, sustain the hope, and let people know what they could do to help.

Second, after receiving so much support from the public throughout these past twenty-six years, both Jerry and I felt it was important to reconnect, so they could hear our voices and know a little of what we were going through. We knew they cared about us, and we wanted people to know we were just as stunned and confused as they were.

Jerry had patients the next morning, but he planned to be back for the conference at 12:15 PM. I stayed home and tried to get myself emotionally prepared to talk to the media. I was full of nervous energy, so I decided to test my own theory and prove it was impossible to be mean, angry, and vindictive while baking homemade chocolate chip cookies. This was a true test, so I made a double batch.

As the final trays of cookies were coming out of the oven, people began to drop by the house. Alison arrived early with two other staffers from JWRC to lend support and help coordinate the media. While we mingled and waited for Jerry to arrive, Alison asked if she could serve some of my cookies to the throngs of reporters now gathered at the bottom of our driveway.

"Sure," I said. "That's a great idea."

We piled the warm cookies on trays, and Alison brought them outside to share with the waiting crowd. It was a perfect diversion for Jerry, who parked at a neighbor's house and avoided walking past all the reporters by sneaking through the woods behind our house.

When it was finally time, Jerry and I held hands as we started the long, slow descent down our driveway. As I looked out at the dozens of reporters, I saw many familiar faces—people who had been our friends and helpers for over twenty-six years. At the same time, I also noticed the fresh faces of some younger reporters, who probably hadn't even been born at the time Jacob was kidnapped.

Jerry took the podium first. He started by thanking everyone for being part of our very long journey. He acknowledged the huge roles that law enforcement and the media played in getting us to this point, but also thanked the public for their important role as well. "No one plays a more important role than you, everyday citizens, and reporting that little piece of information, when added to other pieces of information, will solve the puzzle, and bring Jacob home."

Next it was my turn. As I stepped up to the microphone, I tried to sound more confident than I felt. "I, also, want to thank you for being with us for twenty-six years. That's such an amazing length of time, and the reason we wanted to do this here is because this is where it happened."

I thanked Jared and all the Paynesville victims for coming forward to help and encouraged people to keep turning in information. I explained how we'd been caught off guard, just like everyone else, but I refused to be silent.

"We still don't know who took Jacob. We have as many questions, or more, as all of you. We will let law enforcement, and the courts, and the process continue, and we'll watch impatiently for answers. But the one question that we've asked for twenty-six years is . . . where's Jacob? *Where* is Jacob?"

I would be leaving for NCMEC the following day to continue my work as board chair and to keep fighting for the world Jacob knew. I stressed that it was up to all of us to recognize the problem of child pornography so we could prevent something like this from happening to another family.

When I finished, the reporters were silent. The press conference had lasted only six minutes, and Jerry and I didn't take any questions. Instead, we turned around and walked arm in arm back to the house.

Once inside, we joined our friends and watched the live TV reports being filmed outside our home. Many reporters noted that neither Jerry nor I had mentioned the name "Danny Heinrich" in our statements.

I was glad they noticed.

Some of the reporters talked about my cookies. It was funny how that had been such a random moment in my day, yet somehow, those cookies ended up being the perfect thing that tied us all together. Because of those warm chocolate chip cookies, I got the feeling these people could see us for who we really were, or at least who we used to be. We were just normal people in a normal house who did normal things—like eat chocolate chip cookies fresh out of the oven—until that one horrible day in 1989 when nothing was ever normal again.

They got it. Without a doubt, we could feel their collective compassion, and we knew these reporters had our backs. They were ready to dig in and were willing to move heaven and earth to help us find our son.

{ Chapter 49 }

Several weeks went by before we finally got a chance to connect with Joy. Since Heinrich's arrest, she had been inundated with requests for media interviews, but had respectfully declined, wanting to keep the focus on Jared and Jacob. It wasn't until she was contacted by a reporter from the Minneapolis *Star Tribune* who told her they were doing a story on the Paynesville victims that Joy finally agreed to do an interview. For the first time, one of these young men had agreed to go public with his story, and Joy wanted to show her support.

One by one, she began reaching out to other Paynesville victims to let them know about the upcoming article and to ask if they would also like to be included. Several agreed, so Joy passed along their contact information to the reporter for follow-up.

The article, which covered almost two full pages, ran on Sunday, November 15. It included interviews with several of the victims Joy and Jared had talked to over the past two and a half years, and though they had already shared their stories on Joy's blog, this was the first time any of them had ever spoken publicly, without concealing their identities. Only one chose to remain anonymous.

As Jerry and I read the article, we were overcome by its intensity and emotion. These young men had been silenced and voiceless for almost thirty years. Now they were speaking out, and we could feel their pain intertwined with ours.

All shared similar stories. Even though each of them had reported their assaults (or attempted assaults) to police, none had received any kind of follow-up from either the Paynesville Police Department or the SCSO. These boys had been terrorized and left with permanent emotional scars from their attacks, yet the lack of response from law enforcement had left them feeling like they were expected to just "get over it" and move on.

Now, thirty years later, they were angry. They felt that if someone—anyone—had just listened to them and taken these incidents seriously back in the late 1980s, maybe Jared and Jacob's kidnappings never would have happened. Like Jared, they were now coming forward to share their stories publicly, in an effort to help find Jacob. They were revisiting their pain in order to help us. It was truly powerful, and we were so grateful to these young men for their bravery and strength.

Later that evening, Joy stopped by for a short visit and Jerry asked her what she thought about the article on the Paynesville victims.

"I thought it was good," Joy said. "But I just feel so bad for the town of Paynesville. They've been through a lot."

The first wave of publicity had come a year earlier, when Esme Murphy had discovered Joy's blog. Now the onslaught was back in full force, with reporters anxious to learn more about Danny Heinrich.

So much had happened in that small community, and there were so many child victims of sexual assault who were now adults. Some had been victimized by Duane Hart; others still didn't know who their attacker was. Was it Hart? Was it Heinrich? Was it someone else? Nobody knew for sure. The only thing we *did* know was that these boys had all been victimized and no one had taken them seriously.

"I feel like we should do something," Joy said. "A town meeting or something."

My eyes lit up. "Jerry and I were just talking about that!"

After reading the *Strib* article earlier that day, Jerry and I had discussed the possibility of having some kind of healing gathering in Paynesville. We wanted to meet these young men and thank them for their support. Both of us felt a true connection to them, and we wanted them to know we were all in this together.

Joy liked the idea of a healing gathering, but envisioned something bigger—a town hall kind of meeting, with representatives from the Paynesville Police Department and the SCSO who could also update residents on the investigation and encourage them to come forward with tips. I found it amazing that *Joy* was the one to point out the opportunity to ask for the community's help in finding Jacob—Jerry and I had been focused on the needs of the victims.

The idea began to take shape. I suggested having representatives from JWRC there, so they could provide resources for victims and their families.

I also offered to contact the director of the Central Minnesota Sexual Assault Center. Joy suggested having the event at the Paynesville High School auditorium, a facility that held up to five hundred people. She also suggested banning media from the event, in order to protect the privacy of the victims and give Paynesville a break. This was still a big and emerging story, and we knew if the media caught wind of it, they would want to be there.

The next day, I contacted Pam Jensen at the SCSO and Paul Wegner, the police chief of Paynesville, to float the idea past them and get their input. They both liked the idea, but Chief Wegner surprised me by saying he would actually *like* to have media present, at least for part of the meeting. He felt it would give them an opportunity to show Paynesville in a positive light. He suggested banning media during a private Q&A session at the end, so people would feel more comfortable speaking up. He also suggested calling it a "community information session" rather than a "night of healing" so it was more inclusive. He wanted to make sure the whole town, not just victims, knew they were invited to attend.

We liked his suggestions and decided to move forward at full steam. We planned the date for Monday, November 30, 2015, but as luck would have it, there was a blizzard that day. The chief called me to report that roads were impassable, so we made the mutual decision to cancel the event. We rescheduled for a Sunday evening the following week, December 6.

As luck would have it *again*, there was heavy fog and freezing rain on the evening of December 6, but we didn't feel we should cancel again. We decided to go with it.

The car ride from St. Joe to Paynesville was long and tense. It was normally about a thirty-minute ride, but on this night, the fog was so thick we arrived later than we intended. A heavy mist hung in the air, and the lights of the high school cast an eerie orange glow as Jerry and I inched across the icy parking lot. Everything felt cold, dark, and heavy.

When we entered the auditorium lobby, Joy immediately came over to greet us with a warm hug. She pointed out Jared and his mom, then told us Chief Wegner wanted to meet with us briefly.

The Paynesville High School auditorium was much nicer and bigger than I anticipated for a small rural high school. We found Chief Wegner up toward the front, speaking to Captain Pam Jensen. After some quick introductions, we went over our game plan and decided who would speak in which order. I was immediately impressed by Chief Wegner and the way he presented himself. He was young, about Jacob's age, and highly motivated to make his community better. He was calm and controlled, and I was happy to follow his lead.

The auditorium was beginning to fill with people, and I could see at least a dozen TV cameras and reporters lining the back wall. I forced a mild smile and waved at many of the familiar faces.

We chatted with Jared for a while. He introduced us to one of the survivors of the Paynesville attacks, and I recognized him as one of the contributors to the recent *Strib* article. I thanked him for his willingness to come forward and felt an instant connection to his pain.

Joy also introduced us to a few of the moms of Paynesville survivors. Each of them told a similar story. They had immediately reported their sons' terrifying incidents to police, only to be disregarded and forgotten. How could this have happened, over and over?

Amy and Carmen arrived safely from the Cities. I was also relieved to see Alison and Jane from JWRC, who quickly set up a booth in the entry with brochures and other information.

Finally, it was time to start.

We walked back into the auditorium, which had now filled with about 150 people. At 7:00 PM, Chief Wegner opened the meeting. He thanked everyone for coming and then briefly explained why we were all here. "Almost thirty years ago, the community of Paynesville was shook to its core with a series of heinous attacks against the young boys of this community."

He described the attacks in general terms, then moved ahead to 1989 and spoke briefly of the eerie similarities between Jared's and Jacob's cases, and the Paynesville attacks.

As the chief spoke briefly of Danny Heinrich's arrest and the possible connections among all these cases, he then skillfully turned the spotlight back on Paynesville.

Lost in all the media hype and speculation are the victims, their families, and lives of the people of Paynesville.

We cannot change what happened so many years ago. The heinous, unforgivable attacks of almost thirty years ago will be part of our history forever. Those impacted by the attacks will live with the scars and memories as long as they live.

The attacks, however, do not define who you are as a person

or who we are as a community. The community of Paynesville is strong, resilient, and supportive, and the Paynesville Police Department is committed to the safety and security of all residents and visitors to the city.

I have personally watched this community come together in difficult times and persevere. Together we will continue to move forward and make Paynesville an even better, safer community to live in.

After thanking Jerry and me for hosting the event, and Joy for helping to make the arrangements, Chief Wegner introduced Pam Jensen from the SCSO. She was brief but cordial.

"If you had a personal relationship, know about vehicles, party spots, anything of that nature regarding Danny Heinrich, or if you have any other information about other cases, please come forward," she said. "We'll talk to you about those also because those cases don't get solved unless people like you come forward. I know it's a hard topic, but it's important that we're all on the same page."

We appreciated her appeal for more leads, but for many in the room, her comments landed on deaf ears. So many of these victims *had* come forward but were never contacted by Stearns County. These men were in their early to mid-forties now. Just like Jacob, many of them had been with friends when they were attacked. They had all lived in fear, not knowing who would be next.

As Captain Jensen finished her remarks, Jerry took the podium. He talked about the connectedness we now felt with the Paynesville community and explained how we'd been "hit in the face" with Heinrich's arrest. Now, just like everyone else, we were waiting impatiently for the wheels of justice to turn. If Heinrich did take Jacob, we needed him to talk. Jerry encouraged people to fill out the tip sheets and assured them we would read each and every one. If they felt more comfortable taking a tip sheet home and mailing it to us anonymously, he encouraged them to do that as well.

Finally, it was my turn. I could feel the energy in the room, which included a fair amount of bitterness and resentment toward law enforcement.

"One of the things that happens when you're a victim is you feel very isolated," I said. "That's the purpose of this meeting—to give victims a chance to talk to each other and to law enforcement." I tried to assure them that, while denial may have kept reports of the Paynesville assaults from being investigated more seriously in the 1980s, things were different now. "You are blessed to have this chief who gets it, and who has promised this would never happen today," I told them.

I kept my comments brief, and when I was done, Chief Wegner asked the media to step out into the hallway so we could continue with a private Q&A portion.

It was then we heard the true anguish of this hurting community. Their comments were raw, candid, and sometimes heartbreaking. It seemed everyone in the room either was a victim or knew someone who was a victim. These were parents, spouses, siblings, neighbors, and friends. As Joy carried the wireless microphone around the room fielding questions, I did my best to respond. Sometimes all I could say was, "I'm so sorry."

While many people took the opportunity to vent their frustrations, others offered more concrete information, including suggestions of where Jacob might be buried. I cringed when I looked over and saw Amy's and Carmen's reactions. This was all so hard.

We had promised to keep the meeting to about an hour, so I was grateful when Chief Wegner interrupted to say it was almost 8:00 PM. I made a few final remarks.

"Thank you so much for coming tonight in this treacherous weather," I said. "We want to help Paynesville heal, and if there's anything we can do to help, please call the Jacob Wetterling Resource Center, and we will get back to you as quickly as possible. Thank you from the bottom of our hearts."

Jerry and I drove home that evening, exhausted and sad, but still with hope in our hearts. We felt we'd done what we could to promote a sense of healing, and we also felt united with all those who had attended. At the very least, maybe those young men who had been brave enough to share their stories would now find some validation and peace. I hoped so. Their voices had strengthened me, and I hoped everyone who attended that meeting was able to walk away with just one clear message.

We hear you, Paynesville, and we are so grateful.

{ Chapter 50 }

When Danny Heinrich was arrested on October 28, 2015, we were not only thrust into a new world of horrible possibilities, we were also thrust into a world that was completely foreign to us—the US court system.

Jerry and I knew very little about the court process or what was next. At sixty-seven and sixty-six, neither of us had ever served on a jury or even hired a lawyer. Now, I felt like I'd been dropped onto another planet.

Heinrich had already made two court appearances. On October 29, he made his initial appearance at the US Courthouse in St. Paul, where the judge charged him by criminal complaint, advised him of his rights, and appointed a team of two public defenders. On November 4, the judge held a preliminary hearing and found probable cause to move forward with a trial. At the hearing the judge interviewed the prosecution's sole witness, FBI Special Agent Shane Ball, who went through all the evidence in great detail. Heinrich was denied release from jail at the preliminary hearing and put into the custody of the US Marshals.

Next was the indictment (scheduled for December 16) and the arraignment (scheduled for February 9). I had no idea what either of these things were.

At the indictment, Danny Heinrich was formally charged with twenty-five counts of felony child pornography offenses, including seventeen counts of possession and eight counts of receipt of child pornography. It spelled out each count in full detail. Throughout the rest of December, there was a flurry of motions, orders, continuances, and extensions. It was maddening, especially because it all had to do with the pornography charges, not Jacob. We knew there would be continued pressure to get Heinrich to talk, but all of it would take time—and patience—which was not my strong suit.

On January 8, Pam Jensen called to tell me she was retiring. Pam had been our family contact at the SCSO since 2000, and even though we hadn't always seen eye to eye, I knew she cared. At times, I sensed her hands were tied, and she could do only what the sheriff allowed. Other times, I got the sense she felt I should be sitting back with my feet up, sipping an umbrella drink, and enjoying retirement. I don't think she ever truly understood the urgency I still carried.

Four long months after the arrest, the arraignment (first scheduled for February 9, then pushed back to February 22) finally took place. After being made aware of the charges against him, Danny Heinrich pleaded not guilty to all twenty-five counts of child pornography. The whole thing lasted four minutes.

The judge also pushed back the date of the jury trial—from March 14, 2016 to July 11, 2016. We had been preparing ourselves for a trial in less than a month; now we would have to wait another four months. Again . . . maddening.

Throughout the spring and summer, Heinrich's defense team continued to file motions and extensions for more time. In April, they filed a motion for a change of venue, arguing that Heinrich couldn't get a fair trial in Minnesota because of all the recent media attention and the notoriety of Jacob's case. They also filed motions to suppress Heinrich's original statements and to throw out all items found in the July 2015 search of his house, claiming it was an illegal search and seizure. Yet again, it was all so incredibly maddening.

The judge approved another extension at a hearing on May 24, 2016, and truly, I was going crazy. In my own head, this man had already been granted plenty of extra time by simply being free for the past thirty years. Now he was being given more time so his defense team could come up with some plausible reason as to why he had all that child pornography in his home?

As the court continued to push back the schedule, Jared was also struggling to resolve his own anger and sense of injustice. He continued to call us with his weekly Sunday-night check-ins, and it was often hard to listen to him rage on about Minnesota's statutes of limitations that prevented him from bringing criminal charges against Heinrich. All Jared had ever wanted was the chance to confront his attacker and get answers to the questions that had plagued him for so long. Why him? Why Cold Spring? Was Jacob's case connected to his? Were the Paynesville cases connected? He wanted Heinrich to admit his wrongdoing and be punished for it. It was that simple.

In May, Jared received an unexpected gift when he learned about an update to the Minnesota Child Victims Act. While the original law was enacted in 2008, a new subdivision was added in 2013 that provided a three-year window for adult victims of childhood sexual abuse to file civil lawsuits against perpetrators, regardless of the statute of limitations. The law stemmed from the decades-long abuse that had been recently uncovered within the Catholic Church, but it also provided Jared and other childhood survivors like him the opportunity to bring civil charges against their abusers.

Jared did not have the funds needed to hire a lawyer. But he had developed a close friendship with Esme Murphy from WCCO-TV, and she offered to call a few of her legal contacts to see if any of them might be interested in taking on his case pro bono. With Esme's referral, Jared was introduced to Doug Kelley, a prominent Twin Cities lawyer from the law firm of Kelley, Wolter and Scott.

Doug helped Jared file a civil lawsuit against Danny Heinrich on May 11, 2016, just two weeks before the act's provisions expired. They charged Heinrich with one count of sexual battery and one count of false imprisonment, and they sought damages in excess of $50,000. Jared was well aware that Heinrich had no money, so even if he won his civil case, he would be highly unlikely to receive any kind of monetary award. But that didn't matter to him. Jared just wanted his day in court, and finally, he would get it.

Doug Kelley explained to Jared there was something else this civil case could do. It would provide them the opportunity to subpoena people and have them testify under oath. This could include suspects, victims, known associates of Danny Heinrich, and even former law enforcement officers. In turn, this might help us in our own quest for answers in Jacob's case.

Once again, Jared was on fire. Doug needed a list of people they might want to call to testify, so Jared and Joy put together a veritable "who's who" of Jared's case, including names and descriptions of Danny Heinrich's associates, Duane Hart's associates, Hart's victims, the Paynesville victims, and any former law enforcement officers who had worked on Jared's case from the very beginning.

By summer, Doug was ready to discuss strategy. He asked Jared if he would be willing to set up a meeting with Joy, Jerry, and me. We invited everyone to meet at our house on Saturday morning, July 9, 2016.

Doug Kelley had worked on several high-profile cases, including a Las Vegas casino bank fraud deal involving the Mafia. More recently, he had been appointed to manage and liquidate the personal assets of Thomas J. Petters and five codefendants after they were convicted of the largest Ponzi scheme in Minnesota history. He was clearly a top attorney.

As for us, we only knew of Doug because of his kind reputation. The highest compliment came from Jerry's cousin, who was an auto mechanic and had worked on Doug's car over many years. He couldn't say enough good things about the man.

As Doug Kelley arrived at our house on that warm summer morning, the first thing I noticed was his calm, easygoing nature. He had a soft, reassuring voice, a wonderful smile, and bright blue eyes that reflected kindness and understanding. I was incredibly grateful to him for his generous donation of time and talent on Jared's civil case.

After everyone was settled, Doug got to the point. "It's clear you're all very important to Jared, and I'm going to need your help putting together his case."

He explained what was necessary to win Jared's civil case against Danny Heinrich. They would need testimony from witnesses who could share pieces of the pain he had lived—a divorce, lost opportunities for promotion, and his recent unemployment due to anxiety and stress that caused him to be too distracted to work.

"What he did affected my life," Jared affirmed. "There's not a day that goes by that I don't think about this guy, and I want him to pay for taking away my childhood."

Joy, Jerry, and I all voiced our willingness to testify on Jared's behalf. Given what he had gone through to help us in our search, it was easy to say yes.

Shortly after Joy and Jared left, Doug paused and said, "Do you have one more minute? I have something I'd like to talk to you about."

He explained that he had recently been in contact with Andy Luger from the US Attorney's Office. Andy told Doug that he would be more comfortable sharing information regarding developments with Heinrich if Doug were to formally represent Jerry and me. When Doug offered to represent us pro bono, we gladly accepted.

Summer of 2016 remained busy, which kept us happily distracted from the slow-turning wheels of justice. In mid-July, Joy joined Jerry and his group of backpackers for the Twenty-Third Annual Wilderness Trek for the Jacob Wetterling Resource Center. She'd never attempted any kind of mountain climbing before, but with Jerry's encouragement, she decided to give it a whirl.

Joy added a whole new dimension to the trek. From her daily Facebook posts, live video feeds, and a detailed blog post after she returned, it was fun for me to see and feel what the group went through during their week out west. The trek was hard, and while Joy gained a new appreciation for Colorado's "Fourteeners" (mountain peaks of 14,000-plus feet), I gained a new appreciation for her spirit of adventure and willingness to jump in. Together as a team, the Trekkers raised over $16,000 in pledges for the Jacob Wetterling Resource Center that year—a new record.

As August arrived and summer started to come to an end, our family got together for our annual vacation at Leech Lake in Walker, Minnesota. As always, it was another fun week of swimming, kayaking, paddleboarding, biking, fishing, bingo, s'mores, kickball, a family photo shoot (with a new color-coordinated theme each year), and of course, the annual cousins' dance show, choreographed by Auntie Carmen.

As we sat around the campfire on our final night, Trevor turned to me and quietly asked about the investigation.

"Anything new I should know about?"

"Not really," I assured him. "There's nothing new to tell."

I paused a moment before adding, "I just really hope it's not him."

Trevor looked at me knowingly, then turned back toward the fire.

I didn't want our perfect vacation to end on a sad note, so we changed the subject and the rest remained unsaid.

Although the end of summer always triggered memories of Jacob's kidnapping, I still looked forward to the crisper days of fall. The sumac was already starting to turn bright shades of red, signaling shorter days, the return to school, and the start of Vikings football.

On Monday night, August 29, Jerry had just gotten home from work and we were trying to figure out what to do for dinner when we heard someone knocking.

Jerry ran down the stairs to open the door, and I heard him say in surprise, "Doug! What's up?"

It was Doug Kelley. I shut the refrigerator door and walked over to the top of the stairs.

"Sorry for the surprise visit," Doug said. "Do you guys have a few minutes?"

{ Chapter 51 }

Everything shifted. I remember Doug's visit and the eight days that followed as if I'm still living them in real time.

My mind is spinning as we sit around the kitchen table. Doug says he tried calling Jerry and me on our cell phones a few times, but couldn't get ahold of us. That's why he's here. He needs to talk to us, so he just got in his car and drove to St. Joe.

Doug tells us he received a call from US Attorney Andy Luger earlier in the day. Luger wanted to meet with him—right away.

Doug asked him, "You mean I should set my pen down and walk over to your office right now?"

"Yes," Luger told him.

Doug explains that the two assistant US attorneys have been negotiating with Katherian Roe, the head public defender. They've reached a tentative plea agreement with Heinrich, but nobody wants to go forward unless we are in favor of it.

"This is all very confidential," Doug says. "There's some convincing evidence, but if there's a leak, Heinrich might back out of the deal. We need to do this quickly before he can change his mind."

"What convincing evidence?" I ask.

"Heinrich has known for ten months that he's basically facing life behind bars if he's convicted on all twenty-five counts of child pornography," Doug says. "His options are running out, and with the trial only a month away, he's suddenly willing to negotiate. But he has a volatile personality, and he could change his mind again at any moment.

"The broad outline of the deal is that Katherian Roe will make a proffer of evidence which would tell the feds where Jacob's body is. If they find the body, then Heinrich would confess to Jacob's murder and to sexually assaulting Jared."

I recoil from the shock of his words. *Jacob's murder.*

"Heinrich will be interviewed by law enforcement and will be required to provide convincing evidence of the crimes. He will plead guilty to one count of child pornography in the federal case and there would be a maximum possible sentence of twenty years. In addition, Janelle Kendall, the Stearns County attorney, would have to agree to not prosecute Heinrich for Jacob's murder."

Doug's tone is gentle, but his words are so sharp I get stuck and have trouble following.

"Heinrich knows he can't be charged for Jared's assault because of the statute of limitations, so Jared does not have to agree to this deal. But the US attorney wants him to admit to Jared's kidnapping as part of the public record so it can be used for civil commitment down the line."

Jerry interrupts. "You said something earlier about a proffer of evidence. What's that?"

Doug explains that a proffer means Heinrich's lawyers would tell the feds the details of what Heinrich would say if he was to be interviewed by law enforcement.

"The purpose of a proffer is that, if the feds don't believe Heinrich, they would withdraw from the agreement and none of the details from the proffer could be used against Heinrich. So, to get the plea agreement, he would have to tell what happened and give convincing evidence."

There's that phrase again. *Convincing evidence.*

"So, if he agrees to tell us what happened, he only pleads guilty to one count of child pornography?" Jerry says.

"Right," Doug affirms. "But he would have to give convincing evidence; otherwise, the plea agreement is off the table."

My brain is fading in and out. I ask a second time, "What is convincing evidence?"

My fear is that all the major players seem to believe Danny Heinrich killed Jacob, but I'm not as convinced. I go back and forth with Doug about a dozen times because I don't know what "convincing evidence" means.

"I don't care if he convinces *them.* He needs to convince *me.* I'm Jacob's mom," I say, choking back tears.

I need to breathe. I leave the table and walk down the hall to the bathroom, where I close the door behind me, bury my face in my hands, and sob.

Doug and Jerry continue chatting. I can't bear to hear any more, but I don't want to miss anything. After another minute or so, I pull myself together and go back to the table.

"What if Heinrich is lying, just to get the plea deal?" I ask Doug. "What if they don't find anything?"

Doug explains. Heinrich is worried about the hair strands the BCA is currently testing. If just one of them is a match to Jacob's DNA, he knows there's a strong possibility he will be charged with Jacob's murder. That's why he's willing to talk.

If we say yes to the deal and they find nothing, the plea will likely go away. That is, unless Heinrich can provide enough substantial, credible information in his interview with the investigators to convince them he's telling the truth.

If they *do* find something—if they find Jacob's body—Heinrich would get twenty years on one count of child pornography, but nothing for our son's murder.

Either way—whether they find something or not—if we say yes to the deal, the search for Jacob would likely be over, since everyone already seems to believe that Heinrich is guilty, including the general public.

On the other hand, if we say *no* to the deal, we'll never get a chance to hear what Heinrich has to say.

Doug tells us Heinrich's lawyers are convinced he has information and is willing to talk. Heinrich knows he'll likely spend the rest of his life in prison if he's convicted on all twenty-five counts of child pornography.

"I've known Katherian Roe for many years, and I trust her implicitly," Doug tells us. "You can take what she says to the bank."

My mind is racing. What if they don't have enough to convict? What if he gets off, or is only given a short sentence? He would be free, and we would have lost our one opportunity to find out.

Finally, Jerry and I tell Doug we're interested. The twenty years is okay. Clearly not enough, but getting answers is more important to us at this point. And given everything Heinrich would be required to admit to as part of the bargain, it's very likely that he would be civilly committed after serving his sentence and kept behind bars for a very long time. My hang-up is still the "convincing evidence." If they don't find Jacob's remains, what else could possibly be "convincing" evidence? Clothing? Photos? A story we can't verify?

Doug steps outside to call Andy Luger. When he comes back inside, he tells us Luger has offered to meet with us tomorrow to further explain the details. He will have all the interested law enforcement people at the meeting, and they've agreed to hold it at Doug's law office to avoid media attention.

After Doug leaves, Jerry returns a call to Amy and sounds amazingly calm. We fry some fish for dinner. While we're eating, Carmen calls. We chat lightly and go back to our dinner. Shortly after, Trevor calls to thank me for the back-to-school shirts I sent to the boys.

The small talk is torture, but we can't share anything with them. If word gets out, all deals will be off. But without being able to discuss this with our kids, we can only guess what they would want us to do. What will this mean for them? What will this mean for *all* of us? After twenty-six years of asking "Where is Jacob?" am I really prepared to hear the answer?

As I get up to clear the table, I have no way of realizing the answer is no. I'm in no way prepared for what we will go through as a family over the next eight days.

{ Chapter 52 }

Sleep is impossible. As Jerry and I watch the minutes tick into hours, we take turns trying to keep each other from falling apart. One moment we cling to each other in quiet desperation. The next moment we pull away, suffocated by the heavy reality of what we are facing. All night long we flip from our backs to our sides, each of us trying desperately to find a moment of respite from our dark and racing thoughts.

It's still dark when Jerry finally gets up. He has patients this morning, so I'm meeting him at Doug Kelley's office at 1:00 PM. I have no idea what to expect. I'm just so glad Doug will be there to help us through this horror.

I have a new tenant moving into my little rental house today, so just after sunrise, I pack the car with cleaning supplies and head to St. Paul.

And this is where I find myself on the first day of the rest of my life—mopping and scrubbing as if my life depends on it. I check my phone to see what time it is. Still early. I pull out the refrigerator to mop underneath, trying hard not to think. Once that's done, I push the refrigerator back into place and pull out the stove. I refill my bucket and move on to the living room, then the bathroom. For reasons I can't explain, the normalcy of house-cleaning calms me, and I find the smell of Mr. Clean oddly comforting.

It's getting close to noon, so I finish vacuuming the carpets and take a final glance around. My little home. My sanctuary. My dreaming place. Our new tenant is a friend of Carmen's, and I desperately want her to love this place as much as I do.

I step into the bathroom and hurriedly change into my black suit. I fluff my hair, put on some makeup, and pin my "Jacob's Hope" button to my lapel. My eyes begin to well up as I stare at the button in the mirror. Jacob's Hope is so real to me. It's what has sustained me and propelled me forward for the past twenty-six years. What now? What if this is really it? Who am I without hope? I don't know what to feel. I don't know how to act. How will I ever get through this?

Google Maps leads me to the Centre Village building in downtown Minneapolis. I park in the ramp and start looking for the elevator when a pickup truck suddenly comes swirling around the corner and almost hits me. Startled, I jump aside. The truck pulls into a parking spot, and I walk back the other direction, still scanning for an elevator.

Now I see the man from the truck walking toward me.

"Hi Patty. I'm Matt Quinn from the Stearns County Attorney's Office." It takes me a second to figure out what to say.

"Thanks for not running me over." I smile awkwardly.

He laughs. "Sorry. I was running late and came up that ramp a little fast."

"Well, if you're late, so am I. Do you know where we're going?"

"Not really. Do you mind if I walk with you?"

I'm happy for Matt's company as we find our way to Doug's twenty-fifth-floor office. The receptionist is waiting for us as we arrive. Not long after, Doug appears and invites me back to his office while Matt Quinn is ushered off to join "the others." I have no idea who "the others" are.

As I enter Doug's corner office, I'm taken in by the beautiful sweeping views of the Minneapolis skyline. The walls are decorated with photos of the many mountains he has climbed. Behind his wooden desk is a wall of dark bookshelves, covered with photos of his family. Another time, I would probably ask him about the photos. Not today.

"Would you like a sandwich?" he asks. Even though my stomach is in knots, I realize I'm starving.

"Sure. Thank you." I take the sandwich and save half for Jerry.

"There are a lot more people here than I anticipated," he tells me. I'm not sure what that means.

Jerry arrives ten minutes late, apologetic and frazzled.

Finally, Doug explains who "the others" are that are waiting for us. Steve Schleicher and Julie Allyn are the two assistant US attorneys who work for Andy Luger. They'll fill us in on all the details of the joint agreement between Heinrich, his defense attorneys, the prosecuting attorneys, and the Stearns County attorney, Janelle Kendall. In order to move forward, the joint agreement needs to be signed today.

"If everyone signs off, the search could happen as early as tomorrow," Doug says.

My God.

"It will all take place in federal court, here in Minneapolis," Doug says. "Under the plea agreement, Janelle Kendall has to sign off and agree not to prosecute with any county or state charges. Heinrich would plead out in federal court."

Doug tells us he has split the participants into two groups so that we won't be overwhelmed by so many people. The feds will be in the main conference room and Janelle Kendall and her party will be in a separate conference room.

When Doug feels we know enough to proceed, he asks if we're ready.

Jerry and I look at each other and take a deep breath. Are we ready for this? *Absolutely not.* We nod and stand up.

We follow Doug into his conference room, and I freeze with fear. Seated at the table is an ominous collection of powerful people.

Andy Luger, US attorney

Julie Allyn and Steve Schleicher, assistant US attorneys

Rick Thornton, FBI special agent in charge of the Minneapolis bureau

Shane Ball, FBI special agent

Drew Evans, BCA superintendent

Ken McDonald, BCA special agent

I'm terrified. My heart is racing. As they begin to speak, I hear their words, but they're hard to grasp.

"We feel we've pushed this as far as we can go," Julie Allyn says. "When we stack up the charges, Heinrich is facing the rest of his life in prison, so he's ready to hear what we have to offer."

Steve Schleicher agrees. "I think we're in a good place. It's clear to us that Heinrich's attorneys believe his story. They believe he wants to provide us with proof so he can serve a lesser sentence in a federal prison."

"He has no empathy, so trying to appeal to his emotions is a waste of time," Julie adds. "This would essentially be an agreement to get answers."

Steve jumps back in. "His lawyers say he's willing to plead to one count of child pornography for a sentence of twenty years, with the stipulation that he not serve time in a Minnesota prison. In return, he agrees to tell us what happened to Jacob and where he's buried. Or, if no remains are found, give us a convincing explanation as to what happened."

I about hit the ceiling with the second option.

"That's not okay," I say firmly. "What if he just tells a story that's not true?

What if he didn't even do it? He gets a lighter sentence for his porn charges and gets to choose where he goes to prison, but we get nothing . . . we still don't know where Jacob is. You all seem to believe he did it, but that's not good enough. He doesn't have to convince you. He has to convince *me!*"

I'm near tears and just not buying into this "convincing explanation" part of the agreement. They explain that, if no remains are found, Heinrich's proffer needs to be really convincing, with substantial details, or the entire plea deal is off the table.

They assure us the joint agreement will occur in steps.

Step One: Heinrich and his attorneys will provide the specific geographic location of Jacob's remains, which could include clothing or other evidence.

Step Two: Based on the location provided to them, investigators from the BCA, the FBI, and the SCSO will begin the search.

Step Three: If evidence is found, Heinrich will provide an in-person interview with law enforcement, detailing what he did to Jacob on October 22, 1989, and what he did to Jared on January 13, 1989. He will plead guilty to one count of receiving child pornography and serve twenty years in prison. As part of his plea deal, neither the Stearns County Attorney's Office nor the State of Minnesota will be able to prosecute for Jacob's abduction, assault, or murder.

Step Four: If *no* evidence is found, Heinrich may still be offered the plea deal, but only if he agrees to still provide an in-person interview and provide enough credible information to convince the investigators doing the interview.

Jerry has a few questions, mostly on process and timing. Soon, they have us both convinced this will likely be our one and only chance to find Jacob. They add that Heinrich's lawyers also feel the time is right—he will talk.

"I don't want this to drag on and on," Andy Luger says. "If we get what we need, we want the first court date to be Friday. We don't want you to have to wait over the long Labor Day weekend."

"We need answers. We'll sign," Jerry confirms.

Doug asks us if it's okay to bring in the Stearns County people to join us, since their county attorney, Janelle Kendall, will also have to sign the agreement. We agree, and he leaves to go get them. When he returns, he tells us Janelle would prefer to have a word with us in private, without the feds in the room. They exit as she, Sheriff Sanner, and Matt Quinn enter.

"This puts me in an incredibly difficult position," Janelle says. "If I agree to sign this, I won't ever be able to press charges against this guy, even if we find new evidence down the road."

I glance at Sheriff Sanner, and he nods in agreement.

Doug asks Janelle whether she has enough evidence to prosecute anyone for Jacob's murder right now and whether she has any prospects of gathering evidence in the future to allow her to bring the charge.

Janelle is clear in her response. "I've got nothing. I can't charge him with kidnapping, because the statute of limitations has run out. I can't charge him with murder, because all I have are the shoe and tire imprints, and the slim chance that Jacob's DNA might show up in the samples we vacuumed from his car. But still, without a body, it would be difficult to get a conviction in court."

I take a deep breath and look at Jerry. We both know she's right.

"I just will not sign this deal without clearing it with both of you," she tells us. "I want to make sure it's what *you* want."

None of this is what I want. But I'm a little more at ease knowing they built in an out. If no evidence is found and Heinrich does not tell a convincing story, the plea bargain is off the table, along with the agreement that Heinrich couldn't be charged by Stearns County or by the state.

"We just want answers," Jerry says. "And it sounds like this is our best shot. So, yes, please sign."

The power players reconvene, and the lawyers collect all the necessary signatures. Janelle is the last to sign. The minute she puts down her pen, someone snatches the paper and hurries off.

Julie and Steve stand and prepare to leave. They explain they will also need to get the judge's signature to authorize the search.

"He's in Europe at the moment," Julie says. "But we've already spoken to him, and he'll be available to send it electronically."

They both thank us and fly out of the room.

We are told sternly by the remaining people in the room that we are not to let anyone know what's going on. Heinrich has not signed the plea agreement yet and could change his mind at any moment. He is volatile. One minute he wants to talk, the next he doesn't. If word gets out, it might scare him, and then the deal will be off.

Jerry and I walk with Sheriff Sanner, Janelle Kendall, and Matt Quinn back to the parking ramp.

Matt promises not to run me over as we all part ways.

Our future now lies in Danny Heinrich's hands.

{ Chapter 53 }

The next morning, Jerry is already at work seeing patients. While I marvel at how easily he is able to disconnect and move forward with his day, I'm also furious and jealous. I don't want to do this day alone.

I fix breakfast and try to eat, but all I want to do is throw up. The knot in my gut is awful. I step into the shower and wish I could just let the warm water cascade over me all day without a worry in the world.

I get dressed. Dry my hair. Check my phone.

Crap. I see a missed call from Julie Allyn at 8:35. I call her back at 9:20. She tells me Ken McDonald was at the Stearns County Courthouse as soon as it opened this morning and got the judge to sign the search warrant. Heinrich directed them to the site and told them where to dig.

"The team is at a farm in Paynesville. They arrived at 8:30 AM and told the property owners they were investigating a crime and had a warrant to search their property. They didn't tell them what they were looking for, but the couple who owns the property has been very accommodating and everything is going well. They're just doing their first inspection right now."

It takes me a second to process what she just said . . . Paynesville. While part of me is in shock and disbelief, the other part of my brain says, of course it's Paynesville.

She tells me to keep my phone close by and promises to keep calling with updates. I thank her and we hang up.

It's only 9:45 AM and my head is all over the place. I worry that they'll find something and I worry that they won't.

Just over two hours later, Julie calls back.

"We found Jacob's jacket."

My heart stops. I can't do this. I'm not ready.

I call Jerry's office and ask to speak with him.

"He's with a patient," the receptionist tells me. "Do you want me to have him call you back?"

Normally I would wait for him to get back to me when he has a break between patients, but not today.

"It's important," I say.

When Jerry answers the phone, I don't even attempt to soften the message.

"They found Jacob's hockey jacket," I manage to choke out.

"I'll be right there."

He's home within ten minutes. All we can do is stare painfully at each other and try to keep breathing while we wait for another call.

Julie calls again around 2:15 and tells us they found bone fragments and some teeth. Something inside me shifts and I go somewhere else. I'm reminded of all the law enforcement trainings I've attended over the years, and suddenly I'm in response mode. Jacob's dental records are in the database. If they match, I know we could have answers in hours, not weeks or months. We know teeth are important.

My next instinct is to protect our family . . . and to protect Jacob.

"It's a crime scene now," I hear myself saying. "It's going to become public very quickly."

"Everyone here is in plain clothes and unmarked vehicles. It's all very low-key right now, but I can't guarantee it will stay like this forever. Do you want to come out and visit the site before it becomes known to the public?"

"Yes," we answer in unison.

"Steve and I can meet you in Paynesville and bring you over to the site. They want a little more time to keep digging, so how about in an hour?"

Jerry and I drive the thirty-eight minutes to Paynesville. We leave our car at a gas station and hop into the car with Julie and Steve. They inform us our visit is breaking protocol and is causing some disagreement among the agencies involved at the site, but both Julie and Steve strongly feel we deserve a private moment at the spot where Jacob is buried before the public finds out.

It's a short drive to the site, which, thankfully, doesn't look like a crime scene at all. It's a beautiful farm field with cows and calves in the pasture. There are no squad cars. If anything, the group looks like they're helping to put in a new drain field or septic tank.

As we pull into the long gravel driveway, I notice five young boys playing football in the front yard of the farmhouse. Their voices transport me back to the days when Jacob and Trevor would play football with all their friends from the neighborhood. It's all so perfectly innocent, and the boys' laughter strengthens me.

Steve parks the car and we step out. Standing between us and the dig site is Sheriff Sanner, along with Captain Pam Jensen, Shane Ball, and Ken McDonald . . . all in shirts and jeans. I've never seen them like this.

My legs buckle as we start making our way over to them. Steve and Julie grab hold of me and offer their support as we continue walking. They explain that Sheriff Sanner has pulled Pam Jensen out of retirement and deputized her so she could be here today and help finalize the case. As we finally reach them, Steve and Julie graciously step aside to let us be alone with our people . . . the ones who have helped us search so long and so hard.

"It's over," Sheriff Sanner says, his eyes welling up with tears. "We found Jacob." He releases a huge sob, and tears stream down my face as he reaches out to give me a strong hug.

I can see Pam is torn apart too.

"I'm so sorry, Patty," is all she can muster.

Our tears continue to flow as we turn to look toward the site.

The forensic agents with the BCA look up at us briefly. Like the others, they're all wearing regular clothes—T-shirts, jeans, and jackets. No one driving by could possibly imagine the reality of what was unfolding under this peaceful grove of trees, or the gruesomeness it represented for all of us.

"Jacob's jacket was by that first tree," the sheriff says, pointing.

"We don't have a lot yet, but we'll be sending the bones and teeth to the BCA lab this afternoon."

I glance around and find a moment's peace in these beautiful and tranquil surroundings. It's just an idyllic little farm in central Minnesota . . . where a young couple is raising their five young boys, tending to their cattle, growing their crops, and leading happy, innocent lives. All of this is in such stark contrast to the developing crime scene and the heavy air that hangs over us.

"We shouldn't stay," I say firmly as I watch the BCA agents focus on their work. "They really don't want us here."

I can feel it . . . how hard it must be for them to separate their own emotions from the task at hand. They're just doing their jobs, but I realize most of them are probably parents themselves. We've been here only about five minutes, but that's enough. I don't need to see any more.

"Thank you," I say. "Let's go."

Steve and Julie drop us off at our car, and we start heading home.

"We have to tell the kids," I say to Jerry.

He pulls off on a side street, and we call them. They're at work, so we ask them to go home or find someplace private. We'll call back in a few minutes.

Jerry sets up a group call, and we break the news as gently as we possibly can.

"We just came from a farm near Paynesville," he says. "They found Jacob's hockey jacket . . . and some bones and teeth."

All five of us join in uncontrollable sobbing, a chorus of the deepest pain imaginable.

We tell Trevor he needs to come home as soon as possible. The US attorney is still pushing to have the first hearing on Friday. That's in two days.

We beg them not to tell anyone except their spouses.

"We can't let it leak, or the deal may go out the window," Jerry tells them. "Heinrich still hasn't signed the plea agreement. We'll call as soon as we hear anything more."

"We're so sorry," I add, crying again. "He's gone. Jacob is gone . . . "

{ Chapter 54 }

Day 3, Thursday, September 1, 2016

Jerry is at his office by 8:00 AM. I'm much slower to get going, especially today. It will be another long day of waiting and talking to no one. The thought of facing another day like yesterday is too much to bear. Maybe coffee will help. I swing my feet onto the floor and—once again—make the conscious decision to get out of bed.

As I head to the kitchen, my phone rings. It's Julie Allyn.

"Are you sure Jacob's name was on his jacket?" she asks.

Of course it was, I know this. But it's the way she's asking me—with doubt in her voice. It makes me pause and question my own memory.

"Yes . . ."

"Well, are you positive?" she asks. "Because the jacket they found doesn't have a name on it."

I pause, unsure how to process this.

"Just a minute. Let me go look at Trevor's."

I run down to the laundry room, where Trevor's red hockey jacket has been hanging for years. I check, and yes, his name is clearly stitched on the upper left chest of the jacket.

"They got them at the same time," I tell Julie. "I know the jackets are the same."

Still, Julie has her doubts. She wants further proof.

"I have a photo of Jacob wearing the jacket. I'll text it to you."

After we hang up, I find the picture of Jacob wearing the jacket while he proudly holds a fish he just caught. I take a photo with my cell phone, text it to Julie, and call her back right away to make sure she got it.

"Are you sure Jacob wasn't wearing someone else's jacket?" she asks me.

Now I'm exasperated.

"No, he *earned* that jacket, you know. He was so proud of it, and he wore *that* jacket all the time. He wouldn't have been wearing someone else's. He was wearing *that jacket* the night he was kidnapped, and it had his name on it."

"So, the reason this is important," she explains, "is because we just found out the teeth and the bones they found yesterday aren't human."

My heart stops.

What does *that* mean? Yesterday the sheriff told us, "It's over." Now Julie is telling us it's clearly *not* over. What's going on? How could this happen? It feels like everything is disintegrating.

I dial Jerry's office and give him the update.

"I can call a few of Jacob's old hockey buddies and ask if their names were stitched on their jackets," he offers.

I know he's just trying to be helpful, but I'm positive Jacob's name was stitched on his jacket. Now it feels like Jerry doesn't believe me either.

We hang up. An hour later, Jerry calls back to tell me he can't reach any of them. Whatever. It doesn't matter. I know Jacob's name was on that jacket.

Heinrich is supposed to be sitting down with the federal prosecutors today, late morning or early afternoon. According to the agreement he signed, this is when he's supposed to confess and tell them what happened the night he took Jacob. Everyone was hoping the court hearing could take place tomorrow, Friday, so Heinrich wouldn't have a chance to back out of the plea agreement, and we wouldn't have to carry this agony over the long Labor Day weekend. Now it all feels tenuous at best . . . like everything is hinging on whether Heinrich is telling the truth.

Julie calls again and tells me the interview with Heinrich got backed up but will still happen today—probably not until late this afternoon or evening.

"I'll keep you posted," she says.

I decide to go for a walk. As I pass the abduction site, I stop and talk to Jacob.

"Please, Jake, just give us some clues," I beg. "We need help."

I repeat this same trip several times throughout the day. In between trips, I try to do some cleaning and organizing, but there are simply not enough dirty dishes or overfilled closets for me to tackle on a day like today.

Finally, Jerry comes home from work and I have someone to talk to. We distract ourselves by fixing a meal that neither one of us feels like eating. Still, the phone doesn't ring. What's going on?

I hold out as long as I can before finally calling Andy Luger around midnight. I put my phone on speaker so Jerry can hear too.

"Hi Andy, it's Patty and Jerry. I'm sorry to call so late, but can you please tell us what's going on? Are they *still* talking to Heinrich?"

Luger tells us the interview with Heinrich didn't start until after 7:00 PM and had just concluded around 11:30 PM.

"I haven't received the report yet, so I don't have any details," he tells us. "The interview went long and late."

He offers to call us when he gets the report, but doesn't expect it to be done anytime soon.

"Would it be okay if I give you a call first thing in the morning?"

I'm so tired of this.

"That's fine," I tell him.

"The way things stand, the hearing definitely won't happen tomorrow," Andy says. "We're probably looking at Tuesday now, the day after Labor Day."

We hang up and get ready for bed, few words passing between us. I try to sleep, but my thoughts are consumed by dirt and digging, bones and teeth, stitching and hockey jackets.

Poor Jacob.

Damn you, Danny Heinrich.

{ Chapter 55 }

Day 4, Friday, September 2, 2016

Just before 8:00 AM, Jerry leaves for work and tells me to call him as soon I hear from Luger. He's only seeing a few patients and will be home shortly. We plan to leave for the Cities so we can be with our kids and grandkids. It's not long before my phone rings.

"I got the report and we're going back out to the dig site later this morning," Andy tells me. "Ken McDonald is working with the Stearns County Attorney's Office to get a second search warrant and a sealing order. We expect them to start digging again sometime before noon."

"Did they get more information from Heinrich?" I ask.

"Yes, he provided more details, so they're fairly certain they should have what they're looking for later today. They'll have a forensic anthropologist with them on site this time who can identify human remains, so we'll know right away."

I close my eyes . . . take a deep breath . . . exhale.

"When do we get to find out what Heinrich said?" I ask.

"I think the sheriff wants to meet with you. We'll know more later and try to set something up."

When Jerry comes home, I give him the latest update. There's nothing more we can do, so we each pack a bag and leave for St. Paul. Trevor and Trish arrived last night, and we're driving down to see them at Carmen and Kristian's.

It's a long, ominous drive. A little before 11:00 AM, we decide to call Joy to let her know what's happening. Even though we're desperate to keep this secret from getting out, Jerry and I both feel it's because of Joy and Jared that we've gotten this far.

I dial Joy's number and put her on speakerphone so Jerry can also hear.

"Hey Patty!" she answers in a cheerful voice. "How's it going?"

She's at work and completely unaware of what I'm about to tell her.

"Are you somewhere private where you can talk?" I ask.

She pauses. "Just a minute, let me shut my door."

When she comes back to the phone, I tell her that Jerry and I are in the car, headed to Carmen's.

"What's happening?" she asks.

"Heinrich agreed to a plea deal," I tell her.

She gasps, but says nothing.

"They interviewed him last night and he confessed," I tell her. "They're digging on a farm site in Paynesville right now."

We give her a shortened version of the past three days: the jacket, the bones, the teeth . . . the setbacks.

"Is this really it?" she asks.

"Yes," I tell her. "We're pretty sure this is it. You should go home. We'll call you as soon as we hear something."

"I'm so sorry," she says, crying.

I'm crying now too.

"I know. This is really hard. But we wanted you to know."

"Does Jared know?" she asks.

"We're not sure," Jerry replies. "Doug is keeping him up to date."

I can't imagine how it will feel for Jared to finally know that the guy who kidnapped and assaulted him is the same guy who killed Jacob. We're all worried for him.

Joy promises not to say anything, and I promise to call her as soon as we know anything more.

Next, I call Carmen to let her know we're on our way.

"How are you doing?" I ask her.

"Fine," she answers, her voice cold and dull.

"What's wrong?" I ask. She doesn't sound like herself.

"I can't do this anymore," she admits. "I can't carry this by myself. I need to talk to my friends. It's just too much."

I know exactly what she means. I can't do it either.

"It's just so hard to put on a smiley face and act like nothing's wrong when my insides are being cut apart," she says through tears.

"I know," I agree through my own tears. "Just try to hang in there. We should be there in about an hour, and we'll figure out what to do."

"Okay," she replies in that flat monotone.

"See you in a bit. I love you."

I can't stand how this is affecting my kids. I realize they're all grown adults now, but to me, in this moment, they're still thirteen, ten, and eight. More than anything, I just want to absorb all their pain and take it away.

By the time we get to Carmen's, we're grateful to see our friends Nancy and Bill have arrived. They only know a little of what's going on, but they know we need help. They've offered to stay with the grandkids so we can have some adult time to talk and plan. Maizie and Belle love Nancy and Bill, and I'm so relieved to have them there.

As soon as I see Trevor, I walk over and give him a big hug, but it's not his usual warm response. I immediately sense his steeliness. He's angry, and I can tell he's trying hard to hold it together so he doesn't break down in front of everybody. I want to ask him how he's doing, but I'm afraid of what he might say. "Compared to what? Normal people?" Or "How am I supposed to feel when I know there are people digging for my brother's bones right now?"

When Amy and Chris arrive, Lili and Izzi join Maizie and Belle inside while the rest of us jump in our cars and drive to Battle Creek Park in Maplewood. It's a crisp, sunny fall day, darkened only by the reason we're there. We find a picnic table at the top of a hill and pray no one else will come near us.

We chat briefly to get a feel for how they're doing, then we update them with everything we know. Jerry and I share the fiasco of the previous day— how none of the bones or teeth were human, and how Jacob's name wasn't on his jacket. We tell them they're back at the dig site right now, but so far, we haven't heard anything.

Trevor is the first one to speak.

"We have to tell Aaron."

"And Rochelle," Amy adds.

"And Shannon," Carmen says.

I agree. "But please tell them they absolutely *have* to keep this quiet. They can't share with anyone. There's just too much at stake."

Aaron, Rochelle, and Shannon have all been on this journey with us since day one, and we know we can trust them. Aaron was with the boys that night. Rochelle was babysitting Carmen when it happened. And Shannon, our live-in babysitter for many years, is like a big sister to our kids and a daughter to Jerry and me. They're all family.

Jerry and Trevor walk off to a corner of the field to call Aaron and his

parents, while Amy and Carmen head off in a different direction to call Rochelle and Shannon.

I stay at the picnic table with Chris, Trish, and Kristian. They're quiet,
and I wonder what they're thinking. They weren't there to experience everything we went through as a family back in 1989, but I get the sense they're
getting a feel for it now. Jacob's disappearance was truly the crime of the
century in Minnesota. For better or worse, by marrying into this family, our
children's spouses have become public figures, just like the rest of us. I can
see their angst, and aside from the worry they have for their partners, I know
they're also worried about their own kids. How will they tell them? How can
they possibly explain this in a way that makes sense and doesn't scare them?
I wish I could take that away too.

When everyone returns to the picnic table, Jerry and I walk off to call our
siblings while the kids stay and talk. Thankfully, we're able to stay in the park
undisturbed for a couple of hours. When we can't think of anything more to
say, we get in our cars and make our way back to Carmen's. We try to distract
the grandkids with games of Crazy Eights and Candyland, and as afternoon
fades to evening, someone orders pizza for dinner. Still, there's no call.

Finally, around 5:30 PM, Sheriff Sanner calls. They found him. They're
sure this time. The forensic anthropologist has confirmed that the remains
are human. We also learn they found Jacob's soccer shirt with his favorite #11
and "Wetterling" on the back.

No amount of preparation could have possibly softened this blow. After
nearly twenty-seven years, we now know the horrible truth. Our son was
murdered.

{ Chapter 56 }

By the next morning, it's all over the news. Every major Twin Cities TV station is reporting that Jacob's remains have been found, and I'm receiving endless calls and texts from reporters asking me for confirmation.

I don't know what to do, so I call Doug Kelley. "I swear, it wasn't us," I tell him desperately. "We checked with everyone we told, and none of them said anything."

I'm worried the leak will somehow mess up Heinrich's plea agreement, but Doug manages to calm my jangled nerves. He's not sure when there will be an official announcement from the sheriff's department, but he tells me he'll make some calls.

My mind is racing a million miles an hour. We haven't even had a chance to tell our dearest friends, and now they're finding out through the media. Who talked? What if this messes up the plea deal? What if Heinrich backs out? But then . . . how can he back out if he's already confessed? I just don't want him to get off on some kind of technicality. I'm terrified, confused, and sick with worry.

I call Sheriff Sanner, then Andy Luger. They're still waiting for the report from the Ramsey County medical examiner. When that's complete, they'll put out some kind of statement. I get the sense there's some disagreement over who they think should do it—the SCSO, the FBI, the US Attorney's Office, or the BCA. Maybe I'm just being impatient and overly critical, but *what are they waiting for?*

The sadness is really sinking in for our family now. Every one of us has our own set of questions, but we don't ask them out loud for fear of planting more dark thoughts that hadn't been considered yet. Did he suffer? Did he die right away? What exactly happened? What did he say?

Doug calls back and we discuss our options. We decide to put out a very brief family statement, just so we can have a little time and privacy.

The first person I respond to is Caroline Lowe from KARE-11 news. She's covered Jacob's story with compassion and integrity from the very beginning, and I know I can trust her. "All I can confirm is that Jacob has been found and our hearts are broken. I am not responding to any media yet as I have no words."

Next, I dial Alison Feigh's cell number, knowing full well that JWRC is being barraged with calls. "I'm so sorry, Alison. We couldn't tell anyone."

"I know," she says, choking back tears.

Soon we're both crying. Alison—Jacob's classmate—has shared our hope through it all. At only thirty-eight, she has spent her entire adult life working with families of missing and exploited children and had helped us build our vision for the Jacob Wetterling Resource Center. Through our collective work, she knew the power of hope, but also the trauma that comes with answers. She has been through this with other families, but never has it been so personal or so painful.

Alison assures me she'll find a way to put aside her emotions and deal with whatever comes up. She helps me put together a short family comment for my Twitter feed, then reads me the statement she has been working on for JWRC's Facebook page. It's perfect, and by the end, we're both crying again. I'm so grateful for her.

We are in deep grief. We didn't want Jacob's story to end this way. In this moment of pain and shock, we go back to the beginning. The Wetterlings had a choice to walk into bitterness and anger or to walk into a light of what could be, a light of hope. Their choice changed the world.

This light has been burning for close to twenty-seven years. The spark began in the moments after the abduction of Jacob Wetterling, when his family decided that light is stronger than darkness. They lit the flame that became Jacob's Hope. All of Central Minnesota flocked to and fanned the flame, hoping for answers. The light spread state-wide, nationally, and globally, as hearts connected to the eleven-year-old boy who liked to play goalie for his hockey team, wanted to be a football player, played the trombone, and loved the times he spent with his sisters, brother, and parents.

Today, we gather around the same flame. The flame that has become more than the hope for one as it led the way home for thousands of others. It's the light that illuminates a world that Jacob believed in, where things are fair and just.

Our hearts are heavy, but we are being held up by all of the people who have been a part of making Jacob's Hope a light that will never be extinguished. It shines on in a different way. We are, and we will continue to be, Jacob's Hope.

Jacob, you are loved.

Now that the news is officially out, the outpouring of support comes rushing in. Jerry and I are staying at Chris and Amy's house in a suburb north of the metro. Slowly but steadily, friends and family have started to gather.

Our whole extended family is reeling. We've hung in there so tightly for all these years, bound by hope. Now that it's all come unraveled, we feel lost, unsteady, and vulnerable. We sit together in Amy's backyard and try to make small talk as we check our phones and try to gauge how the rest of the world is reacting to the stunning news.

Many news reporters are outside our home in St. Joe, and their reports show the flowers, cards, and gifts that have been placed at the end of our driveway. It's so surreal to see our house on TV knowing we're not there. Our neighbors assure Jerry and me it's best to stay away right now, and even though I know they're right, it still feels strange.

Finally, the BCA announces that the remains found yesterday are, indeed, Jacob's. The Ramsey County medical examiner, a forensic anthropologist, and a forensic odontologist all worked together on a Saturday to provide the expedited results. Later that evening, the SCSO confirms it but provides no further details, saying only that the BCA would be performing additional DNA testing and more information is expected next week.

As the evening wears on, Jerry and I really feel the need to go home. We have a bite to eat from all the generous offerings people have dropped off, share a few more tears and hugs, then make the one-hour drive back to St. Joseph. It's not until the final turn toward home that I notice all the porch lights. As we travel along 91st Avenue, past the neighborhoods, past the streetlights, past the abduction site, we can see that every single house has its porch light on for Jacob.

Jerry makes the turn into our little circle, and we're both relieved to see the news crews have gone home for the day. As he prepares to turn into our driveway, I catch my first glimpse of the mountain of flowers, cards, and gifts waiting for us.

I gasp and my eyes instantly fill with tears.

Oh, Jacob. You were so loved.

{ Chapter 57 }

Day 6, Sunday, September 4, 2016

I'm so tired. Deep-down, bone-weary, beyond-exhausted *tired*. It's the first night Jerry and I have slept in our own bed since Thursday, but we know we can't stay long. We need to get out of here before the media vans show up again.

I hear the front door open and realize it must be Jerry coming back from his morning walk. I check my phone: 7:00 AM. Sigh. Time to get up and figure out how to get through another day.

I pour myself a cup of coffee and stare at the stack of cards piled on the kitchen table. When Jerry and I arrived home last night, we parked the car in the garage, out of sight, then walked down the driveway to examine all the beautiful flowers and gifts that had been so lovingly placed there. We took the cards inside, but the rest we left untouched as a tribute to Jacob.

I start opening and reading the cards. Many are from neighbors and friends, while others are from people whose names I don't recognize. Did they know Jacob? Or are they simply kind strangers who have followed our journey and are now sharing in our pain? Whatever the case, I'm absolutely overcome by this show of support. To me, that pile of flowers and gifts at the base of our driveway represents almost twenty-seven years of collective hope, pain, and love.

By 8:30 AM, we're showered, re-packed, and ready to head back to the Cities. As we pull out of our driveway, I'm relieved to see there are no media vans lining our circle. I'm just not ready to talk. Not yet.

"Can we stop and pick up a paper?" I ask quietly, as we turn on to 91st Avenue. I'm not sure I'm ready to *read* the paper, but I want to see it, anyway. After being sequestered for the past week, I want to see what the rest of the world is seeing.

As we drive along 91st, I see that nearly every house still has its porch light on, even in broad daylight. At the stop sign, we turn left onto Minnesota Street, and there, tied to every single light post along St. Joe's main street, is a white ribbon, just like back in 1989 when Jacob was first kidnapped. My eyes fill with tears, and I stare in wonder and reverence, marveling at all the kindness that St. Joseph and its residents have shown us over the years. Throughout our very long search, Jacob became part of everyone's family, and today it's clear the grief can be felt all across town.

Jerry stops at a gas station, and I stay in the car while he runs inside to get a paper. When he returns, he's empty-handed.

"They're sold out," he tells me.

We head into St. Cloud and try another gas station, but they're sold out too. I shake my head at the absurdity of the two of us sneaking around trying to find a newspaper just so we can find out what the rest of the world already knows. Finally, we find a gas station that still has two copies of the *St. Cloud Times*. Jerry returns to the car with both of them.

"OUR HEARTS ARE BROKEN," the headline reads in huge letters. The picture underneath shows Jacob's smiling, innocent face—his fifth-grade school photo, the one I had to take down from the wall and give to investigators, the one where he's proudly wearing that yellow sweater he loved so much . . . the one people all over the country now know and recognize.

Jacob.

The first four pages are filled with stories about the discovery of his remains, the investigation, the timeline, the reaction of local residents. It's stunning to see it all laid out like this. The headlines jump off the pages, grab at my heart, send me back to October 1989, when the headlines were just as bold and heavy. Those long nights at home . . . waiting for the next newscast, waiting for the next edition of the paper, hoping to find out something more than we already knew. All that waiting . . . wondering . . . hoping . . . praying. I close the paper and shut my eyes.

I can suddenly feel myself sinking into that evil, dark abyss I barely escaped the first time around. I can feel it starting to seep into my soul, trying to freeze out my heart, but I won't let it. I will win this battle, I know I will. But right now, I just don't have it in me to fight the fight. Right now, I just have to make it through the day.

Jerry's sister, Anna, is hosting a Wetterling family picnic at her home in St. Paul. Invitations were sent out weeks ago, which now feels like a lifetime ago. When the news came out about Jacob, we discussed it with Anna and considered canceling it, but then decided maybe it was divine providence. We were all going through the same shock and sadness, so why not just get through it together as a family? Rather than isolate ourselves in sadness, we decided to share it with the ones who loved us most.

We arrive early to help set up, and by late afternoon, the backyard is packed with cousins, aunts, uncles, and a few close friends. The sadness and tension are palpable, and I'm starting to wonder if this was a good idea after all. Nobody knows what to say.

Our conversations are mostly filled with questions.

"What's going to happen next?"

"What will happen at the hearing on Tuesday?"

"When did you find out?"

Somehow we get through it, thanks in large part to Jerry's oldest sister, Judy. When she arrives, she asks Carmen to help fix her hair so it will stay off her face. Carmen agrees and mindlessly fixes Judy's hair in a side ponytail that matches Maizie's and Belle's. When Judy sees herself in the mirror, she suddenly gets the giggles and can't stop. Her laughter is so unexpected, so random and out of character, it seems to magically lift everyone's spirits. We continue to banter back forth about Judy's ponytail all day long, and though none of us can remember much else from the picnic, we all remember Judy's ponytail. It was as if her unexpected giggles gave us all permission to smile a bit.

We drive silently back to Carmen's house, then retreat to our quiet spaces and just try to prepare ourselves for another horrible day tomorrow.

Lili is lying on the couch, and I wonder what's going through her head. I know this is heavy for her. She's eleven, the same age Jacob was when he was kidnapped. She gets it, and no matter how much I want to take the hurt away from her, I can't.

I bend down to give her a hug, and she starts to sob.

I sit, wrap my arms around her, and hold her tight.

"It's okay, Lili. We'll be okay."

I wish I could protect her from all the darkness we've had to endure this past week and all that we'll face in the many weeks to come. I don't want her to feel that same debilitating fear my own kids had to live with. They were so young and so innocent, just like her. I so desperately wish I could take away the pain and the fear, but all I can do for Lili in this moment is just hold her and tell her how much I love her. Over, and over, and over.

"It's okay, Lili. We'll be okay."

{ Chapter 58 }

Day 7, Monday, September 5, 2016

It's Labor Day, Trevor's thirty-seventh birthday. We should be throwing him a party, with presents, balloons, cake, ice cream. Instead, we'll be heading to Doug Kelley's office again to find out what Danny Heinrich did to Jacob.

Doug requested this preview meeting from Andy Luger and Rick Thornton so we don't have to hear all the details for the first time in open court. They agreed and Sheriff Sanner has offered to summarize Danny Heinrich's confession for us.

Soon, all our questions will finally be answered. What brought Heinrich to St. Joseph? How did he come across the boys that night? Why them? Why that road? What happened? Why didn't he let Jacob go?

We're at Amy's again, still trying to dodge the media. Trevor and Trish are at Carmen's. I toss and turn for at least a half hour, then finally decide to just get up and go make some coffee. Maybe Jerry will at least get some rest.

I pour myself a cup of coffee, then start to cry. For the rest of his life, this is how Trevor will remember his thirty-seventh birthday. It's so unfair.

With trepidation, I reach for the remote and turn on the TV. In my strange and surreal new world, I see a national reporter from *CBS Morning News* standing in our driveway and reporting live outside our home in St. Joseph.

> As you can imagine, this has been an emotional few days for this small community. Grief, support for the Wetterlings . . . as well as an outpouring of support and *anger* over the fact that this suspect was questioned multiple times over the years, but never arrested in the disappearance of eleven-year-old Jacob Wetterling.

I turn off the TV, angry. She's wrong. He *was* arrested—way back in early 1990—but for Jared's kidnapping, not Jacob's. They surveilled him, arrested him, and questioned him. But when Jared couldn't pick him out of a lineup, they just didn't have enough evidence to hold him. And even if they did—even if they had somehow managed to bring Jacob's case to trial and find a jury to convict Heinrich with no body—we still wouldn't know where Jacob was. Would that have been better?

I put my coffee down and rub my face with my hands. I'm angry, edgy, defensive. And so, so tired.

Eventually the rest of the household awakens and the day officially begins. It's not long before everyone is pouring bowls of cereal, showering, checking their phones. No one says much.

Shortly after noon, Shannon arrives to watch Lili and Izzi and we make the thirty-minute drive downtown. As planned, we meet up with the rest of the group and take the elevator up to Doug's office. I'm grateful we're all together—Jerry and me, our kids, and Aaron. I draw a deep breath as we exit the elevator and walk through the doors of Kelley, Wolter and Scott.

As always, Doug is the calming force amid the chaos. He meets us with his kind eyes and warm smile, then escorts us back to a conference room just off the reception area. He has coffee, water, and bagels laid out for us, but no one is hungry.

We join Sheriff Sanner, Julie Allyn, and Steve Schleicher around the table.

"As you know," the sheriff begins, "Danny Heinrich was interviewed on Thursday evening, September 1, at which time he gave us the information needed to find Jacob. Throughout the long interview that followed, he gave a detailed account of what happened the night Jacob was kidnapped."

He continues to talk, but I manage to grasp only small snippets of what he's describing.

Heinrich gave no particular reason as to why he chose St. Joe that night. He was just out searching for a young boy to molest.

He drove around until he spotted an opportunity. He saw the boys biking on their way to the Tom Thumb store and decided they must have come from up the hill.

He drove up 91st Avenue and turned left down a gravel road. It turned out to be a farm driveway, so he turned around and headed back toward the road. When he neared the end of the driveway, he parked his car so it wasn't visible from the road. Then, he got out and waited.

Shortly after, he saw the boys coming slowly up the road. With his gun drawn, he walked out onto the road and told them to stop.

"Get off of your bikes and lay down in the ditch or I'll shoot."

He told Trevor, "Put out the flashlight."

He let two of them go, then put handcuffs on Jacob.

"What did I do wrong?" Jacob asked.

He kept walking and pushing Jacob along to his car. He put him in the front seat and told him to duck down so nobody would see him.

He turned right out of the driveway, made his way to County Road 75, then headed west. He got on I-94 heading west toward Albany, then turned off and took some back roads to Paynesville . . . familiar territory.

When he got to Paynesville, he drove to a gravel pit and made Jacob get out of the car. He told him to take his clothes off, then he sexually molested him.

By this time, we're all sobbing uncontrollably.
Still, the sheriff continues.
"Stop!" I yell. "Can't you hear the tears? Give us a moment to breathe."
We pass tissues around as we try to collect ourselves. The heaviness of the silence feels like we might crash through all twenty-five floors, down to the basement.
"Okay," I say, finally. "Go on."

When it was over, Jacob said he was cold and Heinrich told him he could get dressed.

Jacob got dressed and asked, "Can I go home now?"

I break down again. All these years, I had begged to hear Jacob's voice, his last words, and now here they are, as vivid as imaginable. My tears sting and my chest hurts, but still, the sheriff continues.

Heinrich said, "No. I can't take you home."

He saw a police car go by with its lights on and sirens off, heading east toward Cold Spring. He told Jacob he had to take a piss and made him turn around.

Jacob was crying as he turned away.

He pulled a revolver out of his pocket and loaded it with two rounds. He raised the gun to Jacob's head and pulled the trigger. It clicked but didn't go off.

He pulled the trigger again. It went off, but Jacob didn't fall. He raised the revolver and shot him again. This time, he fell.

I stop the sheriff again. Everyone is sobbing uncontrollably. The air feels heavy, thick, and I'm having trouble catching my breath. I have no idea how much time goes by before we're finally able to listen again.

After shooting Jacob, Heinrich left and went home. After a couple hours, he walked back to the gravel pit to bury him. He brought a shovel, but it was too small, and he realized it would take too long. He knew there was a construction company nearby, so he walked over there and saw a Bobcat. He knew where they hid the key, so he started it up, drove it back to the gravel pit, dug a hole, put Jacob in, threw his jacket on top of him, and covered him up.

Then he walked back home.

About a year later, he went back to the gravel pit and caught a glimpse of something red.

Jacob's red hockey jacket had been pulled up to the surface by growing brush in the gravel pit. He went back that night and dug him up. Then he put Jacob's remains in a garbage bag, carried him across the highway to that rural farm property, and buried him under a grove of trees.

This pain is unlike anything I've ever known. My precious Jacob . . . my first-born son . . . the one I labored so hard to deliver, hugged through a million owies, took to the doctor for whooping cough, stitches, and a broken arm . . .

the child I cuddled, rocked, and soothed by rubbing his back until he settled down. I wasn't there when he needed me. I couldn't protect him. No words can ever describe how badly I hurt after hearing what happened. How Jacob asked what he did wrong. How he was sexually assaulted, and shot. How he just wanted to go home.

I don't know what to do with it . . . where to put it, how to make sense of it . . . how to survive it. In this moment, I don't even know how to think or breathe or stand.

I do know one thing for certain. I will never be the same again.

{ Chapter 59 }

Day 8, Tuesday, September 6, 2016

Yesterday was too much. We're still reeling from everything we just heard, and now we have to go through it all over again—this time, in a public court-room. By the end of today, the whole world will know what Danny Heinrich did.

Somehow, I need to make it through this day. One more breath, one more day.

The hearing starts at 1:00 PM at the federal courthouse in downtown Minneapolis. They expect a packed courtroom, so we were asked to submit a list of friends and family who will be attending so they can reserve seats. Jerry's sisters will be there, along with my siblings and their spouses. We've also included Jerry's cousin and his son; Aaron's parents; our good friends Bill, Nancy, Donna, and Kevin; our former neighbor Scottie and her daughter, Rochelle; Alison and Jane from the JWRC office; Shannon; and Joy. Jared has his own list and will also be there. These are the people who have been with us on this journey, and I know we'll gain strength from them.

My heart hurts for Jared, because I know he feels left out of this plea deal. But at least Danny Heinrich will be on the public record admitting that he was the man who assaulted Jared on January 13, 1989.

As I sip my coffee, I also gain strength by reading the comments on a Facebook post Alison put out yesterday. She called us not long after that devastating meeting at Doug's office.

"Everyone is calling and asking what they can do to help. Is there anything I can tell them?"

Honestly, there wasn't one single thing I could think of that would help me feel better. I appreciated her asking, but what could possibly help when our whole world had just been shattered? We were about to hang up when I had a thought.

"Wait," I said. Out of nowhere, I started spitting out a list. "Tell them to say a prayer, light a candle, be with friends, play with their children, giggle, hold hands ... "

"Eat ice cream?" Alison suggested.

I smiled. "Yes, eat ice cream. Create joy, help your neighbor ... "

It was a testament to the world Jacob knew, to the world we all knew before he was stolen from us. Deep down in my soul, I wanted that world back. If I could convince people to do these things in Jacob's memory, I knew it would bring me comfort.

I check the time. It's almost 9:00 AM.

As I get dressed, I pull my official black suit out of the closet, put on the skirt, then pause and rethink. I don't want to wear black. What would Jacob want me to wear? I put the black jacket back on the hanger and pull out my turquoise one instead. It's a bright, cheerful color, probably not appropriate for today's proceedings, but at this point, I really don't care. Blue is Jacob's favorite color.

We've been staying at Amy's the past two nights. Amy, Chris, Jerry, and I ride to Carmen's house in St. Paul, where we meet her, Kristian, Trevor, Trish, Aaron, and his wife, Renee. Then we pile into two vans, navigate to Minneapolis without losing each other, and park together in the private ramp they've reserved for us. Normally this ramp is reserved for judges in the federal courthouse, but today they're allowing us to use it so we can avoid having to walk past all the cameras and reporters lined up at the public entrance. Our security detail marches us up the ramp like a line of schoolchildren, directing us to a private set of elevators. We're taken to the fourteenth floor, then guided to a stark, no-nonsense conference room where we sit and wait. Jared and Doug join us shortly after, and once again I'm grateful for Doug's calm and commanding presence.

Around noon, US District Judge John Tunheim enters the room. Doug has arranged this meeting for us so the judge could introduce himself ahead of time and take us through the courtroom. He's patient and compassionate as he explains what will happen, then he invites us on a brief tour so we'll have a better idea of what to expect. As we enter the courtroom through a door behind the witness stand, he points out the first two rows and explains that's where we'll take our seats after everyone else has been seated. We practice sitting in our spots, then rearrange ourselves so we know how to line up before entering.

Next, he points to a door on the left side of the courtroom and explains that's where Danny Heinrich will enter, along with his defense attorneys. He shows us where they will sit, where our family and friends will sit, and where the federal prosecutors will sit. Media people will fill up most of the remaining seats, and a separate gallery has been designated for overflow. Although no cameras are allowed in the courtroom, the reporters will most likely be texting and live-tweeting as the hearing unfolds, so word will get out immediately. Unfortunately, there's no way around this, he tells us.

After answering our questions, Judge Tunheim ushers us back to the conference room, where we're forced to wait again. I make my way to the bathroom, and as I lock the door behind me, I catch a glimpse of myself in the mirror. My eyes are tired and dull, and I feel like I've acquired a whole new set of wrinkles over the past eight days. As I stare at the old woman in the mirror, I suddenly recall that dream I had about six years earlier: I was pushing Jacob in a wheelchair and running as fast as I could because someone was chasing us. At one point, Jacob looked back at me, and with a surprised look on his face, he asked, "Mom, when did you get so old?"

I wonder about that now as I stare at my reflection in the mirror. Maybe the dream was some kind of premonition . . . some hint as to how long our search would drag on. I don't remember if I replied to him in the dream, but right now, in this moment, I just want to give him my answer.

"Jacob, I got old on the day you were taken from us. I may be sixty-six now, but as of today, I'm officially twenty-six years, eight months, and six days of *old*."

One more breath, one more day.

I put on some lipstick, take one last look, then walk out to join the others.

Approximately five minutes before 1:00 PM, one of the US marshals brings us into the judge's chambers, and we line up in the order we practiced. As the door opens in front of us, we file into the courtroom in complete silence. Aaron and Renee lead the way, followed by Carmen, Kristian, Trevor, Trish, Amy, Chris, Jerry, me, Doug, and Jared. Before I sit down, I turn and see all our beloved friends and family staring back at us. They all look so scared, and I'm worried for all they're about to hear. Please God, help us through this.

All rise.

We stand as Judge Tunheim enters the courtroom and takes his place behind the bench.

You may be seated.

We sit like this, barely breathing, for at least two minutes. Finally, the side door opens, and Danny Heinrich enters. In the dead and eerie silence, it suddenly feels like all the air has been sucked out of the room.

I glance over at Aaron and Trevor and try to gauge their reaction as they catch their first glimpse of this man who has haunted their thoughts for so long. Trevor flinches, ever so slightly, and I wonder if he recognizes Heinrich's distinct walk. I wish I could reach out and hold him, but I can see Trish holding his hand tightly and I know he's in good hands.

I turn back and watch as Heinrich shuffles slowly to his seat, gaze down, shoulders slumped. He looks pathetic, weak, defeated, and much older than his fifty-three years.

As Heinrich finally reaches his seat, Judge Tunheim begins the proceedings.

"Good afternoon. This is Criminal Case Number 15–340, United States of America versus Danny James Heinrich. We are here today for a change of plea."

After a few formalities and introductions, we finally get to hear Danny Heinrich's voice for the first time.

"Mr. Heinrich, how are you doing today?"

"All right, Your Honor."

It's not at all the deep, gravelly voice we'd heard about for so many years. Instead, Heinrich responds in a nasally monotone that seems devoid of personality or compassion.

Heinrich's defense lawyers hand him the plea agreement, and for several long, painful minutes, the whole court waits as he takes his time reading through it.

Just sign it.

The tension in the room grows. It's thick and palpable.

JUST SIGN IT.

Finally, Heinrich signs the plea agreement. He hands it to his lawyer, and she hands it to the judge.

I take a deep breath and exhale. It's done. This is the moment that finally frees us from having to carry this whole experience on our own. No more secrets. Now the whole world will know what he did.

Assistant US Attorney Steve Schleicher leads the questioning. After several questions regarding Heinrich's age, residence, former places of employment, and other mundane matters, he finally gets to the plea agreement and the confession.

In that flat monotone, Danny Heinrich answers questions about the child pornography they found in his home—how he collected and morphed the images, adding heads of classmates from his junior high yearbooks to the bodies of naked children he found on the internet.

Steve Schleicher then asks him about a particular image showing a minor female with long, curly, brown hair. It's from Count 24 of the indictment— the one count of child pornography he's being convicted on.

As Steve goes on to describe this image in more graphic detail, my mom-gut reels with pain and disgust for all that was happening to the poor little girl in that picture. I pray she can feel some sense of justice now.

When Steve is confident he has provided sufficient evidence to the court to convict Heinrich on the one count of child pornography, he gets right to it.

"Sir, as part of the plea agreement, you understand that you're providing a factual accounting for what happened to Jacob Wetterling on October 22, 1989, is that right?"

"That's right."

"On October 22, 1989, did you kidnap, sexually assault, and murder Jacob Wetterling?"

"Yes, I did."

Heinrich shares in horrific detail all the agonizing testimony we heard the day before. My heart shatters into a million pieces as I hear my kids choking back sobs, and I lean tighter into Jerry as I also hear the gasps, groans, and sobs from all our loved ones sitting behind us. Even the reporters have tears in their eyes as they struggle to keep up with all of Heinrich's responses.

When they finally finish with Jacob's portion of the confession, Steve Schleicher moves on to Jared's portion.

"Now, on January 13, 1989, did you in Cold Spring, Minnesota, Stearns County, abduct and sexually assault Jared Scheierl?"

"Yes, I did."

There's a noticeable shift, as if the people in the room can hardly bear to hear any more. And yet, we do. Again, in horrifying detail, we're forced to listen to how Jared was kidnapped, sexually assaulted, and then—for reasons we'll probably never understand—let go.

I don't know how Steve Schleicher manages to keep his poise as he continues to question Heinrich, but he has to get everything they need in the record. This is extremely important. Because Heinrich is being sentenced to only twenty years for the one pornography charge, it's crucial to get his confessions to the other crimes. With two child abductions, two child sexual assaults, and Jacob's murder on the record, it's highly likely he'll be deemed a continued threat and be civilly committed to the Minnesota Sex Offender Program for further incarceration and treatment. This is so important to me. More than anything, I just don't want him to get out so he can harm another child.

After Steve Schleicher finishes his questioning, the rest of the court process is pretty straightforward. The judge sets a sentencing date for November 21, and suddenly, it's over.

All rise.

We stand again as Judge Tunheim leaves the courtroom. As Heinrich is being led away by the bailiffs, we leave the same way we came, out the door behind the witness stand, through the judge's chambers, and back to the conference room, where we all collapse around the large table.

Doug comes in and asks if we're interested in making a statement to the press. They have a room set up downstairs and are having a joint press conference with representatives from the SCSO, FBI, BCA, and the US Attorney's Office.

The thought of standing in front of a bunch of cameras right now is completely overwhelming to me.

"What do you think?" I ask him.

"I think if you want to say something, you should," Doug tells me.

I'm not sure I have it in me to give any kind of coherent statement, but with everyone's encouragement, I finally agree.

Our whole group files down to the conference room together, and after we take our seats, the press conference begins. Andy Luger takes the podium first, followed by Sheriff Sanner. Both talk about the long and arduous process of getting to this point: the investigation, the collaboration, the negotiation. There are many people to thank, and they do.

Then it's my turn to speak.

Jerry, Amy, Carmen, Trevor, and Aaron follow me to the front and stand behind me as I take my place at the podium. I have nothing but some hastily scribbled notes in front of me, so I try to speak from my heart. I want to take the focus off this awful man and put it back on Jacob.

I also want to thank everybody that has been thanked—the sheriff; Stearns County Attorney Janelle, thank you; the BCA; the FBI; the US Attorney's Office; Julie and Steve; the defense attorneys who worked out the deal.

And I have to say a heartfelt thanks to the National Center for Missing and Exploited Children. They do this work every day. They find missing children, and without them, I wouldn't be functional.

I also want to thank the Jacob Wetterling Resource Center. In his name, we've been doing prevention messages for a very long time, and that work will continue.

And I also want to just say . . . to all of you . . . the media . . . you play a huge role in finding missing children. You've been with us for twenty-six years. I view many of you as friends, and I'm incredibly grateful for the kindness that you've extended to our family, and the integrity of your reports. Thank you.

What I really wanted to say today is about Jacob. He's taught us all how to live, how to love, how to be fair, how to be kind—he speaks to the world that he knew, that we all believe in, and it is a world that is worth fighting for. His legacy will go on.

I want to say, Jacob, I'm so sorry. It's incredibly painful to know his . . . last hours, last minutes.

I couldn't do this without my family. I'm proud, so proud, of the lives that they've built and the happiness they've found, and the children and grandchildren that we so enjoy. That is the world. That is what gets us up in the morning. That *is* the hope. That *is* Jacob's Hope. That *is* what we're going to continue to do.

I also want to say one huge shout-out to Jared and Joy. Jared had the courage to stand up and say, "This happened to me, and there are others." And they found the others, and they talked to those others, and many of them will never get that full confession. Maybe it was Heinrich, and maybe it was somebody else, but we know he had other victims. They deserve so much credit for stirring this pot until he was willing to talk. Thank you.

We love you, Jacob. We will continue to fight. Our hearts are hurting. I would love to talk to you all, but I'm just not ready yet.

Because for us, Jacob was alive . . . until we found him.

We need to heal, and we will speak with you. There are a lot of lessons learned, and there is a lot more work to do to protect all of our world's children.

Thank you.

I'm crying as I finish, and Trevor wraps me in a huge hug as we make our way back to our seats.

Jared takes the podium next, and I'm so proud of him, for all he's endured and the strong man he's become. He's a survivor, a friend, and now an advocate for other victims of childhood assault.

Together, we did it. All of us. And though I have nothing left to give right now, I'm just so grateful for all these good people who came together to make this happen.

Someday, I hope to be able to find some peace with all of this, but today is not that day. Today, Jacob, I am just so very, very sorry.

{ Chapter 60 }

The world was suddenly very dark.

My heart, my soul ached for Jacob. All these years, I had so longed to wrap my arms around him again, to hear the sweetness of his voice, to hold him, to breathe in the smell of his sweaty head after a neighborhood football game. My hope was so real, I could still hear him playing with Trevor, cheering on the Vikings, or trying to convince me to buy him a new pair of Nikes. I could still hear his voice.

Jacob.

I couldn't stop saying his name. It was a prayer and a sob. It had all ended so abruptly. After twenty-six years of hoping and praying, it was all over in eight days. Yes, we finally got our answers, but how was this any better? People kept saying they were happy for us because we finally had "closure," but it wasn't like that at all. I hated that word, *closure*—as if we were just supposed to check this off our list and go back to being the people we were twenty-seven years ago.

How would we *ever* move forward? For the rest of our lives, we would have to live with the horrors of Jacob's final hours. Kidnapped at gunpoint. Handcuffed. Driven to a dark gravel pit in the middle of nowhere. Forced to strip down. Sexually assaulted.

He was cold and scared. He begged to go home.

Instead, he was shot. Twice.

Bang.

Bang.

I could both hear and *feel* those shots as they emptied the life out of my son. I could feel the coldness as he was buried in the ground. I dropped to the floor in tears, heaving in sadness. I had failed. I had failed to keep my son safe, and now he was gone. What kind of mother does that? How would

I ever be able to look at myself in the mirror without seeing that image of Jacob crying and begging to go home?

I could feel his fear, his pain, his humiliation, his sadness. I shuddered every time I thought of those gunshots. I hated guns and never let my boys have even plastic ones. Now I sobbed in agony over the image of Jacob being shot a second time because his body didn't drop after the first shot. I tried desperately to make it better for him . . . praying that my son's wonderful spirit had already left his body before those horrible, violent bullets pierced through him. This gave me some sense of calm, knowing that God was with him and lifted him away so he wouldn't hurt any more.

Still, I struggled to make sense of it. In my heart I knew it wasn't God who had caused my son's death, but this did nothing to lessen my struggle.

I spent nearly twenty-seven years trying to find Jacob, praying for his safety and believing, *hoping,* he could be alive. I couldn't help but feel a sense of futility. Jacob was killed that first night, so what was the purpose of this life that I had built around hope? Why, God? What was the point?

And what about Amy, Trevor, and Carmen? How would they survive this? How could I possibly soften the terror of the past week? Would they ever be able to look back on being thirteen, ten, and eight with a sense of safety, security, and love? Would they ever find happiness again? How long would it take? What could I possibly do to make it happen?

I wished I could think of something wise and heartfelt to say that would provide some comfort for them, but I had no words. We were all alone in our own pain. Coping. Processing. Remembering. Mourning. Screaming in agony.

I had tried so hard to be a good mom, always making sure our kids felt loved and cared for. I knew I had a million happy memories buried in me somewhere, but right now, I could only focus on the darkest of the dark. I kept hearing the sheriff describe what happened that night. I kept hearing that horrible man as he said his empty words in court. He had no spirit, no regret. He was just cold, pathetic, and hollow.

I had worked so hard to convince myself of possibilities. Maybe Jacob had escaped but was living in fear of someone harming his family. Maybe he'd built a life separate from us in order to protect us. I knew Elizabeth Smart was threatened, told by her captor that he would harm her sister if she ever tried to escape. I knew Jaycee Dugaard had stayed with her captors to protect her own children who were born in captivity. I knew Shawn Hornbeck had been taken out one night and nearly killed by his captor, but he'd begged for his life and promised to never leave. All of them had survived. I wanted to believe Jacob had too.

I didn't even know who I was anymore. All these years, I had lived on hope. I had also represented hope for other searching families. When I spoke, I could always speak directly to other parents about staying positive, never giving up, and focusing on the hope. But where was hope now? How would they see me now? How would *anyone* see me now? I never wanted to be a sad story, but here I was. The reality was sinking in and despair was settling into my soul. I was just so deeply, profoundly, agonizingly . . . *sad*.

Nearly twenty-seven years of work was tumbling down into a big heap of nothingness. I wanted to crawl under it and disappear.

My life felt wasted.

I'm sorry, Jacob. I tried, but I failed.

I'm sorry, Trevor, for the pain and suffering you had to endure for two-thirds of your life.

I'm sorry, Amy. At thirteen, you were forced to grow up so fast. I couldn't shield you from all the horrors we had to face throughout the years. I relied on your help with everything, instead of just letting you be a teenager.

I'm sorry, Carmen. You called back your imaginary friends to help find Jacob. You told us Ahbee and Ahbba lived in his footsteps wherever he went. I hope you still find some comfort in believing that. Jacob was not alone that horrible evening.

I'm sorry, Jerry, for being the most difficult person in the world to live with. My rage at times, my passion for what I was doing, my commitment to never stop . . . all for nothing. You maintained your focus and your work despite my outbursts—another missing child, another child found deceased, another coach or priest or teacher found guilty of assaulting a child. It was always too much for me to swallow. You somehow learned not to breathe it all in, but I never did. Thank you for being my rock.

Hope had been my lifeblood for so long and without it, there was nothing. I was lost, empty, depleted. And this time, I didn't know if I would ever find my way back.

{ Chapter 61 }

I believe there's a greater power that guides us through life. It's bigger than anything we could possibly imagine, and it carries us through the darkness until we can find some tiny flicker that continues to grow until it guides us back to the light.

That's what happened next.

It all began with a text to Alison Feigh. On that most devastating of all days, the day Heinrich confessed in open court, Alison was just leaving the courthouse when she received a text from a friend of hers at NCMEC: "What was Jacob's soccer jersey number? My nephew and his teammates want to wear his number on their faces when they play their game tonight. Do you think that would be okay?"

Alison called to get our reaction, and her excitement was contagious. A smile from somewhere deep in my heart began to grow at the thought of all those little kids wearing Jacob's favorite number on their faces.

"I love it," I told her.

When Alison and Jane got back to the JWRC office, they expanded the idea. If kids wanted to wear Jacob's jersey number, they felt it should stand for something. They came up with a long list of traits that exemplified the way Jacob had lived his life, then sent it to Jerry and me to help pare it down. Together, we picked the top eleven traits we felt best captured Jacob's spirit.

1. *Be fair*
2. *Be kind*
3. *Be understanding*
4. *Be honest*
5. *Be thankful*
6. *Be a good sport*
7. *Be a good friend*

8. Be joyful
9. Be generous
10. Be gentle with others
11. Be positive

The next day, Alison used social media to spread the word. She put out a post on JWRC's Facebook page and encouraged people to honor Jacob by wearing his jersey number, 11. She also challenged people to help make the world a better place for kids by making a commitment to live out the eleven traits that Jacob stood for. She included the hashtag #11forJacob and encouraged people to share their photos to show how they were living these eleven traits.

In a matter of hours, the #11forJacob movement went viral, and photos came flooding in from everywhere.

Kids were using duct tape to put the #11 on the backs of their shirts.

They added #11 stickers and patches to their helmets and jerseys.

A volleyball team from Princeton wrote each of the traits on their forearms in black magic marker.

A football team from Marshall walked hand in hand onto the field as they carried their team's #11 jersey between them.

Hundreds of students and faculty in Belle Plaine wore blue and gathered in their school gym to form the number 11 for an overhead photo.

A police department from Shakopee wrote #11 on the backs of their hands.

A group of federal legislators in Washington, DC, stood in front of the US Capitol, and each held a sign with one of the eleven traits.

And the movement continued to grow. The next day, Alison received a call from the Minnesota Twins, who wanted to remember Jacob by wearing a special patch for their September 9 home game against the Cleveland Indians. It was a simple red circle with a red "11" inside and the name "Jacob" underneath. Both teams wore the patches, and the Twins also wore special red jerseys that were auctioned off after the game to benefit the Jacob Wetterling Resource Center. The patches stayed on their jerseys for the remainder of the season and became the unofficial logo for the #11forJacob movement.

The Minnesota Vikings soon followed suit and invited our family to join them for their inaugural game against the Green Bay Packers at the new U.S. Bank Stadium on September 18. We weren't sure if we were ready to attend such a big, high-profile event, but they assured us we would be sitting in the owner's booth, out of the public eye. It was a once-in-a-lifetime opportunity, and we knew Jacob would want us to go, so we went. Aaron also joined us, and it felt so good to just watch football and be happily distracted for a bit. The Vikings gave a lovely tribute to Jacob during the game and also encouraged fans to make $11 donations to JWRC via text as Jacob's eleven traits were posted on the scoreboard.

The Minnesota Gophers, the Timberwolves, the Lynx . . . all did special tributes.

A few weeks later, on October 15, 2016, the Minnesota Wild gave an incredibly moving tribute at their home opener at Xcel Energy Center. Before the game, we were invited to meet Zach Parise, the team's star forward. Zach grew up in Minnesota and wore #11 for the Wild. He knew Jacob's story well and just wanted to let us know how much it had impacted him growing up. He presented us with an $11,000 check for the Jacob Wetterling Resource Center, from him and his wife, Alisha. We were all so touched by their kindness and generosity.

At the Wild game later that evening, we were once again treated to a private booth and were happy to be joined by Jared and his family, as well as Joy and her husband, Ross. Just before the game started, our family was invited onto the ice and we were each given an official Wild jersey with the number 11 on the back. As the announcer read each of Jacob's eleven traits, we took turns turning the jerseys around to reveal the "name" on the back: Fair, Kind, Understanding, Honest, Thankful, Good Sport, Good Friend, Joyful, Generous, Gentle, Positive. By the time the last jersey was turned, the entire crowd was on its feet, honoring Jacob with a standing ovation.

As the days and weeks passed, the 11 movement just continued to grow and grow. For eleven days, the I-35W bridge in downtown Minneapolis was lit blue in Jacob's memory. The Ordway Theater displayed a lighted "11" on their building in downtown St. Paul. The Guthrie Theater in Minneapolis displayed the message "11 for Jacob" on their towering vertical marquee.

It was all absolutely breathtaking.

Yet, for all those big tributes that were so amazing and moving, there were also the smaller, more grassroots efforts that really made my heart swell.

A couple from St. Joseph paid to have mile markers installed along a twelve-mile stretch of the Lake Wobegon Trail, each displaying one of the eleven traits. The final sign says "Jacob's Hope Lives," and I feel him come alive in my heart every time I see it while biking the trail.

Kennedy Elementary in St. Joseph retired Jacob's jersey number and hung it in the school cafeteria. To commemorate this honor, we were invited to a school program with the sixth graders, who read poems and sang "Jacob's Hope" and "Listen."

On Twitter, a woman shared a photo of a note she found on the windshield of her car. It read, "Have a cup of coffee on me! Kindness goes viral. #11forJacob." It included a gift card to Caribou Coffee.

And perhaps the kindest and most meaningful gesture of all came from the most unexpected of sources. The man who always pumped our septic tank (the same one who had pumped the tank at no charge when Jacob was first taken) once again came by our house unannounced. Twenty-seven years later, this kind man showed up and did the exact same thing—but this time he didn't do it for free. When he was finished, he knocked on the door and handed me an invoice.

"I gave you a special discount," he said with a smile.

When I looked down at the invoice, I noticed the total: $11.11.

There were so many special moments like this, and as the 11 movement continued to spread, the dark fog that had threatened to consume me began to lift ever so slightly. I would struggle with the darkness for years to come, but in that moment, this beautiful gift of kindness—given by the people who had so lovingly carried us all these years—was a flicker of hope that always brought me back to the light. It proved what I'd been saying for years. There *are* more good people in the world than bad, and when good people pull together, amazing things happen.

{ Chapter 62 }

Dear Jacob,

I want so much to hug you, hold you, and snuggle like we used to. We were always close, and I can sense your presence right now, right here with me.

I'm sitting at the kitchen table as I write this. It's the same table you remember . . . the one the six of us sat around for family dinners, card games, craft projects, and pizza parties. After all these years, we still live in the same house, the same cul-de-sac, the same town. We never moved, Jacob, just in case one day you might find your way home to us. Our hope was that strong—right up until the day they found you.

Facing your abduction was unbelievably painful. From the beginning, I always anticipated you running up the driveway and throwing yourself into our arms in one big, collective hug. But as the weeks passed and that didn't happen, I had to steel myself to do whatever it would take to bring you home.

That's when I started writing letters. Your first missed Christmas. Your twelfth birthday. Weddings, funerals . . . I shared everything that was going on in our family and in the world. In my letters, I begged you to stay strong. "Hang on, Jacob. We WILL find you." Possibly I was screaming at myself to stay strong, because I was the one who was so broken.

Over the years, I wrote to you on whatever I had. Sometimes it was a little notebook I carried in my purse; other times it was a random scrap of paper, a journal, a cocktail napkin, or my laptop. Writing letters to you calmed my soul and eased my heart.

Today, I continue to write to you, Jacob. I carry you with me, just like when you were a baby and I strapped you to the front of me in a Snugli carrier. Writing keeps you close to my heart.

Recently I came across a manila envelope that was mailed to us thirteen years after you were taken. It was from your student teacher, Miss Michele, at Rainbow House Pre-School. Inside was a packet of materials and notes to her supervisor including a "Case Study on Jacob Wetterling." You were four and a half. She wrote about how she fell in love with you from day one. You were thoughtful, smart, athletic, playful, and considerate. She found you fun to be with, and rather magical. She also remarked about your good language skills, but mentioned you had trouble with one word. *Memories.* You always called them "rememberies."

Reading through your teacher's notes brought back so many rememberies of who you were, who I was, and who we were as a family.

Ours was a happy house. We played and laughed and baked chocolate chip cookies together. Do you remember the year we had a lemonade stand and a garage sale to help the starving children in Ethiopia? We were still living above the chiropractic office in downtown St. Joe. We played "We Are the World" on a boom box so neighbors would hear the music, stop over, and buy something.

When we moved to our house in the cul-de-sac, you made neighborhood friends quickly. We made our new house comfy and continued to play games, do crafts, perform skits, and make homemade Christmas gifts. Ours was always the gathering place for friends to visit. If each of you had a friend over, it became an instant party with eight kids in the house. We all loved our full life and busy home.

When you started sixth grade, you suddenly seemed to grow up. You had your own ideas about what was cool, and you liked to have rap music blaring on the boom box whenever you and your friends shot baskets in the driveway. You were definitely coming into your own space.

And then, suddenly you were gone. Everything changed, and overnight, our happy life became forever divided into the "Before" and the "After."

To survive those first few days, we held hands and used the old boom box to play your favorite song, "Listen" by Red Grammer. As the weeks went by, we added Douglas Wood's song, "Jacob's Hope," and then "Somewhere Out There" from *An American Tail.*

The music helped us get by, but it was the hope that sustained us—a hope that I felt in every fiber of my being.

For almost twenty-seven years, you warmed the hearts of people all over the country with your big smile, your bright eyes, and your favorite yellow sweater. We all dared to hope.

Over time, Jacob's Hope became a mantra. I heard from a soldier in Desert Storm who carried your picture with him overseas. It gave him strength and hope that he would return home alive—and he did. Our hope was that real, not just to us, but to everyone. It kept our family strong, united, and it allowed us to seek happiness again. It wasn't that we ever forgot about you, but everything about the way you lived your life gave us strength and courage to do more, to help others, to find happiness in dark times.

It took a long time, but eventually we were able to find our smiles again.

You would be so proud of your siblings. Amy finished college in less than four years, majoring in criminal justice and psychology, then went on to get her master's degree in special education from the University of St. Thomas. She met her husband, Chris, during her senior year at the U of M. He's artistic, smart, and fun. They gifted us with our first two grandchildren, Lili and Izzi, who provided us with love, giggles, and the opportunity to be playful again. Amy is now a special education teacher. She's also a wellness coach and a runner, just like your dad. You wouldn't believe how many marathons and other races she has run. On top of all that, Amy is a wonderful wife and mom. She is so kind and has more energy than anyone I know.

Trevor majored in early childhood development, and I'm sure that helped him understand some of the trauma he's had to live with over the years. He met the love of his life, Trish, in college, and she has been so helpful to him in times of deep pain. Trevor now sells real estate and loves to help families find their new homes. He's good at it, and he's happy. Trevor and Trish have two of the most creative, playful children on the planet. Jake and Finn love to create skits and play video games online with their cousins in Minnesota. They're all so close.

Carmen majored in human development and family studies, specializing in early childhood development. She met her husband,

Kristian, the summer before her senior year of college while
working at Camp Friendship. Today, they both work with adults
with disabilities and help them strive for the best quality of life. Kris
is from England, so the two of them lived there for nearly two years
after they were married. Dad and I went to visit and had a chance
to really get to know Kristian's parents. They're so much fun, and
I know you would love them. After moving back to Minnesota,
Carmen and Kristian had twin daughters. (We all teased her about
naming them Ahbee and Ahbba, but they decided to go with Maizie
and Belle instead.) The twins have grown up to become amazing
dancers, and when people ask them about their mom, they tell
them, "She's always happy." Carmen worked hard at that and is an
inspiration to all she meets. She sparkles.

Your dad was so lost without his fishing and sports buddy—
his first-born son. He was always so proud of you, and we both
marveled at the kind, fun, happy, spirited boy you were growing
up to be. During those busy searching years when I was traveling,
he tried so hard not to miss any of Amy's, Trevor's, or Carmen's
activities. He is such a good dad. We have cried many tears together,
and our love has been painfully fractured throughout many of the
dark days. But we have always managed to find our way back. I'm
proud of us for beating the odds.

Your funeral and memorial service provided us with an
opportunity to connect with many of your old friends. They
describe you as always smiling, funny, welcoming to new students,
athletic, kind. They remember your birthday parties, soccer, and
football games, but they also remember your kidnapping and
the confusion they each went through. "Who would do this to
Jacob?" they asked. Everyone you grew up with had to learn how
to grow past their own fears, and many of your friends committed
themselves to building a life they knew you would be proud of.
Your classmate Alison is now the director of the Jacob Wetterling
Resource Center and still works to build a safer world for children.
George is in health care. Alex is an architect. Scott works in
technology, Jill is in the state patrol, and Jody is a teacher. They are
doctors, teachers, coaches, government workers—all sharing in a
commitment to making the world better. You're still with them in

many ways, and I know your smile will always shine through each one of them.

Jacob, you also introduced us to many new friends who helped us on this very long journey. My sister Barbi always referred to them as "gifts along the way."

Who would have ever thought that our gruffy old sheriff, Charlie Grafft, had the kindest heart and a soft spot for kids? He poured a lifetime of experience into his search for you, and he used his connections to bring together a powerful team of partners. So often, I was caught off guard by the kindness of law enforcement officers and was able to see a far different side of them than the stereotypical "tough cops" most people see. In fact, many of the officers who worked on your case have become lifelong friends.

You introduced us to other victim families . . . some still searching, some rebuilding after their children returned home. Team HOPE, the national parent support group I helped create, now has over 500 volunteers and has reached out to more than 102,000 people, offering compassionate peer support for those who have a missing loved one. Your abduction, and all that followed, gave so many people the strength and courage to go on.

You introduced us to survivors who shared their troubles and challenges with us, but also their successes. So many of these survivors have gone on to lead happy, fulfilling lives with loving families and children of their own. They brought us hope that you might also be one of the success stories.

You brought us our dear friends, Joy and Jared. Joy's curiosity and perseverance led her to Jared and then to the Paynesville victims. Jared knew and understood your fear, and with Joy's encouragement, he summoned the strength to talk about it. Jared shared his story with other victims in hopes they would also come forward to help find you. It worked. Together, Jared and Joy met with victims and their families, and began to uncover more details with every conversation.

Jared and Joy made us rethink everything we thought we knew. Dad and I formed a tight bond with them, and together we became a powerful team. We were driven by something none of us could explain, and our hearts were tied together by an insurmountable commitment to finding you. We planned next steps, dug deeper, and pressured investigators to take a fresh look at your case. With the full team back at the table and the discovery of key evidence, they were finally able to find the man who took you and get a confession. Eventually, Jared won his civil lawsuit against that man. He won't see any of the $17 million he was awarded, but he does get the satisfaction of seeing a proper dollar figure attached to the pain and anguish Heinrich put him through over his lifetime.

It's not the ending any of us wanted, but together, we did it. We brought you home.

For a long time, I was so lost. I had gone from being the mother of a missing child to the mother of a murdered child. Where was the hope in that? I challenged God to help me understand. "So, what was THAT all about?" I would ask. "What was the point?"

But, just as I never lost hope, I never lost my faith in God. It was hope and prayer that carried us.

I still believe in you, Jacob. I still feel you are so close. Your spirit is strong in this physical world, and you are still making a huge difference in so many lives. You became a unifier of hearts all the world around. You showed us how incredibly special each child is, and that love spread all across the globe, uniting hearts in hope. Today, those same people are teaching their own children to love one another, to be fair and to be kind.

Jacob, because of you, I learned so much along the way.

I learned that each and every one of us has the capacity to do more than we ever dreamed, if we just believe we can.

I learned that worry is useless. Nothing I worried about ever happened, and even if it had, worrying about it wouldn't have stopped it.

I learned that hope is a verb. It requires movement and *doing* to make something come true. It carries us and nudges us to do great things.

I learned to not let the worst things in my life define me. Sometimes a short memory is helpful.

I learned to pick myself up—over and over—because my love for you was always so much bigger than anything life could throw at me.

I learned how to accept myself as "just me"—a grandma, a mom, a friend, and a believer in hopes and possibilities.

Jacob, you continue to live so strongly in my heart.

I feel your spirit soar whenever I see an eagle swooping across the sky. I often look up and whisper a soft "Hi Jake" to let you know that I see you. It's that strong.

I feel your hand softly brush away my tears when I'm having a bad day.

I sense you watching when I see a deer stop to stare at me through the woods.

I hear your voice in the wind, reminding me to smile and enjoy the day.

I shed tears when I learn about other children who are struggling.

I smile when I see rainbows.

I still believe in the magic of Santa Claus.

I believe in the power of following your dreams.

I believe in a loving God.

I believe in prayer.

I believe in the power of good people pulling together to do amazing things.

Jacob, you have taught me—and so many others—to do good things, to work to correct wrongs, to fight for a world that is more caring. Your very strong spirit showed us how to love, how to live, and how to never give up. I am so grateful for the many gifts you have given to all of us. I promise to live the rest of my life carrying hope in my heart and sharing it as generously as you shared your love for all of us.

I thank you, Jacob. I love you with all of my heart, and for all of us who knew you, I want you to know that Jacob's Hope is still very much alive.

With eternal gratitude and unending love,
Mom

Afterword

Sometimes a person comes into your life for reasons you can't possibly understand. When Patty and I first started working on this book, Jacob was still missing. We thought we were working on a legacy piece that would bring attention to his case, highlight Patty's advocacy work, and serve as a spark of hope for other families of missing children. We were wrong. It became so much more.

As we worked on those early pages together, we couldn't possibly have known what was in store for us or what our friendship would have to endure. To see it through would mean going there together—through the darkness, the sadness, and the unfathomable grief. Could we even do it? Would people be receptive to it? Would our friendship survive it?

It has been a remarkable journey.

At that charity gala in 2013 when Patty and I first met, I was forty-six; she was sixty-five. I had just given up my dream of starting a new writing career and gone back to working full-time at what I knew—marketing. Patty was a well-known keynote speaker, a child safety advocate, a national figure in Washington, DC, and probably the most famous Minnesotan I'd ever met. She just oozed *drive* and *purpose*. Like everyone else at the gala, I was blown away by her powerful message of hope and her belief in the overall goodness of humankind.

So I was more than a little nervous about approaching Patty that evening and introducing myself as the blogger who had been writing about her missing son for the past two months. *Did she know who I was? Had she been following my blog? Was I making a difference?* I was desperately trying to figure out my own purpose in life and hoped maybe this was it. By writing about Jacob's case and asking people to "think Jacob" with me, maybe I could somehow create change.

It didn't go as expected. Patty saw my writing less as "making a differ-ence" and more "like stalking or something."

We stumbled past this rocky start with the help of Jared Scheierl. He was the catalyst, the icebreaker, and the energy source who kept the momentum going. We were joined along the way by more brave victims who agreed to come forward and share their own stories of similar attacks. Soon we were driven by a force that was bigger than all of us. We all felt it.

Two years after we met, in August 2015, Patty first asked me if I would be interested in helping her write a book. She invited me to her house, baked chocolate chip cookies, and shared some of her earliest writing. She'd started and stopped many times over the years, but she just didn't know how to put her thoughts in order or what people wanted to hear. But as a fan myself, I knew what they wanted. I suggested that people wanted to know who she was and where her tremendous strength came from. I encouraged her to *just write.* Start from the beginning. Tell me about your childhood, your family, your friends, your first job, your first love. Just write.

We clipped along and it was fun. I hadn't known I could admire Patty Wetterling any more than I already did, but clearly I could. The more I learned, the more I marveled at her bravery, her moxie, and her strength. She was the "boot-strappiest" person I'd ever met.

Our friendship grew as I encouraged Patty to tell me more. I learned that in real life she is just as self-deprecating as she appears onstage, so I found myself having to press for more details to flesh out a story. "Describe it to me," I'd say. Or, "How did that make you feel?" Often these sessions devolved into laughter as she described something outrageous and I found myself saying, "You did *what?*"

We caught our groove, took some classes, found a writing tribe, and re-ally started to feel like we were getting somewhere.

And then in the middle of it all—after nearly twenty-seven years of searching—Jacob's remains were found, and the answers came. They came crashing down in such powerful blows, none of us could stand. Throughout the state, as parents, as Minnesotans, we were all stunned into a deep, dark sadness.

I'd never seen Patty so broken. This woman I'd grown to love—this Supermom who led us into battle and carried the flame of hope for so long—was utterly depleted. I feared she would never smile again, let alone be able to write.

I was also struggling. Not only was I worried about Patty, but I also deeply missed her. I hadn't been able to attend Jacob's memorial service on September 25, 2016, because I was in France for a wedding. Missing this ceremony left a huge void in my heart, and my own grief had nowhere to land. At work, I still wasn't able to talk about Jacob without crying, and I couldn't make sense of it. I'd never even met this boy, and yet I felt so deeply that he was somehow a part of me.

And then another little miracle happened. In those thick, inky days, my friend Rosie called me out of the blue. She and her husband had a cabin on Lake Koronis in Paynesville, and she wanted to offer it to us as a quiet place where we could start writing again. I asked Patty what she thought, and she agreed to give it a try.

We met at Rosie's cabin for the first time on October 16, 2018. It had been over two years since we'd gathered like that—just us—and this time, we didn't talk about the book at all. It was like starting over again, not just on the book, but on our friendship. We were different people; Jacob's death had changed us both.

That day, Patty and I both moved forward in our own healing. We cried, and hugged, and tried to process what we could. It was a take-your-breath-away kind of devastation, and I felt horribly guilty for my own role in bringing Patty to this awful place. I reasoned that perhaps *not knowing* was better than *knowing*, but she assured me that wasn't the case. Their whole family needed answers. They needed to know that Jacob was at peace and that no one could hurt him anymore. Yes, it was hard, she told me, but the constant pain of not knowing was worse. Her words brought me some comfort that I didn't know I'd been missing.

Eventually, we got back to writing again, faced with the daunting reality that we now had a whole new story to tell.

Word by word, page by page, chapter by chapter, a book started to take shape. And along the way, our friendship continued to grow. It turns out a lot of life happens in the time it takes to write a book. Through joy, sadness, frustration, and occasional meltdowns, we plodded on.

To take breaks from the writing, we got together with our husbands and played 500 a few times a month. We ironed out the "Iowa rules" versus the "Minnesota rules," argued over whether it was called "nula" or "nullo," then settled into teams of boys versus girls. Sometimes the boys won, sometimes the girls won, but we always had a good time. (The tradition continues to this day. And mostly, the girls win.)

Finally, in August 2021—after six years of hard work—we had a completed manuscript. We found an agent, completed our second draft, and waited with high hopes as our agent submitted *Dear Jacob* to nearly thirty potential publishers. Several were interested in seeing the manuscript, and we ended up with three solid offers. However, none of the interested parties seemed to have a good grasp of the magnitude of this story; instead, they wanted to pigeonhole us into the "true crime" category of their booklist. We decided to pass.

When the Minnesota Historical Society Press came through with their offer in September 2022, we knew that *Dear Jacob* had found its perfect home. MNHS Press understood that this was so much more than a true crime story. It changed Minnesota history, it changed the way we parent our kids, and it led to stricter federal laws for predatory offenders. But mostly, MNHS Press recognized that, in Minnesota, Jacob was everyone's boy. We all grieved for him when he was found, and because of Patty's willingness to share her story with us, perhaps this book could help us all heal a little more easily.

On October 17, 2023, *Dear Jacob: A Mother's Journey of Hope* was finally released to the world.

Suddenly our days were filled with media interviews, TV appearances, and author talks in front of crowds of up to seven hundred. I'd barely wrapped my head around the fact that I was finally a *writer* before realizing I would also have to become a *speaker*.

Patty made it easy. She is so comfortable in front of an audience, drawing on decades of experience speaking as an advocate for children. At our very first presentation, for the Friends of the Hennepin County Library's "Talk of the Stacks" author lecture series in downtown Minneapolis, she was so warm, relatable, and *funny* that she not only calmed my nerves, she also put the whole audience—already electric with tension—at ease. She spoke with effortless simplicity and approached the hard topics in a way that felt like putting salve on an open wound. She didn't speak of bitterness and anger, but of hope and healing. Then, when it was my turn, she handed off the baton with a calming smile and a twinkle in her eye that said, *You got this.* And off I went on my own lap around the track, running confidently only because of the confidence she had in me.

Up until that moment, we had no idea how those presentations were going to go, but that first event set the pattern. We had never practiced and barely had time to review the moderator's list of questions before the next gig. People often commented on how natural our conversation seemed, or how they enjoyed our shared sense of humor. We knew we had a special chemistry, one that had been built on more than eleven years of trust and friendship.

After the presentations, people stayed and sometimes stood in line for over an hour to get their books signed. While they waited, they often shared their own memories of how old they were when Jacob was kidnapped, and how their lives had changed so dramatically. Some had been kids in 1989, afraid to walk to their friend's house or go for a bike ride. Some who were parents began taking their kids to the bus stop and accompanying them as they trick-or-treated around the neighborhood on Halloween. Others, like me, were in our early twenties, but we still did what we could. We paid attention, watched the news, wore buttons, handed out flyers, and prayed. No matter how old we were or what stage of life we were in, we all remembered those initial days of worry and fear.

During the book signings, I usually signed first, so that Patty could have more time to write a personalized message or chat with people. Often, as someone handed me a book to sign, their chin quivered and their eyes glistened; they were barely holding it together. When they finally got their turn to meet Patty, tears flowed openly as they told their own story of struggle or grief. As Patty held their hands and shared encouraging words, it was like a great weight was released from their entire being. Just being in the presence of someone who got it—someone who could recognize their pain—seemed to make a visible difference.

In those horribly difficult days after Jacob's remains were found, I remember Patty telling me how lost she felt, how all those years of searching and advocating felt so futile now because she had failed to do the one thing she had set out to do: to bring Jacob home alive. After a lifetime of representing hope to other searching families, who was she now? Where was the hope now?

I tried to tell her that she *had* made a difference. Her efforts were *not* futile, and so many kids were home safe with their families because of her life's work. But I think it was there, at those book signing tables, where Patty finally started to realize that what I was saying was true, that she still represented hope for so many people.

Patty radiates kindness, understanding, sympathy, acceptance, resilience, and strength. For twenty-seven years, she endured every parent's worst nightmare, and still she came out of it on the other side, without hatred or malice in her heart. She refused to let the man who took Jacob take anything else. She wouldn't let him take her marriage, her family, or her belief that most people in the world are good. Because of her, we are tougher on predators. Kinder to victims. More vigilant for the missing. More protective of the exploited. And more collaborative among law enforcement.

She has found her smile again.

When I sign books, I usually keep it pretty simple, with just one word above my signature: *Believe.* The truth is, I had my own struggle with depression just before I met Patty. I'd sold my business with the hope of launching a new writing career, but I had failed. I gave up on my dream and settled into the notion that maybe I wasn't meant for bigger things. Maybe this was as good as it gets. My kids were happy and healthy. I had a loving husband who did the lion's share of the cooking. I had a good job and made a decent living. I convinced myself I was being selfish and ungrateful for wanting anything more.

But for the life of me, I just couldn't stop "thinking Jacob."

In my heart, I will always believe that this story found me, and not the other way around. Jacob is my light and forever will be. He set my life on a path that was so extraordinary, I could never have imagined it on my own.

As a bonus, Jacob also led me to this unlikely and unexpected gift of friendship. What began with a rocky start between two moms just trying to fulfill their purposes in life has resulted in something so deep, powerful, and life altering, there really are no words to explain any of it. It just *is.*

Patty often says, "When good people come together, amazing things can happen."

In this case, they surely did.

Believe.
Joy Baker

Acknowledgments

As coauthors, we have many people to thank for helping us bring this book to completion.

Together we would like to thank our amazing writing group—Colleen Bell, Jim Bonilla, Kathy Guralski, Sherry Kempf, Katy Perry, Ann Prince, Lisa McClintick, and Mary McCormick. The ten of us met at a virtual writing retreat during COVID, and we continue to meet every other Wednesday. We consider ourselves incredibly lucky to have found such a talented group of friends and cohorts. Thank you for your time and your encouragement.

Many thanks to our beta readers, who read our *very long* first draft and passed along invaluable insight and feedback: Kelly Frey, Heather King, Lisa McClintick, Jane Nygaard, and Ann Prince.

Thanks also to retired FBI agent Chris Boeckers and Minneapolis attorney Doug Kelley, who helped us with fact-checking and remembering during the final stretch; to our agents, Delia Berrigan and Sharlene Martin at Martin Literary Management; and to our incredible editor, Ann Regan, editor in chief at the Minnesota Historical Society Press.

Patty Wetterling and Joy Baker

When I decided to write a memoir, it was in great part to thank all the people who have carried me and my family throughout this very long and life-altering journey. There are just so many people who impacted my life in ways big and small.

I gained much strength from the searching families who came before me and built the platform on which I stood. Through victims of abduction and/or sexual exploitation, and through the support of Team HOPE members, I witnessed incredible strength, stamina, and determination to make the world a better place for all children.

I want to thank our neighbors the Jerzaks—Rochelle for babysitting Carmen that fateful night, Merle who made the 911 call, and Scottie for her unfaltering love and support for so many years. Also Connie Cross and Dave and Vicki Glenn, who were with us when we got the call and offered tons of support and resources, including tremendous assistance from the College of St. Benedict.

A special thanks to the Larson family, who endured the terror and have always been there for whatever we needed. Aaron, we have treasured watching you overcome so much fear and trauma and then grow into an amazing, compassionate, caring man. Jacob would be so proud of who you have become. I know you'd still be best friends.

Thank you to all law enforcement officers who assisted in the search to find Jacob. Special thanks to BCA superintendents Michael Campion and Tim O'Malley; BCA administrator and Minnesota State AMBER Alert coordinator Janell Rasmussen; FBI special agents Al Garber, Steve Gilkerson, Shane Ball, and Chris Boeckers; Hennepin County detective Neil Neddermeyer; all the Stearns County officers—starting with sheriffs Charlie Grafft, Jim Kostreba, and John Sanner; Captain Pam Jensen, our family liaison; Benton County sheriff Frank Wippler; and officers from everywhere else who followed up leads and helped in the search. Thank you for your determination to keep working to solve these horrific crimes against children and to assist families. Bruce Bechtold—the first responding officer on the scene in 1989 and chief deputy when Jacob was found in 2016—said it best: "Everything mattered." Every call you took, every piece of evidence you collected, every suspect interviewed, every person cleared, every search you made . . . mattered. It all gave us the answers we so badly needed.

Thank you to everyone who has ever worked at the National Center for Missing and Exploited Children and especially former CEO Ernie Allen and our case manager, Ron Jones. You kept me alive, hopeful, and purposeful from the first call we made to NCMEC. You are truly a place of hope for all missing kids and for all children who are home safe today. Special thanks to past NCMEC board members and forever friends Colleen Nick, Cordelia Anderson, Karen Tandy, and Dr. Sharon Cooper. You brought so much joy and helped me survive some huge life challenges.

Thank you Alison Feigh for your lifetime commitment to building a better, safer world for children through your leadership at the Jacob Wetterling Resource Center. I love our brainstorming sessions and your ability to make some of my wild and crazy ideas happen. Thanks also to Jane Straub, Suzanne Severson, and all the support staff. You are all so dear!

Thank you to the entire state of Minnesota for leaving porch lights on, tying white ribbons, attending prayer services, searching, turning in leads, distributing flyers, bringing food, and writing songs and poems. Thanks to the media, the sports teams, the corporations and small businesses, the schools, and every community member who showed support, helping in every way imaginable. Thank you for never quitting the search for Jacob.

Deepest gratitude to all the people we didn't even know who supported us. You strengthened my resolve to fight for the world Jacob knew—a world that was kind, where life was playful, fun, and happy. Without clinging to how life should be, what it could be again, I would have crawled into a shell and never returned. You gave us a light to turn to through your support, prayers, and continuous acts of kindness.

Thank you to all the children who sent pictures and precious notes of support. You are a constant reminder of hope and innocence. Your notes telling me to not give up still carry me when my spirits are down. Thank you to the teachers who encouraged these letters, in schools and religious instruction classes. We are all one family, and we need to pull together more often. Jacob would like that.

Heartfelt hugs to our lifelong friends Nancy and Bill Bronson, Kevin and Donna Blanchette, Vic and Fran Larson, Dan and Mary Kay Carle, Jim and MaryAnn Graeve, Judi Novak, and Jeff Friesen and Lee Aberle and to so many new friends who bring joy to our lives. Your continued thoughtfulness and generosity help us to pick ourselves up again and again.

And Jared. I will never, ever forget our first meeting and how strong you made me feel. Yet, *you* were the strong one. You stayed in touch, and when we met again years later, you were convinced you could help. You sacrificed your own privacy to help us find answers. I absolutely loved it every time you stopped by for a hug. I treasure your friendship.

Doug Kelley, thank you is simply not enough. After offering to help Jared, you shared your wisdom and generosity with our family, guiding us through the land of lawyers and courts, plea bargains and hearings. I felt like a little kid lost in the forest, and I gained strength through your steady hand, holding us up and guiding us through. You rescued us when we hit rock bottom and didn't let go until we could stand on our own again.

A huge thank-you goes to our families who held us tight, no matter what was going on. To my siblings and their spouses: Peg and Glenn, Nancy and Cliff, Russ and Linda; and to Jerry's sisters Joan and Anna (and her best friend Byron); and all of our nieces and nephews for prayers, hugs, meals, volunteerism, encouragement, and sustenance throughout this journey. We are so lucky to have such strong families, and you all have blessed us with happy family gatherings and memories that gave us the love and encouragement to go on.

And to our family members who are no longer here—Mom and Dad, Erv and Lil, Judy and Dick, Barbi and John—thank you for holding Jacob in your loving arms until we can hold him again ourselves.

Jerry and I thank God every day for our most amazing children and grandchildren. My heart swells with pride and love for Amy, Chris, Lili, Izzi, Trevor, Trish, Jake, Finn, Carmen, Kristian, Maizie, and Belle and our special babysitter daughter, Shannon. Thank you for giving me the love, support, and purpose to work so hard on seeking solutions to the problem of missing and exploited children. You are the reason behind everything I do. I love you more each and every day.

And huge hugs to my dear husband, Jerry. We've weathered so much throughout the past decades. I couldn't have survived this without you and look forward to many more years of happiness together. I love you dearly.

This book would never have been completed without the dedication, research, and skills of my coauthor, Joy Baker. Her love and promise to Jacob came from a source bigger than both of us. I am forever grateful for her teaching, coaching, encouragement, and commitment to helping me tell my story. I truly believe that Jacob chose you to help me write this memoir. Thank you. I treasure our friendship.

My sister Barbi described so many of you as "gifts along the way." Thank you for your smiles, your hugs, your kind words and deeds—and mostly, thank you for sharing the hope with me.

Patty Wetterling

First, I must thank my husband, Ross, for putting up with me for so many years while I blathered on about dreams, purpose, and starting a writing career. While I'm sure you questioned my sanity at times, you never lost faith in me. Thank you.

Thanks also to my friends Betsy Bonnema and Jane McLaughlin, who were the first to tell me, "Take the leap and the net will appear." When, in fact, the net did not appear, it was always my BFFs (the YaYas and the Janes) who showed up to pick me up, dust me off, and push me off the cliff again. Thank you.

In 2010, the net finally began to appear when I started a blog called *Joy the Curious*. To everyone who ever subscribed, left a comment, or sent a message of encouragement, please know how much that meant to me. Your kind words made me feel like a real writer. Thank you.

To Jared Scheierl—how can I ever thank you for agreeing to meet me over pizza and a beer that first time? You talked to me and shared your story. Who knew that meeting would lead us on such an epic journey? Sometimes the universe throws people together at exactly the right time, and I deeply believe that's what happened here. We were both dealing with big life changes and searching for purpose. No doubt in my mind, it was a God thing.

From there we met Brad, Danny, Kris, Mark, Troy, Nathan, and other Paynesville victims who also agreed to step forward and bravely share their stories. You are *all* the true heroes. Your courage and your willingness to speak up truly made the difference. Thank you for your powerful voices.

And finally, a huge thank-you to my friend and coauthor, Patty. Thank you for sharing Jacob with me. You had no reason to trust me, but you did. Our deep friendship has been an unexpected gift on this winding journey, and I will be forever grateful to you for believing in me. I am in awe of your wisdom, your compassion, and your strength. Thank you for being the light for so many.

I dedicate this work to my sons, Jordan and Cole. Dream big, boys.

Joy Baker

About the Authors

Patty Wetterling is a national advocate, visionary, and educator on the prevention of child abduction and exploitation.

Joy Baker works as an independent marketing consultant, professional copywriter, and writing coach.